A Layman's Faith

By

Peter Slot

As Preached in his Parish Church and Elsewhere

1982 To 2012

Grosvenor House
Publishing Limited

Peter Slot is hereby identified as author of this
work in accordance with Section 77 of the Copyright, Designs
and Patents Act 1988

The book cover picture is copyright to Inmagine Corp LLC

This book is published by
Grosvenor House Publishing Ltd
28-30 High Street, Guildford, Surrey, GU1 3EL.
www.grosvenorhousepublishing.co.uk

A CIP record for this book
is available from the British Library

ISBN 978-1-78148-797-6

A Foreword

My faith has been a long time coming. I was born in December 1932 to loving parents, who were Jews by birth, but had no particular religious belief. My father, when asked, said he simply did not know whether a God existed. My mother believed, I think, in a God who was good, but saw no need to do anything about it. My elder brother and I were sent to Church of England schools, because our parents thought that the education there was the best that could be found – and I was taught the basics of the Christian Faith by good teachers, who taught that the history and the beliefs were true. I grew up thinking that this was so. I sang in choirs as a schoolboy and continued to do so in adulthood: and so attended church regularly. I asked to be confirmed when I was seventeen and was formally baptised a fortnight before the confirmation service. My parents did not object at all – but were not, as I remember it, particularly interested either. I had been taught that it was right to go to church on Sunday mornings – and my brother and I often did so.

When I came down from Oxford University and began to read for the Bar, I was living with my parents in a flat in South Kensington and began to attend church on Sunday mornings at Holy Trinity Church, Prince Consort Road, just behind the Albert Hall, where the Parish Priest was the Reverend Douglas Cleverley Ford, whom I found to be a brilliant preacher. I have always reckoned that I learned more about public speaking from listening to him than from any other source. I learned to listen to his sermons, gained much from them and realised that a good sermon was a true work of art. I wanted to be able to speak like him.

Years passed. I fell in love with and married a wife, who despite having a considerable mind of her own, fully supported me in everything I did, sang soprano and was also a churchgoer. When we started a family and moved to live in Surrey, we both sang in

I

the village church choir and have done so ever since and attended church regularly. I have been a communicant member of the Church of England now for sixty three years: and, inevitably, over time, I have thought deeply and carefully about the things that I truly believe – and, at the same time, the things that I truly reject. I practised as a barrister for twenty three years and, at the age of forty seven, was appointed a Circuit Judge, a position which I held until I retired at the end of 1997. In 1982, not long after my appointment to the Bench, a re-organisation of the Parishes in the area, where we lived, caused a single priest to be responsible for the worship in three churches, including our own at St Michaels, Betchworth: and our new Parish priest, the Reverend Anthony West, asked me if I would be willing to take some non-sacramental services for him and, perhaps, preach at them from time to time. He needed, as he put it, an extra pair of hands and obtained informal permission from the Bishop of Kingston to enable me to do so. Thus it was that I began to preach.

Before this time, I had sometimes spoken about my faith at discussion meetings, but never in detail and never in a formal context: and I found that, if I was going to preach from the pulpit, I was truly going to have to work out with the very greatest care precisely what I believed and why I believed it. It was vital neither to understate nor to overstate the very important things that I believed in: and it seemed to me to be essential to get the message right and to try to make it live. I sought to do this when I started: and, when I was formally appointed a Reader in 1991, I tried to continue to do so. When I was asked by some friends and fellow-parishioners to publish some of my sermons, so that they could have a chance to read them, I thought it a great compliment – so here they are. They were, of course, written to be delivered orally, not as written matter to be analysed and digested – and the material appears here precisely as preached, without any editing and with all faults. Some of them were written and delivered twenty or more years ago and expressed what I wanted to say at that time: and I have not altered them to try to bring them up to date. They contain, as material written to be spoken in public often contains, a considerable amount of repetition, but not, I hope, too much over-simplification. They set out, as best I could do it, the Gospel of Christ, as I believe it to be. Inevitably, a good part of the material in these sermons has been learned from others, from the teachers and preachers who have taught me what I know and believe, and clearly cannot be claimed to come from original thinking on my part. I am greatly indebted to them.

It was only when, after I had assembled the material, I came to read it through, that I realised the extent to which the words I had used, whether original or not, had encapsulated the faith which I profess. I am a layman and feel no call to be anything else – and that is why this volume bears the title "A layman's faith". For that is what it is.

INDEX

Advent Sunday

Isaiah, Ch 2 v 4

Today is Advent Sunday, which traditionally marks the beginning of the new Church year. And two very well-known readings have been appointed for today. Isaiah Ch 2:- They shall beat their swords into ploughshares and their spears into pruning hooks. Nation shall not lift up sword against nation, neither shall they learn war any more. And St Matthew Ch 24:- Watch, therefore, says Jesus. For ye know not what hour your Lord doth come. But know this, that if the good man of the house had known at what hour the thief would come, he would have watched and would not have suffered his house to be broken through.

They shall beat their swords into ploughshares. Nation shall not lift up sword against nation. Neither shall they learn war any more. It is over 2500 years since Isaiah gave the Jews that wonderful prophecy: and now, all these years later, Advent after Advent and Christmas after Christmas, we read it and rejoice at it. But do we believe it? What are we to make of it? I had always thought that the Prophet was foretelling the birth and ministry of Jesus: and that his message was that peace would be the blessing which Jesus would leave for us, that Jesus would be the Prince of Peace. But I do not know whether I think that now.

For He has not been the Prince of Peace for this world of ours, neither, if we look at the record, did he pretend that that was what his legacy would be. I come, he said, not to bring peace, but division. And He has. He has brought division, not peace, to tribes, to nations, to peoples, to churches. For hundreds of years, Christians, devout Christian men and women all of them, killed and tortured each other in His name, burning archbishops to death in public in His name, murdering ordinary folk by the hundred in His name, because the leaders of His Church could not agree about His teaching, could not agree about His message and believed, truly believed, on the basis of what they understood Jesus to have told them, that it was better that these unhappy people should be sent into life with God blind than, with two eyes, to be cast into everlasting fire. They believed that, because that was what Jesus was reported to have told them. For hundreds of years, Christians and Muslims fought one another in the name of the same God, both sides believing, from the bottom of their very souls, that this was what God wanted them to do, that it was better for the infidel, whether he be a Christian infidel or a Muslim infidel, to die in pain and disgrace than to spend eternity in the place reserved for the damned. Jesus, venerated as the Son of God by Christians and venerated as one of God's greatest prophets by the Muslims, is reported as have given different messages to each warring side, so that all sides truly believed that they were right and that everyone else was wrong - and believed this, through thick and thin, through life and death, because of what they truly understood Jesus to have taught them. For nations, for Churches, for governments, Christ has not been the Prince of Peace. He has been the focus for war. You may not like this assertion. I don't like it either. But, unless we are to be misled by our own spin, we have to face it, apply our minds to it and decide what to make of it.

Why is His Church still split over the ordination of women as priests or their appointment as bishops? It is because of what Christ did and said - and what His followers did and said - and did not do? Why is the Church fighting itself about homosexual priests? Because of what Jesus and His followers did and said - and did not do and say. It just won't do to say that it is man's sin that has caused all this horror. It is man's acceptance of what Jesus is reported to have said and of what St Paul, His apostle, is reported to have said. And man has accepted it, not because he is sinful but because he has been told to accept it, because he has been told that it is God's will that he should accept it - and so he has. We have to face the fact that the international legacy of Christ has been war, enormous suffering and heartfelt disagreement: and that, two thousand years and more later, there is no sign that any single sword will be turned into a ploughshare or any single spear into a pruning hook.

If it was God's purpose that Christ should bring a cessation of international war to this earth, we have to admit that that purpose has failed completely. And it is something, which, in argument, in discussion, in our efforts to persuade unbelievers that Jesus offers us the way to eternal life and a good pattern for living, we have to face and answer. We have to answer for the unchallenged fact, that this Jesus, this amazing man who came to tell us about God, to tell us how to live and to conquer death for us, fulfilled His mission without ever writing anything down or causing any contemporary record of his teaching to be made. It must have been Jesus' decision that so long a time would be allowed to pass before any record was made of what He had taught, that, by the time anything was written down, all the eye-witnesses were dead and people's recollections were seriously different: and that the first teachings of His message, with all their faults and uncertainties, would be found in the letters of St Paul, many of which were written as answers to questions put by troubled Church communities and were never designed to be a comprehensive account of the Christian faith at all. We do not know what the questions were, so we cannot tell for sure what the answers mean. So is it any wonder that the messages are contradictory?

I do not pretend to know the answer to all this, but it is possible to look at it from another angle. If Christ's message was a message designed for nations or governments, it was not a message designed for them alone. It was a message primarily for individuals. It was an invitation to you, to me, to individuals. Come unto me, if you are heavy-laden: and I will give you rest. Put your trust in me and I will bring love to your heart. Be my disciple and I will give you something to live for. Do what I tell you and I will be with you always. I will come to you, no matter how far away from me you have travelled. One of these days I will come to you. It may be a surprise. It may be expected. But be ready, for I may come when you are not looking: and, if I do, you may not find me.

Our task in this life, our principal task, yours and mine, is to find our way to God. That is what we were born for. For Christians, Jesus is that way: and it may be a very long journey. There are tens of thousands of people, some troubled, some not, who have found that Jesus was with them without their knowing it and, having found this out, have lived with joy in that knowledge for the whole of their lives. Some of you, I expect, are in that condition. Others of you may be seeking it. Jesus tells you to be ready - to keep your mind's mobile phone on, in case the message comes. If the good man of the house had known at what time the thief would come, he would have watched. If the seeker after God had known at what time Christ would come, he would have listened. If his mobile phone is not switched off, he should hear the message.

But what will the message be? All I can say is that it will be a message for you and for you alone. It may not be the same message that I have received. It may not be the same message that your parish priest has received. It may not be a message which you can wholly comprehend or easily follow. But it will be a message for you. But, whatever it is, I urge you to consider it carefully. If, for example, it is a message to go to war, whether it be to go to war with guns or with words, consider it very carefully indeed. If it is a message that you are right and that everyone else is wrong, consider it very carefully indeed. For it may be a false message.

For this certainty that I am right and everyone else is wrong is the reason why wars occur. This is the cause which has made us spend so much time over all these centuries fighting each other: and it is very dangerous. Our belief (in this Church at least) is that Jesus brings us a message of love and teaches us that the problems of the world are answered by love. To govern the world with love is a very hard, probably an impossible thing - for it is difficult to fight murder or terrorism effectively with love, because you and those for whom you are responsible will be dead before you get anywhere. But, on an individual basis, you can live your life with love, you can treat your neighbours with love, you can (our

Rector does) run your parish with love, you can show anyone who is willing to watch and listen that a loving life is the right life: and that Christians, who love one another, are doing God's work. This is what Jesus told us - and, as individuals, we can try it.

If Jesus had been asked what His followers should do, if they saw peoples of other nations being murdered because of their race or creed, I do not know what He would have said. If Jesus had been asked whether homosexual men, who worshipped Him, counted themselves His followers and, in their lives, loved others deeply, should be allowed to work as priests and administer the Sacrament, I am not sure, but think I know what He would have said. But if you had asked Him, as you probably do when you pray, how you should live with your neighbours and conduct your life, with all its difficulties and dangers, I believe He would have told you to love one another as He loved us. And this, I truly believe, is what we should try to do in this new Church year, which is just beginning. I think, for the moment at least, that it is probably the best we can do. I wish you all a happy New Year.

Advent Sunday (2)

St Mark Ch 13 v 26

Today is Advent Sunday, traditionally the first day of the Church's year, traditionally the day, four weeks before Christmas, when we are encouraged to prepare our minds for the advent, the coming of Christ. The Church, in this context, is not encouraging us to begin our Christmas shopping. It is not encouraging us to stock up the shelves with good things. It is inviting us to reflect on the coming into the world of God's Son, this greatest-ever-in-history event, which we are about to commemorate, to think on what we believe about it and to prepare our minds for it. For Advent Sunday, the chosen readings are usually readings, which refer to Christ's coming and what it means. At Advent, we often read of prophecies and of promises, of the Prince of Peace, of the saving of mankind. But not today. Today the chosen reading is the passage you have heard from St Mark: and it is a difficult passage – difficult for me anyway – which speaks of Christ's second coming and speaks of it in a context, which is very challenging indeed. Today's Gospel reading finds Jesus, apparently, talking to four of the apostles, Peter James John and Andrew, about the end of the world and telling them how, when the world ends, He will return in the clouds with great glory: and that these things, the end of the world and his coming in the clouds, will happen in their lifetime. It is there in the Gospel, clear, it seems, as day: and we have to decide what we are to make of it. We have to decide what we are to make of it, because we know for sure that it did not happen. The world did not come to an end in the apostles' lifetime. Nor did Jesus return in clouds of glory in their lifetime. Two thousand years have passed since the apostles' lifetime and neither of those things has happened yet. We have, it seems to me, to face the fact that, if Jesus said these things, he was wrong: and, if He did not say these things, then the Gospel writers got it wrong. It is an uncomfortable position for someone, convinced of his Christian belief, to find himself in. I do not like it one bit, but I, and you, have to face it. We live in a

6

time when people ask us about our faith, what it is we believe and why we believe it. It is no good asking the intelligent young to believe in Christ's divinity and to come and worship with us, if we do not know what we believe about these things. If we are going to tell them anything, it must be the truth that we try to tell them. Nothing else will do. And, if we cannot trust Christ or we cannot trust the Gospels, how can we know where the truth lies?

I want, as a layman, to share some thoughts with you about this. I have not studied theology and I have no authority to teach you anything. You need not pay any heed to what I say at all. But it is my firm conviction that Christ told the truth to those he spoke to: and the difficulty with this passage arises from incorrect reporting of Jesus' words. St Mark's Gospel, in which this passage appears, was written, the scholars tell us, 30 years or more after Jesus died: and the possibility of incorrect reporting is obvious. It is more obvious still when you consider the circumstances. Mark obtained his information, indeed his own firm beliefs, from the disciples themselves. It is Christ's disciples who are the source of all the information in the Gospels. The Gospels make it clear that the disciples were bowled over, irresistibly attracted, by Jesus' personality, left everything, home, family, career, everything, and followed Him. During His ministry, they understood very little of what He said and, from start to finish, had no idea who He was. Their discipleship was utterly devoted, but, at the same time, blind and uncomprehending. When Jesus was taken from them and crucified, they were totally lost. They fled and went into hiding, having no idea what to do. Christ's message was lost to the world, so it seemed: so it seemed, dead in the water, gone for ever. But then something happened. The man they had revered, the man they had given up their lives for, the man they had seen dead and buried, came back from the dead and pulled them back together. Now, for the first time, they saw the miracle for what it was. Now, for the first time, they understood the message. Now, for the first time, they realised what He meant by The Son of God. Now, for the first time, they had the understanding, the conviction and the eloquence, to preach His Gospel to the world – and they went out and did preach His Gospel to the world, which is why we are here.

But though, through their leader, they had become giants for their cause, they remained human beings also, human beings with human weaknesses. They were utterly captivated by the experience they had had of Him, they were determined to spread His message to the world they knew: and, inevitably, they saw what they thought they remembered of His works and recalled what they thought they remembered of His words, with rose-coloured spectacles and rose-coloured recollections. They had been so convinced by their experiences of the risen Christ that they were, from time to time, prepared to say anything which would convince their hearers of the rightness of their cause – and indeed the scholars tell us that accuracy in the reporting of history was not expected in those days. In consequence, they exaggerated some things and embellished others. We have every reason to believe that the substance of their message was true. But not all the detail is true. They were recalling words which were used and events which had happened many years before – and inevitably, given all these circumstances, they must have overstated some things and mis-remembered others. It would be amazing if this were not so. But, if that is the reality, we have to live with it and acknowledge the truth about it.

When Jesus had this conversation with His apostles, I do not know, I cannot know, precisely what was said. It may be that He said that they would see Him again. It may be that He spoke of people seeing Him in glory. It may be that the lifetime of those listening to Him was mentioned. We simply cannot know. It is unlikely, I think, that He said he would come in the clouds. Throughout history, those who worshipped Gods thought that the Gods lived up in the sky, among the clouds: and the Old Testament is full of that imagery. After all, before man learned to fly, which is a fairly short time ago, no one knew what was above the clouds – for no one had been there. The rain came from the clouds. The sun shone through the clouds. The thunder came from the clouds. To those, who knew nothing of space and the planets, God was thought of as being up there, because the things which God sent came from up there. If Jesus had gone to Heaven, up there was where Heaven was – and the idea of Christ returning in the clouds was a natural thought. If He was coming from the sky, how else would He come? But we know what is up there now. We don't believe any more, do we, that God and Heaven are in the sky somewhere? And, if Christ comes back, we don't expect, do we, to see Him coming down from the sky, like some sky diver or parachutist? And I, for my part, do not believe that He said or promised that He would come in the clouds in glory. A possible explanation of these words, which is consistent with Christ's other teaching, is that He was talking about death – the thing which happens to everyone in his or her lifetime and saying that the apostles might expect to see Him in the course of their dying experience. I have no idea, but that may be a possibility. For, after all, this is our faith, is it not? Christ promised us that He would be with us always and in us always: and our belief is that, when we die, we will find ourselves, by some mysterious alchemy, spiritually in His company and measured for what we may be worth – with our sins hopefully forgiven and joy, to a greater or lesser extent, our final reward. This, I think, is what we mean by eternal life: and this, after all, is the inheritance which our faith tells us that Christ's Advent has bought for us. This, the promise of eternal life, is the difference which Christ's coming has made for us. This is why we rejoice at Christ's coming and rejoice at Christ's birth. This is why we need to have our minds ponder these things as, in this Advent season, at the beginning of our new Church year, we prepare ourselves, our minds and bodies, for the great celebration of Christmas and reflect on what it truly means for us all. Christ is coming. We must be prepared for it. We have four weeks to get ready. I wish you all a very happy New Year.

The Good Samaritan

St Luke Ch 10

St Mark; s Gospel, Ch 1. There cometh, said John the Baptist, one mightier than I, who will baptise you with the Holy Spirit. Jesus will baptise you with the Holy Spirit. He will make all things new - and that is what He did - and today we commemorate it. For today, the second Sunday in Advent, is traditionally known as Bible Sunday, the day when we thank God for our Bible and pray that its use may guide us in the right way. Blessed Lord, who hast caused all Holy Scriptures to be written for our learning, grant that we may in such wise hear them, read, mark, learn and inwardly digest them that, by patience and comfort of Thy Holy word, we may embrace and ever hold fast the blessed hope of everlasting life, which Thou hast given us in our Saviour Jesus Christ. Today's Collect is a rallying call. It tells us to work hard. It tells us to draw strength from Christ's words. We are to read, mark, learn and inwardly digest the material put before us. We are to use our God-given brains for the purposes for which they were given us - and think, yes think, about our faith.

I want to invite you this morning to think about one particular piece of scripture, a very well-known piece of scripture, the parable of the Good Samaritan, as recounted by St Luke in Chapter 10 of his Gospel. It is a passage which shows us Jesus at His best. It tells us of the lawyer, a learned Pharisee and expert in the old Mosaic law, who, in public, set Jesus a trap by asking him a trick question - what is the great commandment in the law? He was, in effect, inviting this new and radical teacher to choose which of the Ten Commandments was the most important. Would it be the first? Or the fifth? The second or the eighth? The Pharisees were agog for an answer and, as we all know, there are hazards in answering awkward questions. But Jesus would have none of it. He chose two commandments, neither of which was one of the Ten. The commandments He chose were written in the law all right. You will find them both, quite well concealed in Deuteronomy, if you look for them. Thou shalt love the Lord thy God, He said, with all thy heart and with all thy soul and with all thy mind: and Thou shalt love thy neighbour as thyself. There is no other commandment greater than these. These two commandments encapsulate everything in the law and the prophets. The lawyer then went on to ask: But who is my neighbour? And that question, also a very difficult one, brought forth the parable of the Good Samaritan, a parable which had great lessons for those who were listening and has great lessons, if we think, for us also.

You all know the parable of the Good Samaritan. It teaches at least two lessons, one plain, another, to us at first sight, less so. A traveller was on the road between Jerusalem and Jericho. He was set upon by robbers, stripped of his belongings and left bleeding in the road. As he lay there, a priest came by, saw him, but did nothing and passed by on the other side. Then a Levite came and also passed by on the other side. Then another person came, a despised Samaritan, a sort of wide boy from Essex perhaps, saw him, stopped, bound up his wounds, put him on his own mule, took him to safety and saw that he was looked after. Who, Jesus asked the lawyer, was neighbour to the wounded man? Why, of course, came the answer, the man who looked after him. Yes, said Jesus, go and do thou likewise. Look very closely at that instruction - Go and do thou likewise. Look at it very closely indeed. The first lesson, that we should look after strangers is clear enough. But there was nothing new in that. There was nothing new, in Jesus' day, in good people looking after strangers. It was expected of them. It was laid down in the law that that was what people should do. But that is not the real point of the story. For there were four characters, not two, in this tale: and we need to look at the other two, the priest and the Levite, who enter and leave the scene so quickly. For what, we ask, was wrong with them? Why did they do nothing, pass by on the other side? Was it that they could not be bothered? Was it urgent pressure of business? The priests and the Levites were holy men. What was it about these two, that they set such a deplorable example?

The answer would have been clear to the Jews of Jesus' day, though it is not clear to us unless we see the story in its historical context, unless we read, mark, learn and inwardly digest the material before us. Under the law of Moses, the law set out in the book of Leviticus in our Bible, all bleeding flesh was stated to be unclean: and, if anyone, let alone a priest or a Levite, touched a bleeding body, he or she became unclean also. The old law, the law of Moses, the law set out in our Bible, forbade a priest or a Levite or any devout man or woman, to touch a bleeding body under penalty of becoming tainted and unclean - and every Jew knew that. So the priest and the Levite passed by on the other side, not because they did not care, not because they had other things to do, but because the law required them to do so. The Samaritan, less concerned with his position under the strict religious law of Moses, handled the bleeding victim and took him away to safety. He helped his blood-soaked neighbour, even though the law of Moses forbade it. And Jesus told the lawyer and all those who were listening: Go and do thou likewise. You go and break this law too, if love for your neighbour requires it. What a very different instruction this "Go and do thou likewise" is now seen to be.

And this is the new dawn, the message of the new light which Jesus came to tell us of. It is the new message of the concept of the loving God, who requires His people to learn to love Him and demands of us that we should love one another. It is the new dawn of a teaching, which says that rigid obedience to the Ten Commandments is not enough without love. Note, if you will, that the word Love does not appear in the Ten Commandments. All ten commandments, save two, are prohibitions - Thou shalt not. The only two positive commandments are that you should keep holy the Sabbath day and that you should honour your father and your mother: and the word love does not appear there at all. Jesus' message, the Christian message, is that this is not enough.

Jesus' message is that we should, with all that we are and all that we have, seek to learn to know and eventually to learn to love, this indescribable and wonderful God, who made us: that we should use our emotions, our physical strength and our brains, our thinking processes, in this task: and that we should love our neighbours, regardless of the old teachings, even though those old teachings still remain in our Bible. The book of Leviticus, in our own Bible, told the Jews that they should not touch a bleeding victim lying in the road. That same law in that same book told the Jews then, and tells us now, that we should not touch a menstruating woman, or a woman who has just given birth to a child, for God has said that they are both unclean. That same law in that same book told the Jews then, and tells us now, that God has said that no one with a flat nose or a crooked back or any physical disability should be allowed to become a priest. Jesus' message, the new message, was that such people should not be treated as people to be avoided, as people who were unclean. His message was that they are our neighbours, God's children, people to be loved. His message is that we do not show our love for God by sticking, without thought or consideration, to the rigid rules of the bygone days, by saying If it's in the Bible, this is what we must do. His message is that, without love, obedience to the law counts for nothing. The Good Samaritan broke the old rules laid down in the books of the law. He broke them out of consideration for a stranger in need, out of love for his neighbour. Jesus told the lawyer - Go and do thou likewise. Go and do thou likewise - and this is what I truly believe Jesus today is saying to us. Blessed Lord, who hast caused all Holy Scriptures to be written for our learning. Grant that we may in such wise hear them, read, mark, learn and inwardly digest them, that, by patience and comfort of Thy holy word, we may embrace and ever hold fast the blessed hope of everlasting life, which Thou hast given us in our Saviour Jesus Christ, that same Jesus Christ, who came to baptise us with the Holy Spirit. Welcome to the new dawn. We have a lot of thinking to do.

Rejoice in the Lord

St Paul to Philippians Ch 4. v 4

TODAY IS the third Sunday in Advent and we are a short two weeks away from Christmas, the time when God's Son, Jesus Christ, came to visit us in abject poverty: and so I see nothing inappropriate in offering you, as a text today, the Collect for Advent Sunday. Almighty God, give us grace to cast away the works of darkness and put upon us the armour of light – now, in the time of this mortal life in which Thy Son, Jesus Christ, came to visit us in great humility. I offer you this text: and, with it, I offer you a second text, from Ch 4 of St Paul's letter to the Christians at Philippi. Rejoice in the Lord always: and again I say Rejoice. Let your moderation be known unto all men. The Lord is at hand.

Give us grace – today- that we may cast away the works of darkness and put upon us the armour of light. The Lord is at hand – today. Here we are, two weeks from Christmas, the day when we celebrate what we Christians believe to have been the greatest event which ever happened in human history, the coming of God in human form on earth, to be with men and share their suffering and their joys, to show us how to live, to show how great God really is, to overcome death, to redeem us from our sinfulness and its results and to bring to each of us the chance of attaining eternal life with God. These are truly wonderful things. If they were promised us in an advertisement, we would never believe them. Now that we have them, we are often curiously reticent about them. But, if anything ever happened to change the world for the better, Christ's coming was the greatest. We are about to celebrate it. The Lord is at hand.

And a little over 2000 years ago, on this same day, the Lord was also at hand. But no one knew about it. In Jerusalem and in Bethlehem, on the Mediterranean coast where the Roman ships lay at sea, on the Sea of Galilee where the fishermen's boats were drawn up on the bank, the Lord was at hand also. But no one knew that their lives were all about to be changed. Everywhere it was business as usual. Herod the king and the Roman governor, Pontius Pilate's predecessor, probably Cyrenius, were in Jerusalem, seeing to matters of government. The innkeeper at Bethlehem was enjoying good business, because the census meant that there were travellers on the road. The parents of the children, then very young or not yet born, who were later to become Jesus' apostles and change the world in His name, were looking after their families and going about their ordinary affairs. The shepherds were out with their sheep on the hillsides. Three strangers were on their way to Jerusalem, looking for a king, they knew not who or what. The Lord was at hand. But no one, save the mother of Jesus herself , knew that anything remarkable was about to happen, let alone what it was; and, when it did happen, nobody realised what had happened or did anything very much about it.

The Son of God was born on earth to live with us, to make the Almighty a living reality, to love us as His own body and to save us for ever. But, amazing though it is, no one was to take the slightest notice. A few shepherds were to hear voices in the sky (no one else did) and go to a shed behind the local inn to see what was going on. The three strangers would arrive, go through a grave ritual which no one understood and go away again, telling, so far as we know, no one at all what they had seen, whom they had found or what they had done or whether it had any meaning or importance. They would come. They would see – and they would vanish. Herod would be led to suppose that there might be treason in the air – and would take political action. But no one else in Bethlehem, no one else in Jerusalem, no one else in Judaea, no one in Rome, the centre of civilisation, would do anything at all. The Lord was at hand. But this great event, this greatest of all events, which was, in time, to turn the whole world order upside down and bring the Roman empire to its knees, would go completely unnoticed and completely unremarked. He would be in the world and the world would know Him not. He would come unto His own and His own would receive Him not. Everyone would carry on with their lives as though nothing had happened.

This was, we must assume, God's will. Had Christ's birth and life been marked by earthquakes or substantial and well-publicised miracles among people who counted in the world, the world would have been told at the time, would have seen, learned, marvelled and, maybe, worshipped. Christ could, when tempted, have commanded that the stones be made bread. He could, when tempted, have thrown Himself down from the pinnacle of the temple in public view and miraculously survived. He could, when tempted, have accepted the kingdoms of the world and ruled them – and everyone would have followed Him and, maybe, no one would have turned to God. We cannot know God's reason. All we know is that the Lord was at hand and the Lord came – and that God saw to it that nobody had the slightest idea what was happening or indeed that anything was happening at all – and, for that reason, that no one took the slightest notice. That is how it was then.

But that is not how it is now, is it? We, you and I. have 2000 years of hindsight, 2000 years of history, 2000 years of Christ's work on earth to tell us what is going on. We have, you and I, our own faith in, and our own knowledge of, Christ, the Son of God. They did not know that the Lord was at hand. We do. They did nothing about it, because they did not know. We know. We know it very well. And, if we do nothing, as they did nothing, we do not have the same excuse as they had. We know what is happening. So what are we to do?

St Paul gives us the answer in the passage from his letter to the Philippians, which I chose as my text. "Rejoice" he said. "Rejoice in the Lord always – and again I say Rejoice. Let your magnanimity be known unto all men. For the Lord is at hand. Be not worn down with the cares of this life. But, in all that you do, by prayer and with thanksgiving, let your requests be made known unto God. And the Peace of God, which passeth all understanding, shall keep your hearts and minds through Jesus Christ our Lord". And, so that we may know what we are to do and how to make and keep ourselves ready for the Lord's coming, his letter continues with words which tell us very clearly what we should be thinking about, what we should be concentrating on and what we should avoid. "Finally, brethren" he wrote. Whatsoever things are true, whatsoever things are honest, whatsoever things are just, whatsoever things are pure, whatsoever things are lovely, whatsoever things are of good report, wherever you find virtue and things that are worthy of praise, think on these things". Think on these things.

I could not hope to improve on these words, though Archbishop Cranmer, in the Collect with which I began, had a good go at it, when he invited us to ask for grace to cast away the works of darkness and put upon us the armour of light – but, like St Paul, he told us to do it now. The Lord is at hand. If we are to be truly ready for His coming, it is to these good things that we must now most urgently turn our minds. We must spend time and thought preparing ourselves for Him. Then Jesus Christ, when He comes, shall find in us – yes, each one of us –a place as worthy for Himself as we can make it: and that is what we must, each of us, now most urgently contrive. We know who is coming – and we know when He is due. We have two weeks to get ready. There is work to be done. Almighty God, give us grace that we may cast away the works of darkness and put upon us the armour of light – now, in the time of this mortal life in which Thy Son, Jesus Christ, came to visit us in great humility – that, in the last day, when He shall come again in His glorious majesty to judge both the quick and the dead, we may rise to the life immortal – through Him who liveth and reigneth with Thee and the Holy Spirit, now and for ever. Amen.

Wicket Gate

Christmas Eve. Collect for Epiphany

We gather here tonight to commemorate the birth of a child, who grew up to change the world. He had, in his working life, no political influence, no money of any significance, no publicity machine, no army – just a small band of followers, who had no idea who He was and, for the most part, did not understand His message. He met no one of any importance, went nowhere of much importance, spending his entire ministry in an unconsidered backwater of the Roman Empire, whose worldly authority he never sought to challenge. Yet, having started with nothing and by preaching nothing but a message of love, He changed the world. Doubters question the detail. Indeed they do – as sometimes we do too. But there can be no doubt, no doubt whatever, that, by reason of what He did and said, He changed the world and overcame the Roman Empire in the process. So it is that, on this special night, the night when we celebrate the birth of this, the Son of God, into our world, the night when we remember that distant stable in distant Bethlehem, I offer you as a text - and not for the first time - the prayer for the Feast of the Epiphany:- O God, who by the leading of a star didst manifest Thy only begotten Son to the Gentiles, mercifully grant that we, who know Thee now by faith, may after this life have the fruition of Thy glorious Godhead, through Jesus Christ our Lord: and I want to couple it with twenty of the best-remembered and most famous words that this remarkable man ever spoke: Ask He said, and it shall be given you. Seek and ye shall find. Knock - and it shall be opened unto you.

Grant that we, who know Thee now by faith, may after this life have the fruition – meet the reality. Faith now, if we can find it. Fruition – reality later. Ask and it shall be given you. Seek and ye shall find.

We live in difficult times. Men and women, old and young, long for the personal fulfilment which will bring them peace of mind. They seek it in work, drive themselves too fast, and fail. They seek it in relationships, which perish because they have no depth. They seek it in drink or drugs, which bring them down in ever-descending spirals and unquenchable flames. Our Church teaches that the way of Christ is the best - some say the only - way forward: and, all over the world today, people are asking: What is this faith you speak of? And how can it be found? And since, as a layman, I have been given the honour of being asked to speak to you tonight, let me tell you how I see it: and, in telling you how I see it, let me, since it is a very special night, come straight back to Christ's birth and to the showing of Christ to the Gentiles, an act of God, beautifully pictured in our crib service today, by the leading of the three wise men by the star to Bethlehem. Let me take you back to that familiar scene and link it with another piece of imagery, which comes from the beginning of John Bunyan's great work, The Pilgrim's Progress, a passage I have shared with you before, a passage which is one of the most vivid ever written of the route to faith, the route which, to a greater or lesser extent, if we are to find the faith we speak of, we all have to travel.

At the beginning of that book, we meet Mr Christian, a man alone, whose plight, like that of so many of us today, is that the night is dark and he is very miserable and does not know what to believe or how to find faith. He comes upon Evangelist, who can be his guide. "Then said Evangelist: "If this is thy condition, why standest thou still?". He answered "Because I know not whither to go. Whither must I fly?". Then said Evangelist, pointing with his finger over a very wide field: "Seest thou yonder wicket gate?" The man said "No". Then said the other: "Seest thou then yonder shining light?" He said "I think I do". Then said Evangelist: "Keep that light in your eye and go directly up thereto. So shalt thou find the gate, at which, when thou knockest, it shall be told thee what thou shalt do." And, as I watched, the man began to run.

Seest thou yonder wicket gate? No. Seest thou then yonder shining light? I think I do. If you had asked the wise men on their journey those questions, I suspect they would have given you very much the same answers. For, when it is dark enough to see the stars, it is seldom light enough to see the ground: and a star is very hard to follow, even when it appears to be moving. And, save that we are not wise, we are all like those wise men, are we not? We spend our lives, as they did, searching through the darkness to find that barely seen shining light, which shows the way to God, scrambling through pitfalls, falling into despondencies, achieving occasional small victories, alone, as it seems, in the darkness, with only the chill of ignorance and the shiver of doubt for company, not knowing quite where we are going or whether we are on the right route at all, but believing, often against all the evidence of what we see and hear, that we are not alone and that we are somehow getting there. This is how it has always been for me. Is it not the same for you?

Seest thou yonder wicket gate? No. Seest thou then yonder shining light? I think I do. Keep that light in your eye and go directly up thereto. So shalt thou find the gate, at which, when thou knockest, it shall be told thee what thou shalt do. I cannot watch the three wise men without thinking of that imagery.

But it does not stop there. For, in this amazing story, the wise men reached their destination and found what they were looking for. And thereby hangs the rest of the story. For what were they looking for? And what did they find? They were looking for a king, whom they should worship. But they found, apparently, nothing of the kind. To the ordinary eye, there was no king at Bethlehem, no trappings of power, nothing worthy of worship, nothing remarkable at all. They found, as the story goes, two weary and travel-stained young people with a very small baby, sitting in some considerable discomfort in an outhouse full of animals. This was not what they were looking for: nor was it what they expected to find. Though the inn was full and the village packed with people, no one, except a few farmworkers, seemed to be taking any notice. No one was celebrating anything. No one seemed to think that anything remarkable had happened at all. Had you or I been there, we would almost certainly have suggested that we go back to Jerusalem to make more enquiries. We would surely have asked a great deal more before we gave our gold away. But that is not what these wise men did. We know what they did. They fell on their knees and worshipped Him, opened their treasures and presented their gifts. Why did they do that? The evidence was that this was not what they were looking for. But their faith gave them eyes to see and hearts to believe more than the evidence disclosed. But for their faith, they would have said: "We have come to the wrong place. There is no king here" and looked somewhere else. So, without faith, would we. But what they did is as good an example of the true meaning and operation of faith as the Bible contains. And once again, save that we are not wise, we are all like those wise men, are we not? I am a lawyer and I believe in looking at the evidence to find out the truth. But faith involves looking beyond the evidence. Faith is the conviction that the evidence represents less than the whole truth, the conviction that the reality is greater than the eye can immediately see or the intellect immediately comprehend.

Yes, we can all be like those wise men. Their faith led them to see that these dishevelled and destitute people were the real family of God, fit instantly and without question to be worshipped and adored. Our faith tells us the same. Just as their faith led them to believe, at once, that they were, there and then, in the presence of the real family of God, so, by exactly the same process, our faith leads us to believe those great truths about the personification of God, Father, Son and Holy Spirit, which we are all about to declare in the Creed. Without faith, those men's pilgrimage would have been a waste of time and effort. They would have turned round, gone away and taken their gifts, their talents, elsewhere. Without faith, my friends, that is precisely what we would do too. Seest thou yonder wicket gate? No. Seest thou then yonder shining light? I think I do. If you ask the way and truly search through the darkness, you will see that shining light. If you follow the shining light, you will find the gate. If you open the gate, you will find what you are looking for. The wise men did just that. So with faith may we. Faith now. Eternal life with God later.

That is the promise which this child grew up to make to us. Ask and it shall be given you. Seek and ye shall find you. Knock and it shall be opened unto you.

My prayer, on this special night, for each one of you, old and young, is that your faith may grow and become a quiet and convincing power to sustain you on this day and in all your days: and may Almighty God, who, by the leading of a star, did manifest His only begotten Son to the Gentiles, grant, by His infinite goodness and mercy, that we, who know Him now by faith, may, after this life, through Jesus Christ our Lord, have the fruition of His glorious Godhead. I wish you all a very happy Christmas.

Christmas Day

Unto you is born a Saviour. St Luke Ch 2 v 11

St Luke's Gospel, Chapter 2: "For unto you is born this day in the City of David a Saviour, which is Christ the Lord". Joyous words indeed, words which we hear with delight at every Christmas. But does it mean anything to you? Unto YOU is born A SAVIOUR. A Saviour is a person who saves you. Do you feel that you have been saved by this child? Do you, to be frank, feel that you have been saved at all?

Christmas is, in this our day, the great family Festival. It is a time when families come together, spend time together, give gifts to each other, eat together, laugh together. It is a time for huge generosity, for the pouring out of love on a grand scale. Those who have the great good fortune to live in families find time and money for a grand show, a grand sharing of affection. It is a good time for us all - a very good time: and, on my own behalf and on behalf of Stephen our Rector and the Parochial Church Council, I wish you all a very happy Christmas. But does it mean anything more to you, anything beyond the gifts and the togetherness and the warmth of family feelings? Is it truly special to you? If so, why? Why, of all places, have we come to Church?

We have come to Church because it is the anniversary of the birth of a baby, at first sight, a rather ordinary baby, born apparently to unmarried parents in conditions of unusual discomfort and squalor. You don't find babies born these days in stables, surrounded by farm animals and visited by inquisitive local residents. You don't find new-born babies wrapped up in blankets, lying in boxes of hay. Yet these are the things we celebrate, the things we sing about, the manger, the oxen, the shepherds. And today you have chosen to leave the comfort of your homes, chosen to leave the presents under the Christmas tree, chosen to leave the joy of your family's coming together at home - you have chosen to leave all these things to come here - to come here to celebrate the birth of this baby 2000 years ago. Is it just habit which brings you here? Or just tradition? Is it simply 'we always go to Church on Christmas day'? Why, of all places, come here?

You know the textbook answer as well as I do. The textbook answer is that you do not come here to celebrate the birth of an ordinary baby. You come here to celebrate the birth of a very special baby, the baby whom we call the Son of God, the baby by whom it is said we have been saved. But is that textbook answer an answer which is real to you? Do you truly feel that you have been saved? Do you really care whether you have been saved? That is a question, to which only you know the answer. And you can only know the real answer, if it is a question which you have really asked yourself, which you have really badgered your brain to find an answer to. So I ask you: Does Christ's birth, the event which brings you here, really matter to you? And if so why?

Since I, a layman, have the privilege of speaking to you this Christmas morning, let me tell you why it really matters. The birth of a baby, whoever it may be, is an everyday event. Babies are born every minute of the day and all over the place. We don't usually hear about it: and, unless the parents are our friends or relatives, we generally take no notice. But the birth of this baby matters, matters fundamentally, to all of us because this baby was special. For we, the Church, assert - and have asserted for nearly 2000 years now - that this was the once-for-all birth on earth of the person of Almighty God, the once-for-all birth of the child who alone was to grow into the one man who would lead a sinless life, the one man who would tell us the truth about God, the one man who, by choosing to die an agonising death in appalling circumstances, would be the one man who would buy for us forgiveness for all our wrongdoing: the one man who would give to each of us the chance to attain eternal life with God, when our lives here are finished. We, the Church, assert that nothing more important than this has ever occurred, will ever occur, in the whole of human history. This was God's once-for-all venture.

There were not going go be any more virgin births. There were not going to be any more sinless lives. Beside this, every other event in history pales into insignificance. It is as important as that. That God should have come to earth for you and me is the greatest thing that has ever happened.

I am in Church today to join with others in celebrating this happening, to give thanks to God for it and to commit my life anew to the man, whom this baby grew into and became. I am not alone in this. I am doing what the Church teaches me to do. I am doing what hundreds of thousands of men and women, old and young, do on many Sundays and on every Christmas day. I am celebrating the coming of Christ, His coming into the world, His presence in my life. I am celebrating the presence of Christ in myself and in all those I love: and I am committing myself anew to Him because of that presence. That is why I am here today. But is it the same for you? Are you here to celebrate the birth on earth of the person whom you truly perceive to be Christ, the Son of God? Are you here because you truly feel the presence of Christ in you? Or are you here just to pay a sort of lip service, with a generalised hope that there may be something in it, but you do not quite know what? If it is the latter, I know how you feel. You are not alone. Hundreds of thousands share your predicament. I have been there: and I know. But believe me. Whether you realise it or not, Christ, the baby born on this day 2000 years ago, is in you, is, through His Holy Spirit, for the whole of your life, a living part of you: and it is that birth, the creation of that presence, which is the true cause of our Christmas celebrations.

The presence of Christ in you cannot be seen, cannot be heard. It is not capable of detection by any of the senses. Awareness of the presence of Christ in you may be instantaneous. It may take a long time to make itself felt. But the truth is that, because of Christ's life and death, the Holy Spirit, which is Christ's presence, is, every day and all the time, whether we realise it or not, at work in each of us, is at work in each of you. It is, if I may borrow words from Billy Elliott, like electricity. You cannot see electricity. You cannot feel it. But you know that, if you turn on the switch, the light will come and the darkness will be taken away. You know that, if you put the plug in the socket, the power will come on and things will be changed. You don't refuse to believe in electricity because you can't see it or hear it. You know, as a matter of experience, that, unless there is a power cut, it will be there when you want it and it will make all things different. Those who have no experience of electricity would laugh at you, if you told them about it. They would refuse to believe in it. But you know better. You believe in electricity because you have experience of it: and you know, know for sure, that those who say it is not there and does not work are wrong. So it is with the Holy Spirit - with Christ, present in you and at work in you. You may be unable to see it or hear it. But those, whose hearts are open to the experience of it, know that it is there just the same. The power and the light are always at hand - for you and for me. It may take time to become aware of it, because God moves in His own way and in His own time. But the power and the light, which are the presence of Christ in your life, are vital for your soul's health. You can live life without Christ, just as you can live life without electricity: but it is very much darker and very much colder if you do. Christ in your life is like petrol in your car. Your car can run without petrol, you know it can. It can run all right - but it can only run downhill.

And it all started on that distant day, two thousand years ago, when this baby was born. No ordinary baby, but the Son of God Himself, the child who was going to bring the power, the child who was destined to bring us the chance of a fulfilled life and a vision of eternity in His company and in God's keeping. I wish you all a happy Christmas therefore. For to you is born this day a Saviour which is Christ the Lord.

Many Sparrows

In the beginning was the Word. St John Ch 1 vv 1-14

I offer you as a text this morning Jesus' words from St Luke's Gospel, Ch 12: Are not five sparrows sold for two farthings, and not one of them is forgotten before God? Fear not, ye are of more value than many sparrows. You are of more value than many sparrows. It seems to be a long way from Christmas. I will come back to it.

Last Sunday at your service of 9 lessons and carols, you heard the ninth lesson from the opening words of St John's Gospel "In the beginning was the word". If you come to St Michaels tonight, you will hear it again. We hear it every Christmas. It has become the climax of every such service with the introduction "St John unfolds the great mystery of the Incarnation" - and that, of course, is what he does. Those 14 verses from the beginning of St John's Gospel, 229 words, more than 200 of which are words of one syllable, are one of the most powerful pieces of philosophy in the whole of our Christian theology. In those few words St John unfolds the great mystery of the Incarnation - and unfolds a great deal more as well.

For a start, he tells us about the beginning. In the beginning was the word. The word is the spirit of God, some say the creating, the communicating spirit of God. Everything that came into existence sprang- springs - from the working of that spirit: and that spirit was the source of the light that illuminates, gives a living soul to, every man and woman born into the world. This is our faith. It is what our Church teaches. It is not a process susceptible to logical explanation. It is a process which explains the magic of the existence and variety of thinking humanity. But this is, of course, not all that he unfolds. For he tells us too that the word, the spirit of God, was made flesh and dwelt among us, was made man and came to live here: and the only begotten of the Father, that spirit made human, was born and lived and taught and died, so that man might see how the light, the living soul, should be deployed by us.

Thus St John unfolds the great mystery of the incarnation - the spirit of God, born as man on earth to teach us how to think and how to live. But that is not all that he unfolds in this remarkable passage. For in it he unfolds also the great mystery of the relationship between God and man, the process by which man, the creature, and God, the creator, are, through the living and teaching of Christ, made part of one another. "He came unto his own and his own received Him not. But unto them that received Him, to them gave He power to become the sons of God". The message is that, despite our God-given free will, we are not just random and futile creatures let loose upon the world. We have, you have, I have, we all have, the power to become the sons of God, the power to build a spiritual relationship with the spirit of God which was responsible for our creation as people, the power to build a relationship which survives physical death, just as it survives the vicissitudes of human life, the power to build a relationship which can bring us to that mysterious and utterly blessed condition, which Jesus called eternal life. This is what Jesus taught us. This is what St John unfolds. This is our faith. This is what our Church teaches.

The message is that we have no automatic right to become the children of God. But we have within us the power to achieve that position: and the issue for us, the issue today and every day, the issue for the whole of our lives, is whether we use, or decline to use, that power, whether we build, or decide not to build, the relationship, which will enable us to achieve that result. We have it in us to live the life, to do the things, which will build that relationship. We also have it in us to refrain from the life, to refrain from doing the things which will build that relationship. We spend our lives deciding, or perhaps not deciding, what we will do in this regard.

How is this relationship to be built? Jesus, who knew the answer, answered it in differing ways. He said that the route was through true commitment to Him - "He that truly commits himself to Me, though he were dead, yet shall he live". He also said that the route was through the things we do - "Not everyone that saith unto me Lord Lord shall enter into the kingdom of Heaven, but he that doeth the will of My Father, which is in Heaven".

There are some who will argue that it does not matter much what you do, so long as you believe - that, so long as you believe in God, accept the divinity of Christ or whatever is asked of you, your sins will be forgiven, what you do forgotten and all will be well. Others will argue that it is what you do that counts, that, if you have never found belief in this life, you will find out the truth when life is over: and your non-belief will be forgiven and your deeds rewarded.

Differing views are sincerely held and many have sound scriptural foundation: and, if there is an answer, I don't know what it is. But, for what it may be worth, I am sure of one thing - and it is this, that the all-pervading, all-creating, all-mighty spirit of God is not to be tied down by human rules or conditional clauses. It is God who forgives. It is God who decides. It is God who knows the secrets of our hearts. Our duty, both to God and to our fellow-humans, is clear.

We are God's creation. It is to us that He has given the power to become His children. Our life span is limited. Our choices as to how we live are, in many ways, limited also. But, whether our lives be long or short, whether our choices are varied or few, it is to us, to you, to me, that the power to become the child of God has been given: and, because we have this power, we are valuable. Without this power, we have little value - five sparrows sold for two farthings. With this power, we are, each of us, treasures beyond price. We have been created by the Almighty with the power St John has spoken of. The hand that made us is divine. Each one of us is, in this sense, a masterpiece.

We may not know much about God as we weave our way about this world. But we know, or think we know, a lot about value. If you have a beautiful picture, painted by a master, you look after it carefully, so that it remains a thing of beauty and keeps its value. If you have a beautiful home, you do the same. The things we value most - family, home, treasures, talents - these are the things we look after best. Your soul, your spirit, is the work of an almighty hand. It is, in City terms, your most valuable asset: and you owe it to God to look after it properly.

And the way to look after it properly, whether we like it or not, is to live right - to do good things rather than bad things, to help others rather than hinder them, to build up others rather than cut them down, to live, in a word, the loving life that Jesus told us to live. "This is my commandment - that you love one another as I have loved you".

We must do the things that Jesus told us to do. We know what they are. We must refrain from the things which Jesus told us not to do - we know what they are too: and we must do this, not because we hope that these practices will bring us to Heaven, but because our souls, the personalities which inhabit these temporary bodies of ours, are made or unmade, are looked after or neglected, are hoovered and dusted or left to rot, by the effect our conduct has on them. Do foul things and your soul is in the end defiled by the effect of them. Do honourable things and your soul is, in the end, honoured, made clean, hoovered and dusted, if you like, by the effect of them: and the result is very probably precisely what you would expect.

You receive Jesus by listening to His words, by prayer and through Communion: and by doing what He says. To those that receive Him has been given the power to become the children of God. You have that power. Whether and how you use that power, that asset, is your choice - yours alone. Are not five sparrows sold for two farthings: and not one of them is forgotten before God. Be not afraid therefore - you are of more value....... than many sparrows.

Alpha and Omega

Revelation. Ch 1 v 8

From this morning's first Reading. I am Alpha and Omega, the beginning and the ending, saith the Lord, the Almighty - the Almighty.

I want to ask you a question. You believe in God - otherwise you would not be here. So I ask you: Do you believe in a God who is almighty? Have you thought about, have you turned your mind to, the almightiness of God and its importance? Do you believe in a God, who can do anything He chooses? Or do you believe that there are things God cannot do? I know what the Christian Church teaches. It teaches the Apostles' Creed, which begins with the words: 'I believe in God the Father almighty': and the Nicene Creed, which begins: "We believe in one God, the Father, the almighty". The Church has always taught, has always asserted, that God is almighty - which means that there is nothing He cannot do: and, Sunday after Sunday, we say it - we say it every time we meet. But have you made up your mind about it and come to terms with it? And do you believe it? Do you believe in the almightiness of God? And, if you do, what do you do about it?

I ask this question because, while I know what the Church has always taught, I sometimes wonder what the Church really believes now. I speak to many people, devout people, priests even: and many of them express doubts about the ability of God to do some things. I know many professing Christians, who cannot bring themselves to believe that Christ was born of a virgin, because (you know how the argument goes) we all know that children are not born like that. I know many professing Christians, who don't believe in the physical resurrection of Jesus from the dead, but believe only in a spiritual resurrection - and part of their argument is that a physical resurrection simply cannot have happened. They say there is no need to believe in these things - you can be a convinced and convincing Christian without believing them: and doubtless you can, I don't want to argue. But do you believe, as you assert in the Creed, in a God who is almighty, in a God who can do anything he chooses? And, if you do, what should you be doing about it?

For what it may be worth, I myself believe in an Almighty God. I believe that God has a will as to what should be done on earth and that He has the power to bring it about, if He chooses - a power, if He chooses, to override the laws of nature and do things as He will. I believe that God can, and sometimes does, communicate directly with human beings. I believe that God can, and sometimes does, cause miracles to happen in everyday life. I believe that God can, and has been known to, bring about a virgin birth. I believe that God can, and has been known to, bring a dead body back to life. I believe this, because I can see no alternative. If you believe in God at all, then either you believe in a God, who is almighty and can do anything: or else you believe in a God, whose power is limited by the laws of nature, which is a logical contradiction. A God, who exists but is limited in His powers, is no God at all. If God exists, He must be a God of unlimited power, a God to whom nothing is impossible. No other sort of God has any meaning at all.

What do we know about this God? Let me tell you what we know. The Church teaches, and I believe, that Jesus was the Son of God: and the Church teaches, and I believe, that Jesus, through God's miracle-working will, rose from the dead. I believe that, if this Jesus, who was to rise from the dead, was indeed the Son of God, then He knew things we do not know: and one of the things he knew, one of the things which he alone knew because of who he was, was the truth about the nature of God: and, so that we might know it, He told us about it, He told us about the nature of God. He told us that we should speak to God in prayer: and He told us what words to use when we do: and, in telling us what words to use when we pray, he gave us a great deal of information about the God we pray to. He told us that God listens. He referred to God as 'The Father'. He told us that God was in a place called heaven. He told us to treat God's name as holy. He told us that God has a kingdom, which we may reach. He told us that God has a will, a will for those of us living on earth, which, day in and day out, we should try to do. He told us that God can cleanse our consciences by forgiving our sins. He told us that God can give us our daily bread. He told us that God can deliver us from evil. He told us that the kingdom and the power belong to God for ever: and that God lives in glory. In teaching us how to pray to God, He gave us all that information about the God we pray to - and in particular, that God has a will for us: and that God has the power, if He chooses to exercise it, to do what needs to be done.

This is what Jesus told us: and we have to believe that he was telling us the truth. Do you believe it? Is there any alternative? Consider the amazing drama of this morning's Gospel reading. Jesus, risen from the dead, faces Thomas who has expressed justifiable doubts about the resurrection. 'Look at me. Feel the imprint of the nails. Put your hand into the gash in my side. Be not faithless, but believe'. Thomas tests it. He responds: 'My Lord and my God': and Jesus does not contradict him. He accepts what Thomas says. He says: 'Because you have seen me, you have believed'. Thomas' words are significant enough. But Jesus' acceptance of them surely means very much more. The risen Christ is Lord and God: and God, through Christ's rising, has shown that there is nothing He cannot do.

God, then, is almighty, the Lord and creator of all things, greater than great, beyond measurement, beyond dimensions. What should we do about it? Human reaction to the presence of God has always been to do what the Church has always taught us to do - to abandon all pretence of the importance of oneself (for we are nothing by comparison with God) and fall down and worship. But is this what we do? All religions, not just our own, teach that we should be silent in awe at the presence of the God we worship: and that no effort should be spared, nothing should be left undone, to show our respect and adoration for this, the greatest of all beings, who is responsible for our creation and preservation and all the blessings of our life. I was, a few weeks ago, in Seville Cathedral - a huge and beautiful structure, full of the most amazing and valuable creations that man has ever contrived, all put together and dedicated to the glory of God. All this was done, over hundreds of years, because nothing less than the greatest that man could contrive could possibly be good enough for God. But is this how we think of our duty to God in the Church of England now? Do we truly stand in awe of God in the year 2001? Do we truly treat God with respect in the year 2001? There was a time when seeking Communion with the risen Christ was viewed as being one of the most important and exciting events in a Christian's life - a huge privilege: and when, before that rich and cleansing experience, hours of prayer and spiritual preparation were recommended. There was a time when at least we were expected to get up early and eat nothing before seeking Communion. Now some (I do not say all. I hope it is only a few) take Communion without a second thought - as though it was no more important an event than coming down to breakfast. There was a time when the use of God's name was a special thing, when it was thought wrong to take God's name in vain. Now it is commonly used as an expletive - and nobody turns a hair. Sometimes we do not appear any more to treat God as great or worthy of respect at all. The Church has somehow given the impression that, since all our sins are going to be forgiven anyway, we need not do much to show respect in our attitude towards God. They recently conducted a survey in a neighbouring parish to find out why people did not come to church very often. The answer was that they were, as they put it, too busy. This is a dreadful thing - no other religion in the world would countenance such an attitude - but no one was surprised at it: and I very much fear that we have lost our respect for the Almighty and that too many of us have been lulled into forgetting just how vitally important Almighty God and our approach to Him is in the conduct of our lives.

I hope it is not like that for you: and, for some of you, I know that it is not. But I fear very much that some of us are falling into bad habits. Jesus taught us that God the Father is a loving God: and it may be good that, through our reading and understanding of the Gospels, we have now come to lose the terror, which our forefathers felt, at the thought of the judgements of God. But we are seriously mistaken, if we allow the loss of that feeling of terror to be turned into a loss of a feeling of awe and wonder, a loss of respect, a loss of the need for worship. No matter how clever we think we are, no matter how strong or how successful, we are, all of us, as dust and ashes in the sight of God - loved dust and ashes maybe, but dust and ashes nevertheless: and God is Alpha and Omega, the beginning and the end, the Almighty, to whom are due, from us and from all His servants, blessing and honour and glory and power today and every day and for ever.

If God is truly almighty: if Christ was truly God's Son: if God truly overrode the natural processes and raised Christ from the dead: if we are truly given the chance of attaining eternal life with that Almighty God through Christ's death and resurrection: if all these things are true, then surely we must put God first in our lives and strive to obey Christ's first commandment, which was that we should love God with all our heart and soul and mind and strength: and perhaps those of us who need it should make a new start in this by trying to get back to the idea of treating God with that awe and respect which is truly due from the creature to his creator. So I ask: Do you believe in an Almighty God? And if so, what do you do about it?

Were the whole realm of nature mine, (we have all just sung this verse with gusto) that were an offering far too small. Love so amazing, so divine, demands my soul, my life, my all. Well, doesn't it? And how much do we give?

When they Had
Opened their Treasures
Epiphany. St Matthew Ch 2 v 11

Today is the third Sunday after the Epiphany - and the Epiphany is the day when the Church celebrates the showing of Christ to the world in the coming of the three wise men to the stable at Bethlehem. About two years ago, Dr David Jenkins, then Bishop of Durham, was widely reported as having said that he did not believe in the three wise men and described them as part of the Christmas mythology. His words naturally caused concern to those whose faith is based on the ordinary teachings of the Church. Similarly, a few weeks ago, a Committee of the Church of England published a report, in which they said that they doubted the existence of Hell as a place where people were cast into everlasting fire. This likewise caused concern to those whose faith is based on the ordinary teachings of the Church – and I want, as a layman, to try to face the issues raised by these apparent changes of doctrine. Engaged, as we all are, in the long slow search for faith, should we feel angry or frustrated by these apparent changes of heart? What are we to make of it all?

To address this question, I offer you two texts. First, from St Matthew's story of the three wise men, St Matthew Ch 2 v.11: "And when they had opened their treasures, they presented unto Him gifts". The second text, a long way further on in the Gospel story, is from St John, Ch 14. "Philip said to Jesus: "Lord, show us the Father and it sufficeth us". Jesus answered: "Have I been with you all this time and yet have you not known me, Philip? He that has seen me has seen the Father. I am the way, the truth and the life".

Philip had walked with Jesus throughout His ministry and had been permanently in His company. He was with Him all that time and did not know Him for who He was or the way for what it was. So how are we, who do not physically hear or see our Lord and are not, in ordinary language, in His company, how are we to do better than Philip and to know Him or know the way?

The Christian Faith asserts that Christ is with us always, that, through our baptism and our believing, He is never apart from us or we apart from Him. I believe that. I believe that I somehow speak to Christ when I pray, that I somehow hear Christ when I listen, and that Christ is somehow with me, as a part of me, wherever I am. I believe that this is true for you too. This is my faith, because it is what I have come to believe. It is what the Christian Faith asserts. But what do we say to those, who would like to believe, but presently do not? To those, who cannot hear, because they do not believe yet: and cannot believe, because they cannot hear yet?

If I knew a straightforward way of finding faith, I would tell you what it is. But I do not know of one. Nobody does. To find and follow the faith has never been easy. It is not like learning a new language or attaining a new skill. It is a process of attuning the spirit, so that a belief is gradually created. Faith is elusive, a gradually growing mental process, by which a person comes to be convinced of the truth of facts which are not capable of verification by ordinary methods. A blind man needs faith to believe that a leaf is green. If he had been able to see during his youth and went blind, say, in middle age, the faith would be easier to attain. It will be much more difficult to attain, if he was born blind and has had no experience of what colours are. Developing faith in Christ is, for many people, like that. There are tens of thousands of people, who, just like the blind man with no experience of colour, have, in their adult lives, no experience of God or Christ at all. They have been looking the other way, they have known no need to listen. To their eyes and ears, there is nothing to see, nothing to listen for. They have absolutely nowhere to start.

Faith comes from a variety of sources: and, for each of us, the experience is different. God, either in the person of Christ or otherwise, reveals Himself to each of us in different ways and at different times. Paul met Christ in a blinding light on the Damascus road and the experience was, once for all, utterly convincing. The Roman emperor Constantine, at whose orders the Roman empire adopted the Christian religion, saw a golden cross in the sky and at once believed. For them, and for countless others down the years who have undergone an instant conversion, the impact of the moment entirely overrides the intellect, blows away the doubts and leaves a clear and unequivocal belief, which remains in place for the whole of a person's life. That is how faith is found by some. But, for the rest of us, it is not so easy and not so fast.

It is very often very slow, very gradual. It starts from small things and goes on to bigger things, a gradual accumulation till, probably unbidden, a conviction is created which brooks no denial. The difficulty, so often, is in finding a place to start – and this is where my first text comes in: "And when they had opened their treasures, they presented unto Him gifts" – these three wise men, for those of us in the Western world, part of the traditional Christmas story. Who they were, where they came from, where they went to, whom they told about what they had seen, everything about them is shrouded in mystery. St Matthew speaks of them. The other Gospel writers do not. The Bishop of Durham, when pressed for an answer, said that, on balance, he thought it unlikely that they ever came at all. He may be right – I cannot know. Neither can he. But the point is that they, these three wise men, are part of the traditional imagery, which is, for us, the Christmas story – like the bleak midwinter, the inn with no room in it, the cattle in the stable, the shepherds watching their flocks, the angels from the realms of glory. For myself I believe that, when Jesus was born, God was born on earth – not just a baby, who would grow up to be a great prophet, but God in person, God walking on earth as man, to show us the way – the greatest thing that ever happened in all human history: and I believe that if such a thing, such a miraculous thing, happened, it was and is only to be expected that miraculous events should accompany it – so that the wise men from the East and the angels in the sky pose no intellectual problems for me. I see no reason to disbelieve them.

But the point I want to make is that, for many, indeed I suspect for most of us, those stories, that imagery, are the starting point for our journey from ignorance to faith. Our journey starts there – starts with the imagery, because, for many of us, there has never been anywhere else to start. Until there is a religious cogwheel for the mind to mesh into, the wheels of faith cannot start to turn. Unless there is a religious knitting needle to cast on to, you cannot begin to knit the garment of your faith. The Christian faith is full of imagery. Whether you take the imagery of the Christmas story or the imagery of the Easter story or the imagery of Hell, all of which are devoutly and passionately believed to be true by countless thousands, but are, in part or in whole, historically challenged by others, it is the imagery which sits in our minds as telling us the Christian story: and it is from that imagery that our journey to faith begins.

The imagery is like scaffolding round a building. If you build a house, you put up scaffolding round the structure to support it while it is under construction and to make it easier to lay the bricks, put in the window frames and complete the roof. If you tried to put up the building without scaffolding, you would find it very difficult and might not get very far. The structure might fall down before you had finished. But, when the building is complete, you take away the scaffolding and the structure stands alone, clear to be seen in all its glory. So it is with faith. The imagery is part of the story which those, who were inspired to write the books of the Bible, were inspired to pass on to us: and that imagery has always been, and is now, a valid and natural starting point in our journey into faith. The imagery is the scaffolding round the gradually growing structure of our faith. As our faith grows and our convictions deepen, we can, each of us, as individuals, if our intellect drives us to do it, discard some of the imagery, because, like the scaffolding round the building, we do not need it any more to support the structure. If, through leading lives of study, prayer and dedication, as the Bishop of Durham has done, we find ourselves with a faith, fully constructed and immovably founded on the rock of intellectual conviction, we may be able to discard the imagery altogether, just as the builder, when the structure is complete and will stand free and proud in its completeness, can discard the scaffolding altogether.

But most of us, I expect, never reach that condition. For most of us, the structure of our faith never becomes that complete until the day when Christ comes and takes us to Himself. As St Paul put it in that great passage in his letter to the Corinthians: "Now we see through a glass darkly. But then we shall see face to face. Now, while I live, I know in part. But then I shall know, even as I also am known". Our knowledge of God and Christ, yours and mine, is never likely, in this life, to be better than incomplete – and we will need the imagery still to support us in our journey towards the light. But, if it be the case, as I believe it is, that Bishop Jenkins has got further down that road in this life than you or I are likely to get and can discard the imagery because he has no longer any need of it, I rejoice with him – and so should we all. But let us, you and I, neither despise nor discard the imagery, because it is real to us and we need it. Those three wise men are very important to us. In the imagery of which I speak, they opened their treasures to the infant Lord and presented unto Him gifts, In the real world, in which we live, the imagery, of which they are a part, is a gift of enormous value to us. Let us treasure that gift and give thanks to God for it. Without it, we might well have no faith at all.

Meanwhile let us concentrate, you and I, on the things which really matter – the revealed truth, told us by Christ Himself: "Have you been so long time with me and have you not known me Philip? He who has seen Me has seen the Father".

He that believes in
Me will have everlasting life

St John. Ch 6 v 47.

A story is told of that great Methodist preacher, Dr Donald Soper, who used, well into his seventies, to go and preach, once a week, from a soap box at Marble Arch. One day, he was heckled by a roughly-dressed man, who said: "Come off it Mate. I know your man Jesus. He was a revolutionary like me. He said "Hang all the law and the prophets", didn't he? Hang all the law and the prophets - that's what he said". Donald Soper knew his New Testament. "You are right, my friend" he said. "Jesus did use those words. He was asked what was the Great Commandment in the law: and he replied:" The first commandment is this -Thou shalt love the Lord thy God with all thy heart, soul, mind and strength: and the second is like, namely this: Thou shalt love thy neighbour as thyself. There is no other commandment greater than these. On these two commandments hang all the law and the prophets".

Hang all the law and the prophets. Jesus did say it. It is an extreme example of a misleading phrase, what today we would call a soundbite, some startling phrase, taken out of context and given a meaning it was never intended to have. And I wonder today how many preachers will be seizing upon the soundbite in today's New Testament reading and preaching on Jesus' reported words: "He that believes in me will have everlasting life". How many preachers today will seize upon that passage and preach that faith – that, if you believe in Christ, you will attain everlasting life. How simple it all sounds. But what does it mean? What is it about Jesus that we are asked to believe? And, if we believe it, what, if anything, are we to do about it? Our bishop tells us that the word "Believe" here is not an accurate translation. The original text, I am told, correctly translated, reports Jesus as saying "He that commits his life to me will have everlasting life", which is altogether different. There are some who preach that, if you believe that somehow Jesus is King, that is enough, you don't have to work it out, you don't have to do anything about it, your belief, on its own, whatever that belief involves, will guarantee you eternal life with God. This passage, like many other passages, can mislead us terribly, if they are taken out of context and used as a catch-all description of the Christian Faith.

You see - we are in difficulties here. There are so many passages in the Bible which, if taken by themselves and relied on by themselves, can be used to define the Christian faith and to distort it. There are sayings attributed to Jesus, which can be taken on their own as encapsulating the Christian faith, but which contradict each other. We have to remember that Jesus' words were not recorded at the time, but that they were written down, third, fourth or fifth-hand at best, thirty years and more after they were spoken: and that they were spoken in a Hebrew dialect and translated from that into Hebrew, Greek and Latin and thereafter into English - so that, if we are to be realistic and seek for the truth, we have to accept that we do not truly know precisely what Jesus said or precisely what He meant by it. We cannot use our faith to make us believe that He literally said the English words our Bible attributes to Him because he did not. We use our faith to believe in His divinity and to guide us to the substance and meaning of his teaching. There are many, whose faith leads them to believe that a blind trust in Jesus as King is enough, who go no further and seek to go no further - who stand with eyes closed and arms outspread, intoning "Jesus is King" and closing their minds to everything except what they perceive as His voice. I have no quarrel with this. If this is their revelation of Christ and they truly listen to His voice and this is enough for them, I cannot and will not assert that they are wrong. But I ask, Is it enough? Should it be enough for you and me?

I am worried, when I see adults, in this context, acting apparently like star-struck teenagers seen on the television screen, overcome with wonder at the sight or presence of a David Beckham or a Michael Jackson, engaging in a sort of mindless worship.

I believe that Christ deserves much more from us than some footballer or pop star. God gave us minds to think with: and I believe that we owe it to Him to get our minds involved in our faith, to try to understand what we believe and why we believe it, so that we can explain it to ourselves and go on to explain it to others. The core of the Christian faith lies in Christ's teaching of the two great Commandments, the first of which is, as Donald Soper reminded his heckler, that we should love God with all our heart, soul, mind and strength, which is a very demanding process: and this is something we cannot do with our eyes shut and our minds closed. It is difficult to love God, as we understand the term. Those of us, who have been lucky enough to experience love in our lives, know that love grows gradually, starting from slight acquaintance and moving through time to become a more powerful feeling, which becomes, after time and experience, yes, and understanding of the person concerned, a true, and eventually unbreakable, bond. It is the treasure house of shared experiences, which causes love to develop and grow and become indestructible. To love someone we do not see and cannot measure, someone with whom we seem, at first at least, to have no shared experience at all, seems an impossibility. Yet this, on the basis of the words as presently translated for us, is what Jesus seems to have commanded us to do. Taken literally, I do not think it can be done.

The answer to this problem - and it is a serious one - is, I think, to consider very carefully the meaning of the word "Love" in this context. Love is a word with many meanings. But, if we think about it, in these days, we come to love someone by building a loving relationship with them: and my belief is that Jesus' command was that we should work full-time at building a loving relationship with the God He told us of: and that we should use all our heart, that is our emotional strength, all our soul, that is our spiritual strength, all our mind, that is our intellectual strength and all our strength, that is our physical strength, in that enterprise. It is the absolute core of the faith I profess, that our task in this life is to find our way to God - and the way to God is to work at building a loving relationship with Him. Christ, I believe, does not look for love at first sight. Nor is he interested in puppy love. Nor do I think that He demands unthinking adoration either. What He does seek from us is that we should spend our lives building this relationship, starting, as all such relationships start, from first acquaintance and moving gradually on from there to get to know Him through experiences shared, through problems shared, through happiness shared, through agony shared, through understanding shared, until, in the fullness of God's own time, we come to know that we cannot proceed without His company or do anything worth-while without His presence and His blessing: and that we should do what he requires us to do. That is what is involved in loving. It is a relationship which takes a long time to build - and most of us, in our lives, probably will not get there at all. I hope and believe it is enough that we should have tried: and we may find that the process of dying turns out to involve a very steep learning curve.

But we do not embark on this enterprise on our own. Christ was, we believe, by some miraculous means, a part of God: and this part of God is, through the Holy Spirit, in each of us always. There is, as a result of Jesus' prayers, His promises and His sacrifice, a divine spark in each of us, the divine spark which gives us an immortal soul. The Church teaches that, by God's Grace, a part of the spirit of that divine Christ is in you, that Christ is with you always and His spirit an innate part of you - Christ in you, never absent, never escaped from, always there. This means that, day in and day out, whether you realise it or not, Christ walks on your feet, Christ works with your hands, Christ sees through your eyes, Christ hears with your ears, Christ thinks with your mind, Christ speaks with your voice, Christ works through your intellect. You meet Jesus at the Communion rail. You speak to Jesus when you pray. As Pope John Paul said, on his last visit to England: "It is through prayer that Jesus leads us to His Father. It is through prayer that the Holy Spirit transforms our lives. It is through prayer that we come to know God". It is through these shared experiences of Communion, of prayer and of living with Christ at our shoulder and Christ present, even if unrecognised, in our minds, that our knowledge of God and our loving relationship with God must be built. It is through these shared experiences that we can meet, become acquainted with, become familiar with, become used to talking with, become used to relying on the God, whose existence we believe in. We can never comprehend the mystery. But eventually, if we live long enough and try hard enough, we may finally come to know a little more, to understand a little more and, with that knowledge and that understanding, come truly to love God in the proper meaning of that word.

Hang all the law and the prophets? Believe in the Lord Jesus and you will have eternal life. Belief, whatever it means, may be a start, but surely only a start. For, if we are to learn to love Him, Christ surely asks much more of us than that. For, if Christ is going to be with us, then surely we must strive to be, in heart and mind, with Him also: and we cannot do that, can we, with our minds closed? Well, can we?.

Diversities of Gifts

St Paul. 1 Corinthians Ch 12. v 4

It is a great honour to be invited to come to your Church today to speak to you about the faith which we share: and I bring you warm greetings from St Michaels in Betchworth, not many miles from here, which is the church from which I come. We are a church, well set in the traditions of the Church of England, a different denomination, as the jargon goes, from you. And it is because we belong to different denominations that I have chosen the second reading you have heard today: and it is because we are from different denominations that I bring you the message I bring.

Nearly two years ago, in late December 2007, I watched a small extract on the Television News about religious attendance. We saw a vast crowd, between 400,000 and 500,000 people, men and women, gathered in the open air. They had come, many from a great distance and all at, to them, great personal expense, to pray, in a particularly holy place. The men all wore white as a symbol of purity and respect. No one fought or argued. They were all at peace with one another. There was no shelter from the weather and nowhere comfortable to stay. They knelt and prayed to God that their sins might be forgiven and their spiritual lives enriched. They planned to stay for three or four days. Then they were going to set out, each to their separate homes again. And, at much the same time, on Christmas Eve and Christmas day of that year, 300 or 400 people, men, women and children, attended one or more of our four services at St Michaels in Betchworth, and came to pray to God that their sins might be forgiven and their spiritual lives enriched. Then they set out, each to their separate homes again. Two separate groups of people, one huge, one much smaller, both, it seems, engaged in the same enterprise.

Which brings me to today's chosen reading from St Paul' letter to the Christians in Corinth. There are diversities of gifts, wrote St Paul, but the same spirit. There are differences of administrations, but the same Lord. There are diversities of operations, he said, but it is the same God which worketh all in all. In Betchworth, we saw 300 or 400 people attending Christmas church services – not a bad turn-out for a small country village. Near Mecca, for that was where it was, we saw 400 or 500 thousand Muslims, from all over the world, respectfully dressed and carefully prepared, attending the great Haj pilgrimage, which is a highlight of their religious life, and praying where the prophet Muhammad is said to have preached his last sermon - hardly a bad turn-out either. There are differences of adminstrations, but the same Lord. There are diversities of operations, but it is the same God which worketh all in all. It is the same God which worketh all in all. Or is it? Is it the same God which worketh in Betchworth and in Cheam and in Mecca? Or two different ones?

I am going to tell you a story, which I think is true. I think it was about 25 years ago and on a Sunday evening. I had been watching the television and had, as often happened, fallen asleep. I woke up to find that my wife had gone to bed and the television set was still on. I was about to get up, turn it off and go to bed myself, when the next programme was announced. It was, as I remember it, called the James Whale question and was introduced by a young man named James Whale. I heard him say: Tonight we have in the studio, by invitation, leaders from just about every religion in the world – and he went on to introduce them. The Church of England was represented by Bishop Hugh Montefiore, whom we knew well in our Parish when he was Bishop of Kingston and was now Bishop of Birmingham. A senior English cleric had come from the Vatican to represent the Roman Catholics. There was a senior imam from the Muslim faith, a senior rabbi from the Jewish faith, a leading Presbyterian, a leading Baptist, a Methodist, a Hindu and a Buddhist, every faith was well represented. He introduced them all and added that they had all come to answer what he called tonight's James Whale question. You are all leaders of different faiths, he said, all leading your followers to belief in God. Tonight's question is: Is it the same God that you all worship and believe in? Or do you worship and believe in different ones?

I had never heard this question asked, let alone answered, and I could not let it pass – so, utterly fascinated, I listened. Mr Whale called on them all, one by one, to answer the question – and, one by one, they all ducked it. They stood up, one by one, and, clearly, briefly, eloquently and with deep devotion, spoke of their own religion and the greatness and goodness of the God they worshipped. But the question – was it the same God that they worshipped - they did not answer – all except one, just one, a small man, as I recall, in a dark suit, wearing a clerical collar. He said, looking round at the group of men assembled there: "I know you, yes and you and you, for over the years we have worked together in spiritual dialogue and on inter-faith matters: and I know most of you well. I know you to be men of deep faith and great spirituality, good men, deep thinkers and true worshippers of the God you pray to. I cannot believe, and will never believe, that you could be as you are and work and worship as you do, unless you are inspired by the same God as has brought my inspiration to me. The only right way for me to worship is the Roman Catholic way, because that is how I have been brought up. We all worship in different ways because we have all received a different religious upbringing. But my answer to the James Whale question tonight is Yes. It is the same God to whom we all pay our worship. There is indeed one True God and only one True God – and all of us worship Him.

Speaking for myself, I had never thought that I would hear a Roman Catholic priest say that. But he went on to explain his thinking on this issue – but how much of this is what he said and how much is my own inadequate gloss on it, I am not sure. God, he said, reveals Himself to different people at different times and in different ways. We all receive our own, differing revelations of the God we worship and we are all striving, as we live our lives, as best we can, to find our way to the God who has thus revealed Himself to us. In this enterprise, finding our way to God, we are, each of us, inevitably governed and guided by the revelation we have received, for it is all that we have to go on. We are all climbing the same mountain and striving to reach the same summit. But because we have received different revelations and also because of our diversities, diversities of birth, diversities of geography, diversities of language, education and culture and upbringing – and, yes, diversities of gifts - and because we embark on this quest at different stages of our lives, we inevitably start that quest from different places and, for that reason, find ourselves following different paths. Some start at the North side of the mountain and seek to climb the North face – for that is where they are and that is where, for them, the path is. Others make their start elsewhere and, for that reason, use different paths. The mountain is covered with rocks and chasms and the vegetation is thick and often impenetrable, so that movement from one path to another is rarely possible. But sometimes, as we press on upwards, we can catch a glimpse of some one on another path and can lift a hand and call out "Hallo, my friend, how are you doing?" and half-hear an answer, blown on the wind: "On the way, thank you. See you at the top, maybe." And then we lose sight of them and struggle on, each on our own path, but ever hoping, by the same God's grace, to reach that same God's holy presence and find, in His presence, the same eternal truth.

Though the difference in the revelations we have received may cause us to believe differing things about the inscrutable God we worship, though the differences in our cultures or our experience of that God cause us to use different rituals and to use differing language, the one true God we worship is one and true and the same. The only way I can worship, he said, because of the revelation I have received and the experience and upbringing I have had is the Roman Catholic way. But I will never be persuaded that the God (he now spoke to his fellow audience members) you and you and you worship is a different being from the God I worship. Your revelation, your experience, has been different from mine. But it is no less real. It is no less true. We all worship the same God. What a pity it is that we spend so much time apparently fighting each other.

Is this right? I asked. Is this the truth? Have I learned something tonight which I had never known before? I turned off the television set and went to bed with my mind in turmoil – and, to, this day, I do not know if I really saw a television programme and heard a senior Roman Catholic priest from Rome say these remarkable things or whether it was truly all a dream. I have thought about it, though, for many years: and, whether I heard it or dreamed it, I feel very strongly that it must be right. But, I ask you, what is the message which the committed Christian ought to send to the hundreds of thousands of devout Muslims on their great Haj pilgrimage? Do we say "I am sorry. You are wasting your time. You are praying to the wrong God?". Do we say "You are the infidel. You can never find eternal life without accepting Jesus as the Son of God. If you do not convert to our way, you will be lost and damned for ever, for God will never hear you?" Or do we say "Let us see if we can join in prayer together – and let us hope, as we pray together to that same God whom we all worship, that all our prayers may together ascend to the same Throne of Grace and be heard?" Our answer to this question may be the most important decision we will make in this century – for there may no peace unless we get it right. So what is the answer to be?

It may not have been what St Paul meant in his letter to the Christians at Corinth, in the passage chosen for today's second reading. But there are diversities of gifts, but the same Spirit. There are differences of adminstrations, but the same Lord. There are diversities of operations, but it is the same God which worketh all in all. It is the same God, which worketh all in all . Or is it? Or is it?

Jesus and women

St John Ch 11 v 25.

Jesus' short ministry, all those years ago in Palestine, is the foundation of our faith. Scholars tell us that he spent his first adult years working as a carpenter in his Father's workshop, living, it seems, an unremarkable life. A day then came, when he was in his late 20's, when he went to see John the Baptist and was baptised by him in the river Jordan, an event where he had a massive and fundamentally important spiritual experience, when God publicly claimed Him as His Own Son. He then went to the wilderness and prayed and meditated alone for forty days. He realised that, because He was who He was, He could do what He liked and exercise His God-given powers, if He chose, for his own aggrandisement. But He made a different choice His choice was to observe a truly strict self-discipline and use those God-given powers for His Father's purposes only. He then came back to the real world and began his ministry, the ministry which created our faith. Today, for us, is the fifth Sunday in Lent: and Lent is a time when we commemorate those forty days of Christ's iron self-discipline and seek to exercise self-discipline ourselves. Lent is not a time just to give up chocolate or smoking. It is a time, we are taught, to exercise a strict self-discipline, which is more difficult.

Self-discipline comes in many forms. There is physical self-discipline and there is mental self-discipline: and I want this morning to invite you to exercise some mental self-discipline and make up your minds about a problem which is affecting our Church and causing a great deal of strife in it. It may be a problem you don't care about. It may be a problem which you do not think affects you. But it affects our Church, affects it deeply and we are being invited to make up our minds what the answer should be, so that our Church leaders know what we think they should do. Two weeks ago, at our Parish meeting we elected three representatives from our congregation to speak for us at the

Deanery synod. And the first task of this newly elected Deanery synod is to tell the diocesan synod whether we, in this Deanery, favour or oppose the appointment of women as bishops. It is a question on which Anglican Christians disagree and about which strong opinions are held on both sides. Our representatives want to know what we think, so that the views of St Michael's may be expressed correctly: and we are being asked to exercise the necessary self-discipline, consider the arguments and let them know what we think. There is no self-discipline in sloppy thinking or in refusing to consider important issues. Our membership of this Church, our faith, require us to give an answer.

Which brings me to today's Gospel reading, the account of the raising of Lazarus, whose body had been decomposing in the heat and had been dead for four days. You may not see an immediate connection between that remarkable miracle and the appointment of women as bishops. But there is an important one and I will come to it. The principal argument against the appointment of women as bishops is that it is contrary to the Church's traditions (which it is) and that Christ chose to appoint twelve and more apostles, none of whom were women. If Christ chose no women to be leaders in His Church, it is said, it cannot be right to say that He was wrong and start appointing them now. The brute fact is that there are many professing Christians in our Church, who will be most unwilling to accept the authority of a female bishop – and it cannot be doubted that the Roman Catholics, who are our brothers and sisters in Christ, would feel, for the most part, unable to do so or accept the authority of any priest ordained by a female bishop. What should our Church do? There will certainly be strife if we go ahead with this: and there will certainly be strife if we do not go ahead with this. What is our Church to do? What would Christ want us to do?

Jesus, we know, chose no women to be leaders in His Church. The culture of the time was such that it would have been absurd to do so. No man, in those days, whether Jewish or Roman, would have dreamed of accepting the authority of a woman in and about the work he did or the religion he professed. It was the way things were at that time: and that was the time when Jesus lived and set up His ministry. But if you ask yourselves whether Jesus thought women valuable as evangelists or important as people to be entrusted with His secrets, their value to Him and His respect for them become immediately apparent. I offer you three examples of the way He used women in His ministry and relied on them to get things right.

Consider today's Gospel reading. Lazarus and his sisters, Mary and Martha, were close friends of Jesus. Lazarus fell ill and died. Mary and Martha asked Him to do something about it – and He did, a most remarkable miracle. But, before the miracle is effected, Jesus tells Martha the true foundation of the faith He came to proclaim, using those famous words which underpin the faith we all profess: "I am the resurrection and the life. He who commits his life to me, though he were dead, yet shall he live – and whoso lives and commits his life to me shall never die". This statement, made to the apostles much later in His ministry, are used by Jesus here for the first time, while speaking to a woman. When it was time to declare this news, to enunciate this fundamental principle, to let the world know who He was, He chose a woman to whom to communicate it.

Consider the Gospel reading a fortnight ago, the account of Jesus' meeting the Samaritan woman at Jacobs Well. They get into conversation, when He asks her for some water. He speaks of living water, which He can supply. She asks for some of that. He starts to speak to her about God and worship and she tells Him; "I know that Messiah cometh, who is called Christ, When He is come, He will tell us all things": and Jesus replies – and it is the first time He is recorded as ever saying it: "I that speak to thee am he". And she goes and tells the people in her village and brings them out to hear Him. When it was time, a first time, to declare the fundamental truth about His true identity (a truth declared to the apostles much later in His ministry and not even then with the same clarity), He chose a woman to whom to communicate it and sent her to tell her world this greatest truth.

And then go on to consider the most important thing that Christ ever did, the greatest moment in His ministry, His resurrection from the dead on the day we call Easter. To whom did He choose to give this great good news first? The accounts of this in the four gospels differ in their detail, but, on one part of the story, they speak as one. All four report that Jesus first disclosed his risen self to Mary Magdalen, and perhaps to other women also: and St Matthew adds Jesus' instruction that they should go and tell the disciples that He had risen. When it was time, a first time, to declare the fundamental truth of His overwhelming victory in rising from the dead, He chose a woman to whom to show Himself, to whom to communicate it: and, in St Matthew's version at any rate, told her to go and tell the apostles, go and tell the men, go and tell the world, what she had seen. And she did – and they did – and so our Church began. – with a message to a woman.

Did Jesus value women as evangelists, value women as important people to be entrusted with His teaching and with His message? Would Jesus think, in today's culture, when women can be and are prime ministers and Supreme Court Justices and do any job in the book as well as any man can, that it cannot be appropriate for women to be leaders in His Church? I, for what it may be worth, have an opinion as to the answer. Do you?

We are the Body of Christ

"We are the Body of Christ. In the one Spirit we were all baptised into one body. Let us then pursue all that makes for peace and builds up our common life". These are words, used by our priest in this church at every Parish Communion service, when we begin that most important part of the service, known as "The Liturgy of the Sacrament". They are words which are very familiar to us. We are the body of Christ. If anyone asks "Who are the Body of Christ?", the answer is "We are".

Jesus was born to teach us the truth about God: and He died in order to reconcile us with the God he told us of. His purpose was to bring all people into His family, all people into Communion with the one true God. He never claimed that it would be easy. He never said it would be quick. In today's Gospel reading, He is recorded as telling His disciples that men would hate them for being His followers: and he warned them that those who killed them would think that they were serving God in doing so: and there are clearly those abroad to day, wealthy and powerful men, but not very many of them, who heartily believe that God is served by the killing of those seen as the infidel. Nevertheless our Church teaches that, because Christ lived and died as He did, we, His followers, are all one body and, as His Church, are Christ's living, continuing presence in the world. We are, as St Paul put it to the Ephesians in today's epistle reading, no more strangers and foreigners, but fellow-citizens of the household of God. Every time we come to this building, we assert that we are one Body, the Body of Christ. Our present and urgent task is to realise that we are Christ's presence in the world, grasp at our unity and turn it to more effective purpose. But we cannot do that unless we are, and fully persuade ourselves that we are - one united body with one identity and one aim. My assertion is that we are: and I want to tell you why.

You may have heard this story from me before. But, if you have, I tell it you again. It is a tale of a chance meeting, which radically altered my thinking. Some years ago now, while Apartheid was still prevailing in South Africa, I met a priest from that troubled country at supper. He was an Englishman, nearly 60 years old, who had been ordained in England in his youth and had gone to work in South Africa thereafter and had spent all his ministry there. He was now between parishes and was visiting friends. His last parish, the one he was leaving, was an all-black parish. No white people ever went to his church. They went to another parish, 20 miles down the road. He was now to be moved to a white parish, where white people attended the church and local black people went elsewhere – to another church down a different road. I asked him if this separation did not sadden him and his reply taught me a great deal. I can only summarise what he said. "I don't like the way things are in the church in South Africa!" he said "It is a shame there is so much separation between the tribes. But there is no law which stops black and white people worshipping together. The principal reason why they do not worship together is simply the difference in their language. In my black church, I held all the services in the Zulu language in accordance with a ritual which the Zulus had developed over the years. The white people do not speak the Zulu language and do not feel at ease in worship in the Zulu language or in the Zulus' ritual. The black people do not speak English and are not happy in worship either in the white language or in the white ritual. I wish it was different, but that is how the world has been made". And he pointed out that many white people in S. Africa speak only English and that many speak only Afrikaans: and that, while the Zulus speak the Zulu language, there are many other tribes who speak their own traditional languages – and the undermanned Church seeks to cater for all races and languages by developing forms of service in the tongue and according to the usages of each group. But the same Body and the same Blood of the same Christ is at the heart of the worship of them all.

Different tribes, different races, different languages, different rituals – but all one body. Are they united? Or are they disunited?

Some would say: "They worship in different places, use different words and follow different rituals. There is no unity there. For, if they were truly united, they would speak the same language, worship together and follow the same ritual". But that view would be entirely superficial and surely wrong. The Communion rail in the Zulu church and the Communion rail in the English church are one and the same Communion rail, where worshippers kneel at the same altar to worship the same God. The Father, Son and Holy Spirit worshipped by each congregation are exactly the same, though the words and the approach may be different. The Zulu will find the worship and the ritual in the white church different and disturbing, just as the English worshipper will find the worship and the ritual in the Zulu church different and disturbing – not because they are disunited, but because, for each, it is different from what he is used to and the language is unfamiliar. But all these worshippers, however they worship, are worshipping the same God: and they are all part of the same body.

And so it is with our Church, is it not? There are evangelicals, who want to take out the pews and dance and clap their hands in praise of God. They are one limb of the body. There are others, of a fundamentalist opinion, who see the Bible as the revealed word of God and can face no deviation from it. They are another limb. There are others, more sedate, who favour a 1662-type service. They are another limb. There are those who have rejoiced at the ordination of women to the priesthood. They are another limb. There are those, who, after deepest prayer and consideration, remain unwilling to believe that a woman can stand in Christ's place at the Eucharist – they are another limb. There are our brothers and sisters in the Roman Catholic Church – they are another, vital and hugely important, limb – and our brothers and sisters in the Free churches – yet more limbs. Just as, in the body, each limb and organ does different things and serves different purposes, just so, in the Church of Christ, each active, devoted, worshipping group serves a different and valuable purpose within it. Like different parts of the body, each group should be free to serve as it feels called to serve, and should each consider the others to be free to serve as they feel called to serve, not as a symptom of disunity, but in reality to widen the catchment area of the unified fellowship of which each is a living and serving part. For, whether we like it or not, we are all different – different in temperament, different in culture, different in education, differing in our feelings and experience and in the way we approach the problems and blessings of this life, differing too in the route by which we have come to our knowledge of Christ and in the revelation we have received of the God we worship. Some are true extroverts and will feel comfortable in a more extrovert form of worship. Others, who are perhaps quieter in their souls and more introverted in their spirits, will only feel comfortable in a more personal form of worship. It is not that those of us, who adopt differing forms of worship, are wrong. It is simply that we are different: and the Church has to cater for us all – the old, the young, the noisy, the silent, the outgoing, the shy, the achiever, the non-achiever, the articulate, the inarticulate – and it provides a large house with many chapels and many alcoves to bring us all in and enable us all to serve God's purposes.

For remember this. We come to church, you and I, to achieve a purpose: and it is vital to remember what that purpose is. The purpose is not to impose our own brand of discipline on our fellow churchgoers and coerce them into compliance with our own practices. The purpose of our coming here is to enable each one of us, as an individual, properly, effectively and reverently, to worship Almighty God: and the object of that worship is to carry the spirit, in a truly reverent and receptive frame of mind, to the Throne of Grace to be pardoned and strengthened and sent on its way rejoicing. It is to achieve that end that we come to this building, to worship for ourselves and to take part in corporate worship with others. It was to achieve that end that the great churchmen of the past and present have designed our forms of service and our rituals. It is the same purpose for each one of us, whatever ritual we follow and whatever we precisely believe. We must keep our eyes fixed on the Cross of Christ, which is the common heart of all that all of us believe – and we should, thus equipped, adopt the language, the company and the ritual which is the most likely to bring each of us, frail vessels that we are, to that state of humility and reverence as will make us fit to approach the Almighty in our worship. You should feel no shame, if you do not feel at home, or your spirit is unquiet, in a church where the language or the minister or the forms of worship make you uncomfortable. For, like the tribes in Africa, that is how we are made. We are all members of God's household, the Church, even though we enter the house from different directions. If you are unquiet at the language or the practices of the church near your home, you owe it to Christ to be like the churchgoers in Africa and go to the same altar and the same Communion rail in the other church down the road: and, if you truly seek Him there, that is where you will surely find Him.

No matter how far you travel, it will be the same altar and the same Communion rail. It is the same altar and the same Communion rail, whether the church style itself Anglican or Roman Catholic. It is the same altar and the same Communion rail, dare I say so, whether the officiating priest be a homosexual or a heterosexual – and, wherever there is the same Communion rail, there is always the same Sacrament, there is always the same Christ, the same tolerating, bleeding, forgiving and finally triumphant Son of God, pleading with us to lift our eyes from our private foolishnesses and foibles and try to do His work and build His kingdom. When it comes to the crunch, Christ wants your heart. Whether He finds it in a low church, a high church or a Roman Catholic church, or even in a shack on a piece of wasteland miles from anywhere, His spirit will rejoice and so should we all. For we are, you see, the Body of Christ. In the one Spirit, we were all baptised into one Body. Let us then pursue all that makes for peace and builds up our common life.

Shake the Dust off your Feet

St Mark. Ch 6 v 11.

On a day about fifteen years ago, I was walking towards Victoria Station in London and I passed a young woman, sitting on the edge of the pavement, begging. I had been lucky and had had a good day: and I stopped and asked her why she was begging and what was the matter. She told me that she had run away from home and come to London, but, finding nothing here but further misery, she was trying to raise the fare to go back to Rotherham, where her home was. I asked how much the fare was. It was many years ago: and I think she said sixteen pounds or something similar. I gave her the money, suggested she go and buy a ticket and wished her good luck. As I walked away to catch my own train, I looked back. She was still sitting on the pavement begging: and I wondered whether I had done the right thing. Now, whenever I see a young person begging, I remember the girl from Rotherham and wonder what became of her. I had salved my own conscience (for I had been lucky and had had a good day), but had I truly helped her? I will never know. I will come back to her later.

Let me start with Jesus' words to his apostles, from today's reading from St Mark's Gospel, when He sends them out on their first venture to spread the faith on their own. At any place where they will not receive you, He said, shake the dust off your feet as a warning to them. Give a warning to those who did not receive you – a warning of what? Today's Gospel reading, from the New English Bible, does not tell us. But, curiously enough, the Authorised Version of the Bible spells it out precisely, for it contains an additional sentence omitted from today's version. The Authorised Version reads: Whosoever shall not receive you, shake off the dust under your feet for a testimony against them. Verily I say unto you. It shall be more tolerable for Sodom and Gomorra in the day of judgment than for that city. And we know what happened to Sodom and Gomorra. The book of Genesis tells us. They, because of their inhabitants' wickedness, were utterly destroyed by fire and brimstone and all their inhabitants, except two, killed. The original Greek text, I think, on which the Authorised Version was based, contains this additional sentence. The Latin text does not, but simply refers to it in a footnote. The editors of the New English Bible chose not to include it. I don't know why.

Jesus, according to Mark's account, sent the apostles out in pairs to heal the sick. He told them to take nothing with them – just sandals and a stick. No food, no money, no spare clothing, nothing. Find people to take you in and live off them, he said: and, if they don't do it, shake the dust off your feet as a testimony against them – and God will destroy them, destroy them, for their lack of concern. This is today's appointed reading. What on earth are we expected to make of it? We preach, in our Church, a Gospel of a loving God. We are offered today what appears to be the opposite, the stuff of nightmares. So long as we don't think about it, it's just fine. But, if we do think about it (and surely we should think about it) what on earth are we to make of it? How does this threat of destructive vengeance square with the message of the loving God and the all-loving , all-sacrificing, Christ, whom we speak of in this church?

And it is not a unique passage, a statement out of accord with the rest of Jesus' message. There is the passage in St Matthew Ch 25, where Christ tells us that the King, when He comes, will divide the sheep from the goats. The sheep are the good people, who fed the hungry, clothed the naked, visited the sick – and it is they, who will inherit the kingdom. The goats, who did not do these good things, are cursed. They will not inherit the kingdom. Indeed, they are to be cast into everlasting fire. This is what Jesus is reported to have told us. These as-they-seem-to-be threats appear in the Gospels more than once. It would be comfortable to ignore them - and many people do. But, if we are to tell the truth (and it cannot be God's will that we do anything else), we have to face them.

The message of our Church today is that God is a God of infinite love, that Christ, who was a man of infinite love, is part of that God: and that Christ's command is that we should love one another. Jesus gave us a promise of access to eternal life with God, if we do His will. But He warned us that, if we do not do God's will in this, or in any other regard, that access may be denied us. Not everyone, Jesus said, that saith unto me Lord Lord, shall enter into the kingdom of Heaven, but he that doeth the will of my Father, which is in Heaven. Whether we attain to eternal life or not depends upon what we do, not upon what we say or upon what we profess: and the decision as to our future in that regard is God's – and God's alone.

Christ sent His apostles to spread the word and heal the sick. He sent them in pairs and He sent them with nothing. He made it clear, in this and countless other ways, that to do his work and to spread His word needs no worldly riches and will bring you no worldly riches. He told us indeed that it was easier for a camel to go through the eye of the needle than for a rich man to enter the kingdom of God. He gave us His promise that the kingdom of God is there for us and that eternal life with God is attainable for us. But He warned us that some will get there and that some will not. What becomes of us if we get there, we do not know. What becomes of us if we do not get there, we do not know. It is hidden by the veil we cannot see through. It is part of the great mystery. We cannot know what awaits any of us. We can hope for the best. We can pray for the best – for ourselves and for others. But none of us, none of us, has a right to enter God's kingdom and no one can negotiate that right for you. Do you remember Jesus' remarkable parable in St Matthew, Ch 20 about the labourers in the vineyard? The owner hired some men to work in his vineyard and offered them a stated wage, which they agreed to. They began early and toiled all day. Others came and joined them, some at twelve o'clock, some at two o'clock and some in the hour before sunset: and, at the end of the day, he paid the same wage to them all, even to those who had just arrived When those who had worked all day complained that this was unfair, the owner said they had no cause. You agreed the wage, he said, and you have received what you agreed. It is my right to pay what I like to whomever I choose: and Jesus said: That is how it is in the kingdom of Heaven. God is the owner. We are the workers. The reward is a place in the Kingdom: and God will grant it to whom He chooses, whether they work all day or only start in the hour before sunset. It may very well be that the hour before the sun sets on our lives will include a very steep learning curve. I do not know because I know no one who has come back from it. But it is something which, sooner or later, we will all learn.

Meanwhile, what are we to do? The answer is, must be, that we are, each of us, to try to find out God's will for us and do the work he requires of us. It demands of us that we ask what Christ would do, if He were where we are. It requires us to use our minds, to strive to get to know Christ in our lives and to build a loving, yes and a working, relationship with Him: and, at the same time to love our neighbours in the way that Christ meant it. Habitual churchgoing is useful – but it may not be enough. Regular prayer is useful – but that may not be enough either, unless we use our minds in what we do. We have to use our minds to develop an informed and right-thinking conscience: and then to use our minds to act on its dictates in every decision we make. Shall I make this remark? Shall I answer back? Shall I discipline this child? Shall I criticise this decision? Shall I fight against this apparent injustice, even though my family may suffer, if I do? Shall I make this profit, which may be at the expense of others? Shall I spend money on this venture? Or on that venture? Shall I spend my time on this cause? Or on that cause? Or on something else altogether? We make these decisions every day and they affect other people every day. Will it be for good or for ill? For me or for them? We need to use our minds to make our decisions and to make them with love in our hearts and love as our motivation: and we need a loving and informed conscience to keep us whole in this.

Which brings me back to the young woman from Rotherham. Some years ago, the head of the Social Services in London asked the public not to give money to young people begging in the streets, because they simply spent the money on drugs, causing themselves further infinite harm. Let the professionals, who know them and their real needs, help them, he said: and things will be better done, for you and for them. I salved my own conscience by giving her that money. But did it do her any good? I will never know. My conscience may have been a loving conscience to make me do what I did. But was it a loving and informed conscience? I suspect not. As would-be followers of Christ, we face these questions many times in every day: and we can only do what we, as individuals, truly think is right. Faced with the same problem, you may think one course right and follow that: and I may think another course right and follow that: and we may both, in God's eyes, be doing the right thing. There is no universal answer, no book of rules to follow. We can do no more than our best to get it right. If we use our minds to give it careful thought and work it out with love, we are unlikely to go far wrong. But that careful thought and that loving heart, is surely what we must, every day and every hour in every day, have, use and show. That, surely, is how we, as professing Christians, must live today and every day – and every hour of every day. There may still be those who will shake the dust off their feet as a testimony against us because we have not done what they think we ought to have done – and they may be right. But, if we have given it careful thought and have tried our best to follow the dictates of an informed and loving conscience, we should have reason to hope that we have been doing Christ's will – and that is what we must strive for. Can we truly be loving our neighbours, if we do less than that?

Go and Search Diligently

St. Matthew. Ch 2 v 8

St Paul, who, in today's first reading, told the Galatians, and now tells us, how he was converted and how he found Christ, did not go looking for Christ at all. He was a devout orthodox Jew, enraged, as many devout orthodox Jews then were, that the faith preached by the upstart Jesus of Nazareth was beginning to spread among the orthodox Jews of his time. St Paul was not looking for Christ at all. He was looking for Christ's followers, so that he could denounce them and have them killed, as the martyr Stephen had been killed in Paul's presence and with his agreement. It was for that purpose that he had gone to Damascus: and it was while he was on his way there, that Christ found him and denounced him, showed him a light his eyes could not bear, temporarily blinded him and so drew him to Himself. St Paul was not looking for Christ, but found Him. We are looking for Christ, but can we find Him? For this reason, today, when our chosen reading invites us to think about the conversion of St Paul, I offer you two texts, both familiar passages which we are more used to hearing at Christmas than in the Trinity season. The first is from St Matthew's account of the coming of the wise men, Herod's famous words: "Go and seek diligently for the young child: and when you have found him, bring me word again, that I may come and worship him also". The second is from the first Chapter of St John's Gospel: "He came unto his own and his own received him not. But, as many as received him, to them gave he power to become the sons of God".

Go and seek diligently for the young child. Herod's command to the wise men is the same as Christ's command to each of us. "Go and seek diligently for me in whatever form you may find me. Seek for me diligently: and, when you have found me, tell Herod, tell others, so that they may come and find me also. For - and this is St John's message -, when you have found me and received me for what I am, then you will have inherited the power, you will find that it is in you, to become one of the children of God. This is the promise at the heart of the faith which we profess. This is what we stand to win or lose. The end of this search is the beginning of our destiny.

We are engaged, you and I, in a lifelong search - to find our way to God. That quest is what we are born for. Our lives should be spent in building our relationship with Christ, in a continuing growing-closer-together. God reveals Himself to each of us in different ways and at different times - that is why we sometimes disagree with each other and why bishops sometimes say things we do not like very much. To some (and St Paul was one of them) God makes Himself known in some sudden blinding revelation. Others go through a gradual process of learning to believe and learning to trust. To some, God's revelation of Himself is plain and easily understood. To some, the revelation is distant, unrecognisable and unrecognised. Some never hear the word or see the truth at all, usually because they see no need to seek for it, sometimes because, through education and upbringing or the lack of them or by reason of personal disposition, their eyes and ears are closed or they are looking the other way or listening to other messages. Some never learn the language. Others have not seen the truth, even when it came out of the grave and spoke to them. But, for you and me, who would not be here if we were not seeking for the truth, the message is clear. Go and seek diligently for the young child: and when you have found him, take word of it to Herod, that he may come and worship him also.

Easily said: but, like so many of the important things in life, not so easily done. In this context, Herod represents for us the largely unlistening and possibly devious world, which surrounds us, just as Herod's authority surrounded the wise men. When, where and how are we to search? And how do we bring word again to the Herods of this world, so that they will listen to us and come and worship too. It is easy to put your hand on your heart and say: "I have found the light". But, when you face the task of bringing the word to Herod, he will ask for more than that. You will have to explain what you have found, where you have found it and why you think it is the light - and you have to think it out, because you will not have the courage of your own convictions, let alone the factual and philosophical basis to enable you to face and persuade a sceptical and unbelieving Herod, unless you know what it is that you have been looking for and what it is that you have found. It may not be enough to say "I believe". You will have to tell him what you believe and why.

It has always been God's promise that, if you truly seek Him with all your heart, you will find Him. You will find that promise in the Old Testament. You will find it in the New Testament. It is God's promise and Jesus' promise: and it will not be broken. But we must seek with all our heart, we must seek diligently. We may not be called upon, you and I, as those wise men were, to leave our homes, pack our belongings and physically trek through the desert for months on end, following a star which we can barely see. That may have been their route to God. It is not necessarily ours. God may call you to a vision on a mountain top and may deny you the vision till you get there. God may confront you on your own Damascus road and show you the truth in a blinding light, as he did to St Paul and to many others since. I do not know how God reveals Himself to you. I only know how He has revealed Himself to me: and I share such of it as I can with you in the hope that it will help. It is something I have shared with some of you before.

I cannot remember when it started or where it started or why. I have a memory of starting to worship as a young schoolboy and of lessons about the Bible from devoted teachers, of a gradual assimilation of a message, of vivid pieces of imagery recalled from childhood and adolescence, of learning of a deep faith as part of the lives of people I respected, of coming gradually to be able to pray with a growing consciousness that I was being listened to, of listening to people talking about their faith, in churches and elsewhere, in words that stuck in the mind and seemed to make sense, of coming gradually so to tune my senses that I seemed to be able to listen to a communicating source of virtue outside myself, of a gradually growing realisation of the presence and importance of what I have come to perceive as Christ as part of my life and the lives of those with whom I live and whom I love, of a gradually growing trust which has become a true reliance, of a gradually growing faith which has slowly become a conviction, of a real sense of never being any more alone because Christ is always there. It has never been quick. It has never been sudden. It has always been gradual, usually unrealised at the time. Yet from nowhere, over all my years, I have come to be in this pulpit, to be where I stand now. It may have been, it may yet be, similar for you. It may be different. God reveals himself to each of us in His own way and at His own time - and whether we see and hear and whether we seek, either diligently or at all, is a private matter for each one of us to decide. But God's command is the same for all of us. Go and seek diligently for the young child: and when you have found Him, bring word of it to others, that they may come and worship Him also.

How is this to be done? I can only say this. First: The only ways I know of searching for the young child are to listen and to pray. The wise men show us, symbolically, what we should do. They opened their minds and their eyes to something new, exciting and unheard of. They saw a light, reached out across the deserts of the unknown, followed the light wherever it led and found what they were looking for. You and I listen by being silent and by opening our minds and our eyes to the message which God brings to us: and we pray by reaching out with our senses across the void of ignorance and uncertainty and seeking the light - and by repeating this process with diligence and regularity, until we know that we have got there. It took a long time for the wise men. It may take a lifetime for you and me.

Second: we bring word again to Herod by living our lives in a way consistent with the faith which we profess. We are judged, in this regard, not by what we say, but by what we do. Words are easy: actions are more difficult: but the true evangelist uses both. If you live your life in the way that Christ wants you to live it and, when you get the chance, say why, then Herod may see your faith for what it is and come and worship also. Most of us can do no more than that. But that, or an effort at that, is what Christ looks for from us.

Third: I am entirely convinced that God wants your heart. He will seek for you, just as you diligently seek for Him: and your gradual coming together will be the source of the greatest joy you will ever experience.

And the prize? The end of it all? "As many as received Him, to them gave He power to become the sons of God". That power is, can be, yours, if you seek it .It can be yours. So go and seek diligently for the young child: and find Him - and bring me word again that I may come and worship Him also.

Palm Sunday

We gather here this morning on Palm Sunday to commemorate the day when Jesus entered Jerusalem – the irrevocable step, which led Him into the arms of His enemies, the step which he purposely took, knowing it would lead to the Cross. He knew His enemies were waiting – so He could have kept away. He knew He faced only crucifixion – so He could have kept away. But He did not keep away. He came into Jerusalem – sitting on a donkey, as foretold in the prophet Zechariah and in accordance with a plan devised by those who had planned it ("Go into the village. You will find a colt tied. Loose him and bring him hither"), knowing exactly what was going to happen to Him. And the people.... What of the people? The people...rejoiced, not because of His impending death, of which, of course, they knew nothing; not even, probably, because it was Jesus, rather than anyone else, coming into the city; but rejoicing, probably, because it was a public holiday commemorating the Passover, when crowds of people annually gathered in the city for the Feast and for general celebration. So the people rejoiced: and St John reports that they took palm branches and went out to meet Him.

That is what we commemorate – and, like them, we hold palms in our hands as a symbol of our participation in that day. The question for them (though they did not know it) was: "You welcome Him now with palms. You rejoice now in His coming. What will you do to Him in five days time?". And this question, every Easter, is the same for us. We know what they did, those good people in Jerusalem in their day. They welcomed Him today with palm branches and cries of joy – and crucified Him five days later with cries of hate. What will we do in our city and in our day? Will we welcome Him with palms today and crucify Him tomorrow? Or will we welcome Him today and make Him ever welcome? It is not what we do with our palms which counts. What counts is what we do with our hearts and minds and hands tomorrow – and tomorrow and tomorrow and in all the tomorrows which will come after.

The great Russian composer, Sergei Rachmaninov, was a devout man, deeply versed in the rituals of the Russian Orthodox Church: and he wrote, I think in 1913, a song entitled "Christ is risen". But the words of the song are not what we might expect from a poem of that name. For they do not celebrate the joy of the risen Christ. Rather do they portray the despair of Jesus, crucified in agony and now risen from the dead, looking back to the world with all its horrors and its continuing thoughtlessness and cruelty and asking: "Did I, the Son of God, come to earth to die for this? Is this the best, really the best, you can do for me? "And today, in your name and in your church, I say: We have hearts and minds and hands, you and I. Is what we are doing the best we can do with them? Or should we do more and better? Christ has died for us. Christ has risen for us and opened for us, if we choose it, the gate to eternal life with God. What are we doing in return?

I want to try to get right down to the heart of the matter. We profess the Christian Faith, you and I. That is why we are here. We hope to find our way to God and we rely on the Faith derived from the Gospels and on the love of Christ, as revealed to man in His own day and since, to get us there. Our task is to find out what God's will is – for us and for the world – and try to get it done. As Jesus is reported to have said: Not everyone that saith unto me Lord Lord shall enter into the kingdom of Heaven, but he that doeth the will of My Father, who is in Heaven. We have to do God's will – work out what it is for each of us and then do it. My belief, the Church's belief, is that God's will for us is that we should follow Christ in the way we live and in all we do, as best we may. That is not easy, but it is our appointed task. As Christians, we should surely have no other. But there are difficulties in the way, difficulties we all know about. For we do not know what Christ would do in many of the situations we find ourselves in in this life: and we realise that to do what Christ would do, even when we think we know what it is, would very often demand a greater degree of exposure than we are willing to risk. Our world is different from his and we have commitments, as well as irresolutions, of our own.

We do not know what Christ would have done in many of our situations in life because we have no record of him ever being in those situations. We don't know what Christ would have done with riches, if he had a family to keep – because He never had either the one or the other – or what He would have done in abject poverty and great hunger, if He had a family to keep, because He was never in that situation. He always had enough, supplied by someone, though He had no surplus. We don't know how He would have treated rebellious employees in the workplace or the office, because He never had any. We don't know what Christ would have us do, when we meet a beggar in the street, particularly when those, who know the beggars and try to look after them, ask us not to give them money, because they will go and spend it on drugs which will make them worse – because, when Christ met a beggar in the street, He touched him and changed His life, which is not in our power. We do not know what Christ would do in a testing matrimonial situation, because He never married: and we don't know what Christ would have done, if He had been caught up in a just war, because He never was. And we don't know what Christ would have done, if a devout homosexual priest came and truly wanted to serve Him: and we don't know what He would have done, if a ten-year-old boy murdered a two-year-old boy, because he thought it was fun and was doing no harm. We can only consider. We can only guess. Our belief is that He would have acted with integrity and with love, because that was what He taught and that was how He behaved when He met the problems which were, to Him, the orthodox problems of the world He lived in. But how do you act, in the face of these problems, if you act with integrity and love? What do you do? Do you say Yes? Or No?

Christ is in each of us. He is in you. He is in me. His spirit is there with us all the time and in everything that we do. Instinctively, as we make progress in listening to His voice, we come to know what His will is – and, when we do it, the angels rejoice: and, when we don't do it, we crucify Him again. Our duty is to do what He would do. But our difficulty is that we so often do not know what that is. And, when we don't know what His will is, we have to think and try to work it out. To recognise the problem and then run away from it is not enough. We owe it to Christ to pray and to listen and try to work out what love and integrity require us to do. What do we do, what do love and integrity require us to do, if we are summoned to fight in a just war? Or in an unjust war? What do we do, when we are asked by teenagers for advice about sexual activity outside marriage? Do love and integrity, in these days, require us to recommend abstinence, with all the problems which that may cause? Or to recommend the use of contraceptives, with all the problems which that may cause? What do we do, when an utterly depressed friend or relative wants, more than anything else, to die and be relieved of the pain of continued living and cannot do it for himself? Do love and integrity require us to show compassion and help him to die? Or do we insist that life is a gift from God and must not be interfered with? What do we do, when a devout man or woman, who has been born with tendencies and desires, which are homosexual, wants to serve as a priest? Do love and integrity require us to say No, because the Old Testament, whose writers and lawmakers knew nothing of chromosomes and the physiology, which makes people naturally homosexual, said it was an abomination to the Lord to live like that? Or do we use the knowledge of these things that our God-given brains have given us to say that they can serve Christ just as well as anyone else? What do we do, what do love and integrity require us to do, when an ordained priest, of this religious denomination or that, is found to have sexually abused adults or children in his charge? Do we tell Him to mend his ways and send him to another parish? Or do we forbid his further participation in priestly activity and keep him away from children, insofar as we can? Christ taught us to forgive. But what does Christ want us to do, if forgiveness will, or might, put other vulnerable people in danger? Do we know what our answers to these questions should be? Do we think about what our answers to these questions should be? Or do we say it is none of my business. Others, maybe those, who do not have or value the influence of Christ in their lives, must answer them for us?

For, make no mistake about it, these are some of today's vital questions. These are some of the questions which, in our day, fundamentally affect the values, the purpose, the reputation of our faith. What Christ would say in answer to some of these questions is something which we need to work out, which we need to pray about and think about. And we do not answer them or solve them, if we turn our backs on them and leave their solution to others. My fear is that every time we do nothing, give it no thought, leave it to others, probably people with no background of faith in Christ to guide them, to be solved by them, we are driving another nail into the cross. We are the body of Christ, we say. In the one spirit, we say, we were all baptised into one body. Let us pursue, we say, all that makes for peace and builds up our common life. That is what we say. But what do we do? What is it that we truly pursue? We are the Church. It is for us, our Church community, to think and form opinions, tell other people what they are and live in accordance with them. Can we truly be living in accordance with Christ's will, if we don't try to do that? I believe that we are trying to do that. What I am asking is whether we think that we are doing enough.

Today we gather here with palm crosses in our hands. Let us keep them as a symbol of our resolve to find out what Christ wants for us in our own lives and to try, in our own small way, to build His kingdom in this world, which is what we are bidden to do. Almighty God, who gavest Thine only Son to suffer upon earth for our redemption, send Thy blessing upon us and sanctify to our use these crosses of palm. That all, who shall take them in Thy name may enjoy the freedom of Thy kingdom and serve Thee today and every day in all good works. Through Jesus Christ our Lord. Amen.

Love one Another

St. John. Ch 15. v 12

From today's second reading - St John's Gospel, Ch 15, verse 12. This is my commandment, that you love one another as I have loved you. The words are very well known - but often overlooked, particularly so when people become enthusiastic that churchgoers should follow other Christian disciplines. But this was Jesus' last command: and it was also his greatest commandment. Love one another as I have loved you.

To love without conditions is the highest perfection to which human nature can attain. That is how Jesus loved us - without conditions. That is how he taught us to love one another - without conditions. To love without conditions, without reserve, is the Christian ideal. But it is not generally in our nature to love in this way. As humans, we are not generally very good at it. If we were good at it, the world would be a better place. But, when we find this love, this unconditional love, we should cherish it and work at it. For we do not find it often. For those who have fought in war, we know that it is sometimes found in battle - the love which asks no questions, the love where a man will lay down his life for his friend. But, if you look at the ordinary incidents of life, unconditional love is found most frequently in marriage and in parenthood and in a true commitment to those relationships - this loving without reservation or condition, which is the Christian ideal, which is human nature at its highest. This is why the Church views Christian marriage as important - not because it is socially convenient, not because it tidies up the complications which arise from relationships, not because it provides respectability and a basis for permanence, though it does all of these things - but because it is in marriage and in the parenthood which follows from marriage that we come closest to the Christian ideal of unconditional loving and the unconditional giving, which goes with that state of mind. Look at your own relationships - think of them now as you sit here - and, if you have been lucky, even for a short time, you will know what I mean.

Christ, who set the Christian standard, could have done anything, gone anywhere. He could have ruled the world, been master of the universe. He chose to live otherwise - to live humbly and to die in pain - to die for his people, so as to save them for ever: and he made that choice out of unconditional love for those who were to become His Church, unconditional love for you and me. We cannot match that love, you and I. We cannot hope to, though the Mother Teresas of this world have a go at it. But, though we cannot match it, we should at least recognise it and strive for it - because it is the unconditional nature of Jesus' love for us, which is the legacy of His ministry and the foundation of our faith.

We see that love at work most poignantly on Palm Sunday, the day of Jesus' entry into Jerusalem. The story is familiar - but we miss the point if we do not look behind the story. An arrangement had been made - for a donkey to be made available, so that the man, who could have been the King of the world, could ride into the Holy City. The way would be strewn with palm leaves and the people would be cheering. It would look like a triumphal welcome. But Jesus knows it is almost certainly nothing of the sort. Jesus knows almost certainly what lies in store for him in Jerusalem. He knows, almost certainly, that, once he enters the City, he will never come out of it until he has been put to death and risen. He knows, almost certainly, that the shouts of joy will turn to cries of hate, that the triumphal entry will turn into the road to Calvary, that he has a last supper to attend, last rituals to arrange - and flogging, humiliation and unbearable pain to face. He knew that all this was almost unavoidable - he had known it from the beginning. He had seen it as just about inevitable ever since he had turned the devil down at the outset of his ministry. He had expected it every day, when he chose to do God's work rather than serve some other master - and he chose to come to Jerusalem, chose to face what lay ahead for him - and he made that choice out of unconditional love for you and me, out of unconditional love for all of us, out of that unconditional love which we cannot match, save perhaps in our dearest and closest relationships, out of that unconditional love, which marks Him out as the one and only, unique person we believe him to have been.

And that is why we worship Him, you and I, in this contradictory, argumentative, uncertain, indeterminate, unbelievably irritating Church of ours. We do not worship Him because he was peace-loving and kind to children. We do not worship Him because he healed the sick and performed miracles. We do not worship Him because he walked about in a white robe and blessed people or because he was a revolutionary, who sought to change the world. We do not worship Him because he was a remarkable man, who did and said remarkable things. We do not worship Him for any of these reasons, thought they are all true. No. We worship Him because He was God's son and He loved us: because God's love for us is unconditional and, coming from God, He brought God's unconditional love for us into the human dimension and loved us with that same unconditional love through all the days He spent with us in this world. That is why we worship Him. We worship Him because, as God's son and knowing the nature of God's love, He came to be with us for a season and spent and gave His life in showing us just how unconditional God's love for us is. And now today, when we come to Communion, when we take part in the ritual He so lovingly set up for us in his last day after he had come to Jerusalem this last time, we use the system he provided for us to plug into the power source of that unconditional love that Jesus personifies for us - and so be enabled ourselves to love a little and pass on some light to others. This is, for us, the power source of love - and we, you and I, have access to it. We have it at this altar rail and at every altar rail we visit. Every time we come to this altar rail for Communion, we are given the strength to love and go on loving. We must strive, through its power, to learn to love one another and to practise loving one another. The light of Christ's love is in us and has been made a living part of us. We must use it, revel in it and show it, by the way we live, to those we meet today and every day. It is the least, and perhaps the most, that we can do. "This is my commandment, that you love one another as I have loved you".

What Manner of Man is this?

St Luke Ch 8 v 25.

Who then is this that the wind and the sea obey him? In your dream, you are standing at the top of a long field, looking down the hill into the shallow valley beneath. You are alone, the sun is shining. You are waiting for something, you do not quite know what. As you look down this hill, you see Jesus approaching, coming towards you, walking slowly, but purposefully. Who then is this? Who then is this?

Sometimes, in life and in history, a question is asked and an answer is given. A question is asked in today's reading. Jesus and his disciples were in a boat on the lake. A very severe storm came up, so severe that the disciples, some of whom were professional fishermen, were terrified, feared for their lives and asked Jesus, who had been a carpenter and had never been a fisherman, for help. Jesus did help - he calmed the waters, a story told in the Gospels of Matthew and Luke, as well as that of Mark from whose Gospel today's reading came. They asked the question, as we now ask the question: Who then is this, that even the winds and the sea obey him? Jesus gave them no immediate answer. But he did give answers later - and much more than once - one occasion being recorded, towards the end of His ministry, in Chapter 14 of St John's Gospel. On that occasion Jesus, seeking to explain Himself to the Apostles, used those famous words: "I am the way, the truth and the life. No man cometh to the Father but by me": and Philip, who did not understand, said "Show us the Father and that will be enough": to which Jesus answered: Have I been with you all this time and have you not known me Philip? He who has seen me has seen the Father". Question and answer: Who then is this? He who has seen me has seen the Father. Who then is this? He who has seen me has seen the Father.

Who then is this? Consider what we know. This is a man who spent his life doing good, a man who gave us the Sermon on the

Mount, which is the finest description ever given of how life should be lived. This is a man who, through all his life, sought nothing for himself, but served others tirelessly and asked no credit for it. This is a man who healed those, whom the medical science of the day could do nothing to help. This is a man, who foretold his own death and, knowing what lay in store for him, went out and suffered it without complaint, forgiving those, who killed him, even as the torture was being applied. This is a man who, after his death, came back from the dead and was seen by hundreds of people and proved, even to doubters, that his resurrection was a reality. And this is a man who said "Have I been with you all this time and have you not known me, Philip? He who has seen me has seen the Father".

Who then is this? Here is a man (and these are not my words) who was born in an obscure village, the child of a peasant woman. He worked in a carpenter's shop until he was thirty, and then, for three years, was an itinerant preacher. He had no credentials but himself. While still a young man, the tide of popular opinion turned against him. His friends ran away and left him. He went through a mockery of a trial. He was nailed to death in public on a cross between two thieves. When he was dead, he was taken down and laid in a borrowed grave through the pity of a friend. Yet I am well within the mark when I say that all the armies that ever marched, and all the parliaments that ever sat, and all the kings that ever reigned, put together, have not affected the life of man upon this earth as has this one solitary life. His ministry lasted just three short years and was conducted entirely in an unremarked and unimportant backwater of the Roman Empire. The Romans were masters of the world: and Jerusalem was an unconsidered place, a posting nobody wanted. Yet this apparent nobody, working alone in this nothing of a place, achieved all this. Who then is this?

Who then is this? Is He just a great prophet, as the Muslims believe? Is he just a remarkable man, who did remarkable things and used remarkable words? Or is He more than that, which is what the Christian Church teaches and has always taught and believed? Is it the case, as the Christian Church teaches and has always taught and believed, that those who had seen him had seen the Father? Is it the case that this man was the Son of God, a part of God, another face of God? Is it the case that, in answering Philip's question, this man also answered ours? I ask this, because we have to make a choice, to make a decision: and the whole pattern of our lives, beliefs and hopes may depend upon the choice, upon the decision, we make.

We are not dealing in fiction here. That Jesus lived is historical fact and no one contradicts it. The evidence about how He lived is clear and incontrovertible. So is the evidence about the substance of what He said. We have to ask: Is it possible that a man, who lived as Jesus lived, and preached as Jesus preached, a man who lived a life and preached a message of unimpeachable purity and probity, could claim to be the son of God, as He did claim, and then go on to be seen as rising from the dead, as He was seen, is it possible that such a man could be anything other than what He claimed to be? For, if He claimed to be the son of God and was not, he must have been a blasphemer and a charlatan of the worst order: and it simply cannot be that a man, who lived as He lived and taught what He taught, could be such a thing. Either He was a fraud and we cannot believe a word He said: or else He was what He claimed to be. I do not think there can be any halfway house between those two conclusions - and it was all done, all set up by a young man with no connections and no influence within three short years. No PR expert, no spin merchant, in today's language, could possibly dream of achieving such a result. Yet the Christian Church is the result he achieved. Who then is this?

He who has seen me has seen the Father. That is what our Church teaches. You may be convinced of it. You may not be convinced of it. I am - but you may not be. It is your business. To reach a conclusion on the question takes many people many years. It takes some a lifetime to find the answer. But thousands upon thousands of people run away from the question, refuse altogether to turn their minds to the question - and that is something you cannot sensibly do. To run away from the question is like going to a restaurant and refusing to look at the menu. If you refuse to look at the menu, you cannot know what is available, what is there for you: and you need to know whether there is anything there for you and, if there is anything there for you, what it is. For, if Jesus was wrong, there is nothing to live for, no long-term purpose in life, no prospect of anything hereafter. We live in the gloom of knowing that our time here is short and that the end of it is the end of everything. But, if Jesus was right, if the God he told us of exists and if God saw to it that His son, a part of Him, came to this planet and lived a human life in order to bring us to the salvation which He promised us, then everything is changed. If the gate of glory has been opened for us and death is seen as the pathway to that gate, then we can rejoice in the assurance of God's love and at the prospect of something new, when life is over. With this sure belief, we can, and we should, live our lives with the clear and perceived purpose of finding our way to the God, who has done this for us. We can, and we should, keep our eyes fixed on Christ, trust Him and live our lives on the basis that He is at our side. As we go about our affairs day by day, either Christ is with us and in us - or else He is not. It ought to make a huge difference. The Church teaches that He is and it does. I believe that too. Do you?

In your dream, you are standing at the top of a long field, looking down the hill into the shallow valley beneath. The sun is shining. You are alone, waiting for something, you do not quite know what. As you look down this hill, you see Jesus approaching, coming towards you, walking slowly but purposefully. Who then is this? Who then is this? And, as you stand there in your dream and ask yourself that question, it may be, it just may be, that you will hear, at the back of your mind, at the very edge of your perception, a still small voice: Have I been with you all this time and have you not known me, Philip? He who has seen me has seen the Father - and you may find, you may just find, that, all of a sudden, it hits you and you know.

Easter 2000

Blessed be the God and Father. First Epistle of St Peter, Ch 1 v 3

Today, the first Sunday after Easter, I offer you, as a text, the opening words of Chapter 1 of the first letter of St Peter, well known words, frequently set to music and frequently quoted at Easter time. Blessed be the God and Father of our Lord Jesus Christ, who, according to His abundant mercy, hath begotten us again unto a lively hope by the resurrection of Jesus Christ from the dead, to an inheritance incorruptible and undefiled, that fadeth not away, reserved in Heaven for you". "Hath begotten us again unto a lively hope by the resurrection of Jesus Christ from the dead".

Thus wrote St Peter, who, unlike you and me, had seen, known, touched, dined and spent time with the risen Christ after His resurrection. There are those today (there may be some among you) who doubt the reality of Christ's resurrection and talk of the lack of sound evidence and the improbability of it all. By all means doubt if you choose - doubt is a necessary and altogether healthy step on the road to intellectual conviction - it is after all your business and you have to make up your own mind. God gave us brains to think with: and we cannot do His work properly if we leave our brains behind. But it is worth remembering that, unlike you and me, St Peter was there. He saw and felt what happened. He saw and felt the risen Christ: and there is not much of a basis for arguing with him. Argue with the Rector or with me, if you like. You can have a go at the churchwardens any time you fancy. But don't try arguing with St Peter. He saw what he saw, touched what he touched - and based his life and went to his death in his utter conviction of the truth of the fact of the resurrection, which he had personally witnessed, of Jesus Christ from the dead. He did not tell us of a spiritual resurrection. He did not mince his words or talk of ghosts or virtual reality. He saw a dead man risen, experienced His physical presence and was transformed by this event from an inarticulate and uncertain blunderer into one of the greatest leaders and spokesmen of his age, who spread the gospel by telling the world what he had seen and done and passed it down to us in the words with which I began this morning, which is one of the most powerful encapsulations of the Christian faith to be found anywhere in the history and literature of our Church.

Easter has been a time for gifts and I expect that many of you gave and received Easter eggs, which are a symbol of new life. But the greatest gift, which we all of us receive at Easter, is the reminder of the gift arising from Christ's resurrection, described by St Peter as 'An inheritance incorruptible and undefiled, that fadeth not away, reserved, where God is, for you'. Easter is the annual reminder to us all that, through Christ's sacrifice, that which we call eternal life is, if we opt for it, reserved, where God is, for each of us: and there can, in this world or the next, be no greater gift than that.

The Christian faith teaches that Christ was not just a remarkable man who used remarkable words and did remarkable things. He was a remarkable man and he did remarkable things. But that is not the sum of our faith. If that was the sum of our faith, we would believe nothing different from the other great religions of the world. All the great religions of the world teach and accept that Jesus was a great prophet, who used remarkable words and did remarkable things. Our faith is the one that goes further. It is our faith that, by some inexplicable alchemy, Christ was a part of God Himself, who came to earth in human shape with human bones and human flesh and with a human mind: and that by dying and then rising from the dead - and by what He told us about His dying and His rising from the dead - He showed us that death was and is no more than a doorway leading to a greater experience and set up the chance for each of us, should we choose it, of attaining what we call eternal life. The reality of Christ's resurrection is thus the foundation on which the Christian faith is based. As St Paul put it in his first letter to the Corinthians: 'If Christ be not risen, then is our faith vain'. If we do not believe that, there is nothing to believe.

This great truth is affirmed by every denomination of the Christian Church, Anglicans, Roman Catholics, Methodists, Baptists and all branches of every one of them. We may, we Christians, disagree about many things - about how our worship should be conducted and about how our lives should be led - but, on the great truths of the divinity of Christ and the reality of His resurrection, the Christian church is entirely at one: and it is my prayer, and the prayer of many of us as we make our way through the 21st century, that we should turn our minds to the great strengths which we share, to the great truths which unite us, rather than allow ourselves to be diverted by the more insubstantial matters, so much more attractive of publicity, which remain bones of contention between us. Like most bones of contention, they have great power to irritate. But the fundamental truths, which unite the Christian Church all round the world, are of far greater importance: and we must, we truly must, turn our eyes and ears to them.

Take, for example, though I don't want to talk about it today, the much vexed question of the ordination of homosexual men and women to the priesthood. Many firm believers in our Church are in favour of it. But many will not have it and many Roman Catholics would take a similar view. Supporters of both views have reasons which they consider persuasive. This is sad. But, while it is a question which we must think about and make up our minds about, it is not something we should dwell on for too long. Our task, yours and mine, is, each of us, in our own way, to find our path to God. That is what we were born for. This is what we are required to spend our lives doing. We, in our faith, seek to do this by prayer at a deep level and by Communion with Christ at a place and in circumstances where our hearts can be at peace and where our consciences can be cleansed. Whether that place, those circumstances, are found in this Anglican church or that - or in this Roman Catholic church or that - it is the same Communion rail, the same sanctuary and the same Christ to whom we come. Those who worship in a different way from us are not our enemies. They are our brothers in Christ, from whom we stand at a short distance, not by Christ's will, but through man's weakness and intransigence. If a man or a woman feels closer to Christ at the Communion rail in a Roman Catholic church, that is not a defeat for the Church of England - nor, I would suggest, should it be a matter of regret for anyone. If a crisis of conscience brings a worshipper closer to God than he or she was before, the crisis may have been painful. But the result is a triumph for Christ.

What, then, shall we say to these things? The Easter egg is a symbol of new life. Easter is always a time for a fresh start. Let us, in our own small way, those of us who are here, resolve to try anew. The Church of Christ is a huge influence for good in this world. But it would be a far greater influence for good, if its outward show, that which the world sees, were to present to the world a great single force united in Christ, rather than a series of splintered sects, squabbling over things on the periphery. The Creed they are reciting in the Roman Catholic church at Mass today is almost word for word identical with the Creed which we are about to affirm here today. The forms of service are strikingly similar - and the fundamental truths are the same. We may, some of us, live our lives differently and perhaps ascribe to different moral imperatives. But God is above all that. As St Paul put it in his letter to the Ephesians : "There is one body and one spirit - one Lord, one faith, one baptism, one God and Father of all, who is above all and pervading all". We are one Church, expressing one faith and celebrating one Lord. Before we put our Easter rejoicings behind us for another year, let us rejoice by showing the world, by what we say and by what we do, that this one Church is what we truly are.

It is a piece of imagery I have used before, but I do not apologise for repeating it. The Roman Catholic Church and the Anglican Church are like two brothers, each standing on a bridge and looking at a river. One is facing downstream and one is facing upstream. The one facing downstream says:" I know what this river looks like. I have a good view from this bridge. I have been standing here for years and the view is very familiar to me - for I can see both banks and my vision extends as far as the eye can see. I tell you - I know this river". And the one facing upstream says:" I know what this river looks like. I have a good view from this bridge. I have been standing here for years and the view is very familiar to me - for I can see both banks and my vision extends as far as the eye can see. I tell you - I know this river". Like the Anglicans and the Roman Catholics, they use the same words and are looking at the same river. They are also both telling the truth as they see it. The trouble is that these two brothers, though only a few feet apart as they stand on the bridge looking at the river, have been standing back to back. But, if they turn round and embrace one another in love, as Christians and brothers should, then they will both see the whole vision - and maybe, by God's grace, see things slightly differently.

Though we and our friends in other Churches worship in different places, though we adopt marginally different rituals, though we use marginally different words, we are all one in Christ - and, when it comes to the crunch, the truth is this. No matter who you are, Christ wants your heart. That is what He died and rose for. Whether He finds it in this Church or in another, God and His angels will rejoice - and so should we all, shouldn't we?

Blessed therefore be the God and Father of our Lord Jesus Christ, who, according to His abundant mercy, hath begotten us again unto a living hope by the resurrection of Jesus Christ from the dead - to an inheritance incorruptible and undefiled, that fadeth not away, reserved in Heaven for you.

My Father's Business

St Luke Ch 2. v 49

Isaiah Ch 25 v. 8. "He will swallow up death in victory: and the Lord God will wipe away all tears from their eyes". Today, the first Sunday after Easter, we can, once again, look back on it all - the disaster and the triumph, the killing and the rising again: and we ask, as we always ask: What was it all for? What was Jesus really doing here? And one of the best answers is that he was going to swallow up death in victory and see to it that the Lord God wiped away all tears from our eyes. I will come back to Isaiah and his prophecy later: but meanwhile I want to turn to Jesus and to today's second reading. a passage from St Luke's Gospel, Ch 2, which tells us the first words which Jesus is recorded as having spoken during his brief life on earth. He was twelve years old, his parents had brought him to Jerusalem and he left them without telling them where he was going, so that he might go to the temple on his own. They looked for him everywhere and found him in the temple. When they upbraided him for running off like that, he said: "Knew you not that I must be about my father's business?".

Knew you not that I must be about my Father's business? What was His Father's business? What was Jesus' mission on this earth? And the answer, I think, is that Jesus' purpose was to teach us who and what God was and to reconcile us to the God he told us of. Since man had, over the thousands of years since the world began, rejected God's love and chosen his own way, Jesus' purpose, his Father's business, was to reveal to us, by his life and by his teaching, the nature of God's love for us, the joyful and wholly remarkable truth that God loves us without reserve. This love was a love, of which the Jewish Scriptures then, the books of the law and the prophets, told us very little. Jesus came to make the new message of that unqualified love known and proclaimed. He wanted us to learn of that unending and unequivocal love. He wanted us to change our ways because we now knew of it.

He wanted that love to overwhelm us. He wanted us to find that love irresistible. So, in the light of that love, he lived as he lived and taught as he taught, emphasising that one message, as St John put it in his letter, that God is light, continuing light, and in Him there is no darkness at all.

But the love that Jesus told us of did not overwhelm us: and we did not find that love irresistible. Indeed, though Jesus was committed totally to this ministry of love, whatever the cost and whatever the consequences for himself, very few people listened and very few people were persuaded. No matter how hard he fought against the darkness and the unconcern, no matter how eloquently he spoke out against the superficiality and the dogmatism of the old way, he got virtually nowhere. It was the Romans who ran the world - and no Romans, apart from the occasional junior army officer, were listening at all: and the leading Jews of the time saw him either as irrelevant or as a dangerous upstart. His teaching was not going to change the world in his lifetime. He was going to plant a small seed - a small, unconsidered, unacknowledged seed, which contained within it the priceless message of God's love - a priceless message of love indeed - but doomed, in Jesus' lifetime at least, to go virtually unheeded.

It is clear from the Gospels that Jesus realised this and foresaw what would happen to him. He had thought through the implications of his mission. But, however we look at it, it surely cannot have been what he wanted. He did not want the message of God's love to be rejected. He wanted it welcomed. He wanted it adopted. He wanted it proclaimed from the housetops. To have wanted anything else would have been totally absurd: and, as he entered Jerusalem on that fateful Sunday at the beginning of his last week on earth, he may indeed have retained some hope that the welcome he appeared to be receiving might mean a happier outcome. But he was soon disillusioned. Other forces came into play. The authorities moved against him. Judas betrayed him. Even Peter denied him. His support simply melted away. He had not wanted to die on the Cross. This is clear from his prayer that that cup be taken from him. But he now realised that he had no choice. Only by his death could his Father's message be brought home to these greatly loved, but, as it seemed, totally disinterested, people. If he was to do His Father's business, it was now necessary to change the emphasis of the message: and it was changed. And so the message became what, since the first Good Friday, it has always been: "My love for you is endless and unequivocal. It is so great that, even when you have killed me, I will go on loving you. I will commend my spirit into God's hands: and He will raise me from the dead and show you, by my rising, that His love is stronger than death, stronger than anything you, or any powers of darkness, can put against it: and that message will overcome the world". And we did kill him: and he did rise again: and that message did overcome the world. The triumph of that message is the measure of Jesus' victory.

And what lessons there are for us here. As Jesus bore, for those seemingly endless hours, the unspeakable agonies of a man crucified, he must have looked down upon the small world of his living ministry and seen emptiness and failure. Viewed from the Cross his mission lay in ruins. He had come with a message: and that message had been thrown back in his face with pain and humiliation. Everything he had worked for had gone for nothing. Like it or not, he had for the moment failed. He suffered the most appalling physical agony: and, at the same time, he had to bear the pain of what must have appeared to be the total failure of his mission. This was pain indeed. By contrast, the pain we suffer in our lives is nothing, nothing at all. But pain can take many forms. Sometimes it is evident and dramatic, like ill-health or torture or the effects of war. More often, for you and me at least, it strikes at a different level. It takes us by surprise. We cannot prepare for it. We suffer bereavement: or we are abandoned by someone we love. A son or daughter is taken seriously ill. A lifetime's hopes are suddenly frustrated. We find we have lost our skills. Our lives suddenly come to seem pointless and unfulfilled. We suddenly seem to be quite worthless. We are suddenly overpowered by the pain of these things. We suddenly find ourselves totally lost.

But we are not lost. For the pain of these unlooked-for, unexpected calamities brings us precisely to where Jesus was on the Cross, to where Jesus always is for us, to where, even if we kill him, he will go on loving us. Jesus did not die on the Cross in pursuit of some subtle strategy. He was broken, shattered, helpless, stripped of everything, left without recourse - just as we, in our own time of failure and disappointment, are left broken and helpless, stripped of everything, left without recourse. When Jesus found himself in this condition, he abandoned himself totally to God, instinctively knowing that God would raise him up: and similarly, when we are in that condition, so can we. When things for him were at their darkest, his words were: "Father, into thy hands I commend my spirit". When things for us are at their darkest, we can commit ourselves to Christ, who is there with us and has been there before us, and commend our spirits to him. When he did that, God raised him up. Jesus' promise, the message it was His Father's business that he should bring, is that, if we commend our spirits to Christ, if we put ourselves in his hands, then the God he told us of, in his unending, unequivocal, infinite love, will raise us up also: and our faith tells us that, even from the deepest depths of our darkest despair, we will somehow be thus raised by Him. Jesus' defeat was swallowed up in victory. So, in our darkest moments, will ours be also. For Isaiah was right. Death is swallowed up in victory: and God, perhaps soon, perhaps later, will wipe away all tears from our eyes.

Road to Emmaus

St Luke Ch 24. v 15

Some of you may well remember Canon John Montague. He died shortly after Easter thirteen years ago. He had been a much-loved Rector of Buckland, a Canon of Southwark Cathedral, a most experienced and well-read priest, who was in charge of teaching the true Faith to ordinands in this diocese. He knew his theology. As it happened, his last sermon was preached in this Church: and in it he asked a very important question about the resurrection of Christ. On that day, as it was today, the reading had been about the two disciples' encounter with Jesus on the road to Emmaus: and John Montague asked:- If you had been standing beside that road on that day and seen Simon and Cleopas, those two disciples, who said that they had met Jesus on the road and talked with him, would you have seen (ie physically seen with your eyes) two men or three? - a fair and necessary question, to which he gave the (to me) surprising reply that, in his opinion, the answer was probably two. That same answer, probably two, is given today by many thinking Christians. But I was surprised by the answer, because my answer would have been three: and I believe that I would have seen three men, because I believe that there were three men on that road, Simon, Cleopas and Jesus: and that I would, had I been there, have seen all three of them. I still believe that, because I believe that Jesus rose physically from the dead, that is, was there to be seen, touched and handled in body as well as recognised and experienced in spirit. I am absolutely certain that Canon Montague also believed that Jesus rose from the dead. But, if I understood him correctly, his belief was that Jesus made himself visible to those who knew him, those who were attached to him, but not to anyone else: and that is why, had we been there, we would probably not have been able to see him on the Emmaus road. I myself do not see it like that: and I hope you will bear with me if I tell you why, because it is a question we cannot leave lying on the doormat unfaced. For, if we are to be honest with ourselves and to tell the truth to others, we must try to work out where that truth lies.

I believe that Jesus rose physically from the dead as a matter of faith and accept that it can no longer be proved by positive evidence now. There was evidence once. There were witnesses once. But they are not around any more. But it does no harm, no matter how sure your faith is, to look at the evidence: and there is a lot of it. It is:

(1)   His death was established, as required by Roman law, before he was taken down from the Cross.

(2)   His body was entombed for two full days and three nights, after which the tomb was found to be empty. If he only rose in spirit, what happened to the body?

(3)   St John's Gospel lists a whole series of occasions when Jesus was seen, encountered, spoken with and touched by large numbers of people, including Thomas, who would not believe until he had examined Jesus' now living body and handled it.

(4)   St Luke, a man of science, wrote that Jesus showed himself alive after his passion by many infallible proofs, being seen of them 40 days and speaking of the things pertaining to the kingdom of God.

(5)   St Paul, in Ch 15 of his letter to the Corinthians, wrote:" Do you still hold fast the Gospel, as I preached it to you? First and foremost, I told you the facts - that Christ died for our sins in accordance with the scriptures: that he was buried: that he was raised to life on the third day: and that he appeared to Cephas and afterwards to the Twelve and then appeared to over 500 of our brothers at once, most of whom are still alive. Then he appeared to James and afterwards to all the Apostles.

(6)   At least some of the authors of those books, those who spread this news, were writing at a time when eye witnesses, including men bitterly hostile to the publication of anything good about Jesus, were still alive. Those who

spoke of the reality of the resurrection would know that lies would be exposed and exaggeration greeted with derision. Yet they said what they said - and the message did not die out, but spread. Had Christ's body been taken from the tomb and hidden, there were plenty of people in whose interest it was to find it and expose the resurrection for the lie it might have been proved to have been. But nobody did. Consider this after all. It is absolutely clear that the disciples themselves utterly believed that Jesus had risen from the dead. The collapse of all their hopes, resulting from the crucifixion, turned, within days, to a message of exultant triumph. Everything they did and said, after that third day, shows beyond any doubt that they thought that their leader had risen from the dead: and that they thought this was so because they had seen it. And after all they were there.

(7)   As convincing as anything, on top of this, is that, from these improbable beginnings, the Christian Church began. There was no political advantage in being a Christian then. There was no money in it, no status in it, no worldly benefit in it at all. Yet people, ordinary people, went out, as we do not have to do, and died for it. They were nailed to crosses in public for it. They were murdered in secret by their enemies for it. They were thrown to lions to be eaten for it. They were derided, discriminated against, disenfranchised, enslaved, tortured and butchered for it - as we are not. And, if you ask why they did this, they did this because they believed, because they had seen it or heard it from eye-witnesses, because they knew that Jesus had risen from the dead. They put this forward, ludicrous though it sounded, in an intelligent and hostile world, because they knew that it was true: and it is their testimony and their beliefs on which our testimony and our beliefs are founded.

But it does not stop there. You have to ask yourselves, we all have to ask ourselves, what it is that we really believe and where it leads. Do you believe that Jesus was simply a remarkable man, who spoke remarkable words and did remarkable things? If so, there is no reason to believe that he physically rose from the dead. Or do you believe that Jesus was in truth the Son of God, a part of God alive on earth in human form, in biblical terms "The word made flesh", which is what the Christian Church professes? For if you believe that, then there is no reason whatever to doubt His physical resurrection. Both reason and evidence would lead directly to that conclusion. The body in which God chose to clothe himself may have been clearly dead. But God cannot die.

It comes to this. If Christ was part of God, His resurrection was natural, necessary and to be expected. If Christ was not a part of God, then His claims to be God's son and his foretelling of his resurrection were false. The Christian Church professes Christ as part of God. The Jews and the Muslims acknowledge Him as a great prophet, but not as being a part of God. We are here in this building as Christians because our Church, the self-professed body of Christ on earth, has always taught that Christ was and is part of God in person - not just a prophet, not God's representative, but God in person. And the Church teaches, has always taught, that Christ was shown to be divine by the miracle of His resurrection from the dead. If a person does not believe in the resurrection, I do not know on what basis he can believe that Christ was divine. As Archbishop Carey categorically stated: Belief in the physical resurrection of Jesus is not an appendage to our faith. It is our faith. For myself I believe that it is true. It is our duty to proclaim it: and it is worth proclaiming.

But I will add one thing more. There are clearly those in our Church, men and women of goodwill and high intelligence, whose faith in Christ as the Son of God is as strong or stronger than yours or mine, who find themselves unable to believe that this is so. Their route to God is a different route from mine - but their commitment to the Christ whom they know and worship is no less great (is often much greater) and no less sincerely held. They partake of the Body and Blood of Christ at the same communion rail as you and I: and they are part of the body of Christ's church (and just as priceless a part of Christ's church) as you and I. Our beliefs may not be identical. But they are not our enemies and we must not make war with them. For, if a man or woman is not able to believe in the physical resurrection of Jesus from the dead, but is able to believe only in some form of spiritual resurrection (as was, I believe, Canon Montague), that surely should be no reason to think any less of them, let alone to revile them or cast them out. For their belief in Almighty God and in Jesus Christ as the Son and part of Almighty God is just the same and just as valid as yours or mine. Christ did not die for our sins, in order that we might sit round in small circles and moan about it nor that we should form parties and make factions and go to war about it. He died that we might proclaim our salvation from the housetops and revel in the joy, which comes from the certainty of our hard-won immortality - a spiritual immortality which Christ, by his sacrifice and unbounded goodness, has bought for us all.

O God, the King of Glory

Sunday after Ascension Day.

O God, the King of Glory, who hast exalted Thine only Son Jesus Christ with great triumph unto Thy kingdom in Heaven, we beseech Thee, leave us not comfortless, but send to us Thine Holy Spirit to comfort us, and exalt us unto the same place whither our Saviour Christ has gone before, who liveth and reigneth with Thee and the Holy Spirit, one God, world without end, Amen.

That is the traditional Collect for today, the prayer that has been used throughout the whole of the Anglican Communion, year in and year out, on this, the Sunday after Ascension Day, for over 300 years. Today, being the Sunday after Ascension Day, is the one Sunday in the Church's year when we commemorate that peculiar moment, all those years ago, when the world was truly comfortless - that is, bereft of its source of strength - that short period of spiritual emptiness and despair between Ascension Day, when God, in the person of Jesus His Son, went away from us, and Pentecost, when God, in the person of the Holy Spirit, came back to us again. Today is a day when we, in our turn, look back to Easter and what happened then, look back to Jesus' ascension and what happened then, and look forward to Pentecost, which is next Sunday and what is going to happen then: and we ask ourselves what we make of it all and what it means to us.

The Christian Church teaches, in the words of the prayer with which I began, that God, the King of Glory, has exalted his only Son, Jesus Christ, with great triumph into His Kingdom in Heaven. Our Church asserts Christ, the Son of God, risen, ascended, glorified: and that this risen, ascended, glorified Christ is a living part of the God we worship.

Are we right to make this assertion? Is it true? Or are we lost sheep, hopelessly bleating in an empty darkness? Was Jesus truly the

Son of God, who died, but whom death could not hold? Was Jesus truly the Son of God, who rose from the dead and was seen by hundreds of witnesses, witnesses who were later to formulate and preach a Christian faith with a conviction and fervour that made them willing to die for their beliefs? Was Jesus truly the Son of God who, having returned from death in circumstances which we cannot rationally explain, then left his followers in circumstances, which we also cannot rationally explain, and never physically returned? This is what our Church has always asserted and asserts still. Do we believe it? Is it true?

We have to ask these questions, for these questions are basic to our faith. The Church teaches that Jesus rose from the dead, not because he was a remarkable man with remarkable powers, but because He was the Son of God whom death could not hold: and if Jesus truly was the Son of God whom death could not hold, then we know that our future is assured. The Son of God, whom death could not hold, has promised us eternal life with God. "I am" he said "The bread of life. If any man eat of this bread, he shall live for ever". It is you and me he is talking to. It is the bread we eat at this service that he is talking about. If it is true, it is the most wonderful news. If it is not true, but merely a cruel fantasy, then we are all wasting our time here.

I cannot stand here in this pulpit and prove to you that it is true. I wish I could. I can only assert that I have grown over many years wholly to believe it to be so: and that I wholly believe it now. Christ is reported, all over the Gospels, sometimes directly, sometimes indirectly, to have said that He was the Son of God. Men and women, all through history, most of the greatest in Western civilisation, have believed this to be so, proclaimed it and built their lives on the foundation of their faith in its truth. Many have died because they refused to deny it. Who am I, who are we, to disagree? But there are many now, who do disagree: and many more who doubt it: and the reason why so many doubt it is the perceived state of the world and the perceived behaviour of its people. We look at the fighting in Sri Lanka and the Middle East, the starvation in Africa, at hatred the whole world over: and we ask where God is and what God is doing in all this. Where, people ask, is the risen, ascended, glorified Christ in all this? The brutish prosper and the innocent perish. Where is the God of Love, whom Jesus told us of? And what has become of His Justice? It is a wholly fair question. What is the answer?

There are probably many answers: but the only answer I can put forward is simply that it is false thinking to put the blame for our human failings on God. By God's grace, human beings have free will: and they have used that free will to be cruel to each other and to cause enormous suffering to each other on this earth since time began. You don't need to see TV pictures of starving children in Africa. Go to any mental hospital at any time and see what has happened to some of God's children there. Read any history book and you will see that today's human savagery and suffering are quite mild compared to what has been done in the past. The point is that God, through whom man has free will, has made him to use that free will freely - and sometimes to use it for good purposes and sometimes to use it for bad purposes: and it has never been the Christian case, has never been anyone's case, that God will see to it on this earth that all men are comfortable or that all men are fairly treated or that all men will be free from pain. It would be nice if it were so. But it is not so and never has been so. Jesus did not say "Come to me all who are poor, and I will see that you have enough". He did not say "Come to me all that are hungry and I will give you material benefits". Nor did he say "Come to me all who are in physical pain and I will relieve it for you". What he did say was "Take no thought for your life, what you will eat or what you will drink or for your body what you will put on. Seek rather "he said "The Kingdom of God and His righteousness, for it is your Father's good pleasure to give you . . . . . the Kingdom" - not, of course, the material kingdom here and now, but the kingdom of Heaven, which is another and greater thing altogether. He told us, his followers, to care for the poor. He told us, his followers, to look after our neighbours and to do all we can to prevent hunger and thirst. He told us, his followers, to do what we can to ease the sufferings of those in pain, as He did Himself while he was here on earth. But He never promised that there would be a world HERE without poverty, a world HERE without hunger or a world HERE without suffering. Maybe you think He should have done. Some certainly do. But it is plain wrong to arrogate to ourselves the right to tell God what He should do and plain wrong to reject God, because He has not done what we want or what we think He ought to have done.

No. Christ never promised that there would be a world without human suffering. Nor did He die on the cross, so that there might be an end to human suffering. He promised us many things: and He died for many things. But He did not promise or die for that. He died on the cross to redeem the sins of all mankind, so that man's sinful nature should not impede his path to eternal life with God. God is almighty and there is nothing He cannot do. There is no limit to His power to respond to prayer (I believe that firmly) and God's response to prayer is frequent, if unforeseeable. But, subject to that, Christ made no promises as to the quality of human life. What He did promise (and this is the nub of it) was eternal life hereafter - unspeakable joys when this life is done: and if we are assured of that - and we are assured of that - then our worries and our sufferings in this earthly life are seen, by God's Grace, to be transient and bearable. What we have now, for better or worse, we have now - and we use our faith to make the best of it. But our end, when it comes, is to be a new and wonderful beginning for us, just as the ascension of the risen Christ was a new and wonderful return for Him to the place from which He came. He is risen, ascended, glorified. His promise is that, when our turn comes, we too will, by some process we cannot possibly guess at, be somehow brought to the place He has prepared for us, where the Father, who has loved us as His own, will be with us and will care for us, until His further purposes for us are fulfilled.

So it is that our prayer for today is that with which I began:-
O God, the King of Glory, who hast exalted Thine only Son Jesus
Christ with great triumph unto Thy Kingdom in Heaven, we
beseech Thee, leave us not comfortless, but send to us Thine Holy
Spirit to comfort us and exalt us unto the same place, whither our
Saviour Christ has gone before - who liveth and reigneth with
Thee and the Holy Spirit, one God, world without end, Amen.

Behold the handmaid of the Lord - Mothering Sunday

St Luke Ch 1 v 38.

We are thinking of mothers today - old mothers, new mothers, stressed mothers, hard-working mothers, loving mothers- all of them women without whom there would be no joy, without whom indeed there would be no life: and I want to take the opportunity to share with you some thoughts about the woman, who was and is, to us in the Church of Christ, perhaps the most important mother of all, Mary the mother of Jesus, of whom we heard briefly in today's Gospel reading; "Woman, behold thy son". Woman, behold thy son. And, as Mary stood there by the cross, hearing her son speak those words, her mind must have gone back to the beginning and the visit and words of the angel all those years before: "Hail, thou that art highly favoured. The Lord is with thee. Thou hast found favour with God. Thou shalt conceive in thy womb and bring forth a son.The Holy Ghost shall come upon thee and the power of the Highest shall overshadow thee. That holy thing that shall be born of thee shall be called The Son of God. And her reply. "Behold the handmaid of the Lord. Be it unto me according to thy word".

Be it unto me according to Thy word. This act, Mary's acceptance of her destiny, when you consider how young she was and the strict moral standards of her time, can be described as one of the most remarkable acts of faith in human history. That is why she is revered as a saint in the Roman Catholic Church and in many parts of the Church of England. The Christian Church, to which you and I belong, teaches that not only was Mary, the mother of Christ, fulfilling as noble a calling as any woman could receive, but that she gave birth as a virgin, the child Jesus being conceived without any human sexual contact. The Church roundly asserts this and has asserted it for nearly 2000 years. But many people don't, can't, believe it. There are many priests in the Church who say they are unable to accept it, some of our bishops, I believe, among them.

It is said by them to be a pretty piece of fiction, a nice, but unnecessary, piece of icing on the cake of the Christian story, but not essential to our faith, not a necessary part of the Christian Gospel. I have met many good people, some churchgoers, some not, who say that they accept and believe much of what the Church of Christ teaches, but that a virgin birth is just too difficult, too impossible to credit. I want, as a layman with no authority to teach you anything, to take this opportunity to address this issue with you. For there is a real conflict here. Some view Mary, the mother of Jesus, as a shining example of pure living, true faith and godly obedience, the woman blessed among women, chosen by God to conceive, carry, give birth to and nurture the son of God. Others contend that the idea of a virgin birth is pure fiction, designed to explain away the (to some) unpalatable truth that Jesus was born as a result of (what was to the Jews) an untimely, unlawful and seriously disgraceful sexual encounter between two unmarried people - a false tale dreamed up to disguise the fact that Jesus' mother was, by the standards of her time, a loose young woman whose behaviour in and about Jesus' conception and birth was a disgrace.

The first question you may ask - and many do - is: Does it matter? And the answer has to be Yes it does. To be born out of wedlock in those days was a serious disgrace. They were days, remember, when women, found committing adultery, were likely to be stoned to death in public, when the conception of a child outside the bonds of marriage brought public disgrace upon mother and child alike. If Jesus was truly the illegitimate child of Mary and Joseph, then all the talk of a virgin birth and an immaculate conception is simply a deceitful cover-up, designed to deceive and mislead. It means that our faith that Jesus was, in any sense, the son of God is based upon a direct and purposely-spoken series of lies. We have to face this: and I want to face it with you this morning, so that we face it together and hopefully end up facing the same way.

The arguments of those who do not accept the virgin birth are obvious. They say that it is a ridiculous suggestion for which there is no evidence at all. No one knows the truth now. No one knew the truth then, except Mary and Joseph themselves - and, so far as we know, they told no one at all, except perhaps St Luke. It is a fiction, set up long after Jesus died. There is no evidence that anyone mentioned it while the actors in the drama were alive: and it is, in any event, impossible. For we all know how babies are made. Male sperm and female eggs are made to meet one another in a natural and random process, unite, change their shape and start to grow. This is the only way in which a human body with legs, arms, head, face and brain can be made. There is no other way. Jesus cannot have been born in human shape from a human mother unless this process took place. There can be no alternative. If Jesus had been a spirit, they say, and not a human being with bones, flesh and blood, it might be different - but, since there is only one way in which a human being with bones, flesh and blood can be brought into existence, the story of the virgin birth must be fantasy.

These are obviously strong arguments. They are the stronger because they are so obvious. At first sight, they are unanswerable. Many people find them so. But there is another side to the coin - and you can't examine it without asking yourself two other questions first - and they are fundamental questions. They are: Do you believe in God? And, if so, what sort of a God do you believe in? If you don't believe in God, of course, there is no problem. If you don't believe in God, there is no basis for a belief in a virgin birth and no reason to look for one. But you do believe in God, don't you? For if you did not believe, you would not, I imagine, be here. So I ask: What sort of a God do you believe in? For the Christian Church, like the Jews who led the way for them, proclaims an Almighty God, a God whose powers are unlimited and whose ability, if it is His will, to override the natural process and cause miraculous effects is credible, genuine and well-authenticated. Many of the things we see as wonderful in this world are part of the natural process - the birth of a child, the delicacy and smell of a rose in summer, a glorious sunset - these are part of the good things in life which are part of the natural process. We thank God for them. But they are not miracles.

Events for which there is no natural explanation, events which are contrary to the natural process, the things we call miracles, are rare - but miraculous events in the Gospel stories and in the Old Testament and miraculous events recorded in history since then are there for us to consider and are among the foundations for our belief that the God we worship is an almighty God, for whom anything is possible, if He wills it done. If you don't believe in an almighty God, you are in difficulties, because then your belief is a belief in a God, whose powers are in some way limited or circumscribed by the laws of nature, which is almost a contradiction in terms. But if you believe in an almighty God, whose powers include the ability, if He wills it, to intervene in the natural world and achieve results which the natural process cannot achieve, then your belief is a belief in the God which the Christian Church (and just about every other religion in the world) proclaims. If you believe this, you are not alone. You stand with the great majority.

So I come back to the question of the birth of Jesus. If you don't believe in the power of God to override the natural process, then there is no basis for belief in the virgin birth - nor much for believing in the divinity of Christ either. But if you do believe in the power of God to override the natural process, then the virgin birth becomes not only possible and credible, it is seen to be probable and necessary. For if God's Son was to be born on earth, a human being with a divine nature, coming to us for the great purposes of which He spoke, then his birth surely HAD to be a miraculous event because God could not be born on earth in any other way. No child, born of a woman by the natural human process, could have any standing, any recognition, any claim to be the Son of God.

So you make your choice. If Jesus was simply a remarkable man who used remarkable words and did remarkable things, then there is no reason to believe, nor any reason to want to believe, that his birth was miraculous. But if that is all you believe, there is no reason to worship him either. But if Jesus was the Son of God, was a human being whose nature was uniquely divine, if he was the word made flesh who dwelt among us, the only begotten of the Father, full of grace and truth (which is what our Church has always taught that he was), then his birth is to be seen and wondered at as one of God's greatest miracles: and his mother's acceptance of her destiny in this was indeed one of the finest, most fundamental, acts of faith in human history.

Make your own choice. The Church welcomes you whatever your choice is. I have long believed in the omnipotence of God and in the divinity of Jesus. Believing that, I see no reason to doubt, indeed I see every reason to believe, that Jesus' birth was uniquely achieved through the exercise of God's unlimited power in the way the Gospel describes it. Next time you recite the Apostles' creed, consider, when you come to the words in issue, whether you believe what you say. I will believe it. Will you?

Philip and the Ethiopian

Acts. Ch 18 v 27

St Luke Ch 15, v.10. "There is joy, I tell you, among the angels of God over one sinner who repents".

Our task in this life is, each of us, to find our way to God: and we, who are the Church, are called on to help others find their way to God also. Each single spirit, brought home to God from the wilderness, is a victory for Christ: and one of the first such spirits, of whom we learn in the Bible after Jesus' death and resurrection, is the Ethiopian official, about whom we heard in today's first reading.

We don't know much about Philip, who did the bringing home. He came of age as a teacher of Jesus' message very quickly. He was in the second batch of disciples selected by Jesus. He is not reported as saying or doing anything much through almost the whole of Jesus' ministry. Then, suddenly, after a long time in Jesus' company and really not very long before Jesus' arrest and trial, there comes that dramatic confrontation with Jesus, when, together with Thomas, Philip learned the real truth, a truth he had not guessed at or begun to understand.

You know the passage – St John, Ch 14. Jesus says: "I go to prepare a place for you. You know where I am going and you know the way I will take". Thomas says: "We do not know where you are going, so how can we know the way?" Jesus answers: "I am the way, the truth and the life. If you know me, you know my Father too. Because you know me, you have seen Him". Philip, still not following, chips in:" Lord, show us the Father and it will be enough for us". Jesus says: "Have I been so long time with you and yet have you not known me, Philip? He who has seen me has seen the Father" – which means "Has been in the presence of God" – and continues with words of comfort and assurance that have lit the lives of Christians down 2000 years of history. Up till now, Philip had not known what was going on. Now he did.

Within a few short weeks, he went on to witness the last supper, the horrors of Jesus' crucifixion, the despair of the disciples, then Jesus' resurrection and the joy that infused them all, when they saw him again – and then, not many weeks later, he has this encounter with the Ethiopian – and then he vanishes and is heard of in the Bible no more.

The Ethiopian was a stranger, who wanted to know about God. He knew nothing. He was a lost sheep. He was sitting in his chariot, reading Isaiah. Philip asked "Do you understand what you are reading?": and the man replied: "How can I unless someone explains it to me" and asks about the passage he is reading. So Philip tells him about Jesus and the lamb who went willingly to the slaughter – and the Ethiopian was baptised within the hour, asserting a belief which, thanks to Philip, he now held, that Jesus was indeed the Son of God.

How did Philip know what he should do? And how did Philip know what he should say? He knew what he should do, because Jesus had told him to go and spread the Gospel – to feed my sheep. Jesus' instruction to you and me is exactly the same. Philip knew what he should say because he had it from Jesus direct. Jesus had looked him in the eye and told him – just as Jesus, either in person or through others, has looked you and me in the eye and told us. You and I have been the lost sheep of today's Gospel reading. We need a shepherd to help us find the fold. But when we are safely in the fold and truly confirmed in our places there, we are called, are we not, to go out and be shepherds ourselves – to be shepherds and find other lost sheep, to be Philips and find Ethiopians, to be what Jesus called "Fishers of men", not to stand still and stay mute, but to preach Christ to others, as we go about the place. Do we do this? If you meet someone who is curious about Christ and wants to know, what do you say? Suppose you are on your way to church and, at the lych gate out there, you meet a stranger, who asks where you are going and why, what do you say to him?

An old friend of mine, now dead, had that happen to him once. He was talking to some schoolchildren and told them he had been going to church for over 60 years. One of them asked him: "Do you believe all that stuff then?" – and he replied that the fact that you go to church does not necessarily mean that you believe anything and let the matter drop. I was sad when he told me he had said that, but we are often embarrassed to talk about our faith and afraid that we may put in badly, so we shy away from it. But we really ought to be able to do better than that – for God gave us brains and powers of speech and we have been offered every sort of enlightenment: and we should surely try to accept the challenge to use these things sensibly in Christ's service, when we get the chance.

If you go to a modern service of baptism or confirmation, you will find that those who take part are called on to declare: "We believe in one God Father, Son and Holy Spirit. This is our faith" – but, if you say that to the Ethiopian or to the stranger at the church gate, it won't mean much to him. They are words which mean a lot to those who understand them, but not much to those who do not. No. If you are going to tell the stranger what he wants to know, you have to go further than that. It is risky (for you may get it wrong or break down) and it will take time. But Christ requires us to take risks in His service: and, when it comes to the point, we have to know what our faith is.

What is our faith? I can only tell you what mine is. Yours may be different, but no less valid. You may put it in different words. I put it thus. I believe that the world, and the human race, came to be through the decision and the action of some being, who is greater than humanity, a being of unlimited power and dimensions beyond our ability to envisage or describe. That being has a name. We call Him God. Well-documented history relates that God has intervened powerfully and effectively in the affairs of the human race and has chosen to communicate with some people on earth through special interpreters, whom we call priests or prophets. But later, thousands of years after life on earth began and about 2000 years ago, there was a special intervention, when God came to earth Himself, having caused a human being, the one we call

Jesus, to be created by divine intervention, and, while here, did many things which are recorded in the Gospels. Among other things, He showed how a human being can live a life free of offence, according to the way God wishes it.

He also taught us about God – and in particular that He is a God who loves us unconditionally, who cares about what we do and who can, and will, bring to eternal life with Him the spirits of those who do, or try to do, His will. And finally that He chose to die a deeply painful death as a sign that he shares our earthly pain and as a sacrifice to redeem the offences of the human race. God, in the person of His Son, took upon Himself the pain the human race deserved to suffer: and bought for the human race the blessing of eternal life with God, which only He deserved. He gave us the riches due to Him and took in exchange the rags due to us. That is my faith: and it is also my belief that, through what we call the Holy Spirit, Jesus is in us still: and we go to church to give Him the worship He deserves and to be momentarily united with Him in this service which we call Communion. It is this that gives us the strength to face the future with joy in our hearts.

That, my friend (I like to think I would say) is why I am going to church today. Learning about God is a lifetime's study and I could not tell it all in 5 years, let alone in 5 minutes. But come and see and listen – and, maybe, through the Holy Spirit, Christ will talk to you, as I believe He has once or twice talked to me.

We have been going to church for as long time now, some of us. We ought to know what we are about by now. Jesus told Philip: "He who has seen me has seen God. You have seen me – so you have seen God too". Philip believed that and told it to the Ethiopian. So should we. Christ's command to us is to go out with that message and search for God's lost sheep in the wilderness of this world's temptations – and one soul found will make the angels in heaven rejoice. Let us see what we can do.

Trinity Sunday

St Matthew. Ch 28. v 19

I do not want to talk about flowers today, though perhaps I should. I have a friend, whom I respect greatly, who told me that, whenever she sees a beautiful flower, her faith in God is reinforced – and that is no surprise. These flowers are very beautiful and are a great gift from God, as are the human hands that arranged them and, come to that, the human minds which put the hands to work to such wonderful effect. Our minds truly are the greatest engines which God created and, like the flowers and the hands, Christ calls us to use them in His service. These have been used in His service and are a phenomenal display and we give thanks, great thanks, for the love and the skill which went into their presentation. But I do not want to talk about flowers. I want to talk about the God who gave them to us, the God who gave us the hands, the God who gave us the minds, which put the hands to work For today is the first Sunday after Trinity - a day when we think of the Holy Trinity and are invited to stop and ask ourselves who or what it is that we worship in our Church - and why. If a stranger was standing by the gate as you came in and asked you what you were coming here to do, what would you say? And, if he asked you what this God, whom you come here to worship, was, what would you answer? On this issue I offer you as a text the words from today's second reading, Jesus' words from the end of St Matthew's Gospel "Go ye therefore and teach all nations, baptising them in the name of the Father and of the Son and of the Holy Spirit".

In the old Prayer Book, the Collect for Trinity Sunday called upon churchgoers "To acknowledge the glory of the eternal Trinity and, in the power of the divine Majesty, to worship the Unity" - a possibly glorious concept, which seems to leave many members of the Church of England completely baffled. What is this Trinity, this Unity? Why, we ask, make it so complicated? Why, we ask, can't you leave me to worship God in peace? But, if we are to know what it is that we are doing: and if we are to give an answer to the stranger at the gate (or anywhere else, come to that): we have to try to find answers to some of the difficult questions, which grow, like thorny hedges, round the worship, round the churchgoing, in which we engage. It is pretty bad if we do not have an answer for the stranger. But it may be more worrying still if we do not have an answer for ourselves. What is this God we speak of? What are we really doing here?

No one has ever seen God. But Jesus has told us about Him: and there is, I think, no needless complexity. Jesus' only reported mention of what we now call the Trinity is this passage at the end of St Matthew's Gospel and He did not try to explain what He meant. In His ministry, He had taught about God the Father; He had identified Himself as God, His Son, though He called Himself the Son of Man: and He spoke of the coming of the Holy Spirit. But the realisation of the Holy Trinity, three persons in one God, came later. The need for such a doctrine was obvious; and I, for myself, see no reason why we should feel bemused by it. God the Father is God. It has always been so. Christians believe that Jesus was divine, that is a part of God, a man endowed with God's nature: and that, when the Holy Spirit came at Pentecost, that was also God in action. But the thinkers asked, as, since they were thinking, they had to ask: Is Jesus the same God as God the Father? Or is He a different God? If He is a different God, then there is more than one God - and that is contrary to all our teaching. If He is the same God, then where was God the Father, while Jesus was on earth? For, while Jesus was man on earth, he prayed to God the Father, as though He was a different being. To the thinkers, the people who used their God-given minds to answer the thorny questions, this was a problem.

And it is from the search for answers to these questions that the doctrine of the Holy Trinity developed - three persons in one God or, if you prefer other wording, three aspects of the same God, that same God having different identities at the same time: and it is at this point, when we try to say in clear terms what we mean, when we try to put into words what we understand these differing aspects of God to be like, that we run into difficulty. For God is beyond words. As Bishop David Jenkins, the former Bishop of Durham, who loved to make things plain, though he was often very controversial, put it:' The minute we come to try to say something about God, we are up against the limitation of words. For, as we celebrate who God is and how God comes to be, we have to face up to God being the mystery whom it is beyond the human collection of words to describe'. But nevertheless, if we are, as Christians, to communicate to others and amongst ourselves such ideas as we have about God, we find ourselves impelled, do we not, to try and say (and say in words, since we have no other vehicle) what we understand. So let me try.

God the Holy Spirit, the breath of the Almighty in our lives, the voice of the Almighty in our ears, the ever-present means by which this God, this indescribably wonderful all-pervading power, communicates with us and infuses us. As Bishop David Jenkins put it: God the Holy Spirit is God within us as Spirit – within us in the intimacy of our inmost being, God within us, an ever-present influence, whether we are conscious of Him or not, working within us to see our tasks properly done.

Then God the Son. Jesus Christ, ever present in and an integral part of each one of us, never absent, always there, on every field of love and every field of conflict, in every place of work, in every home, on every street corner, at every birth and at every death, the path and the person by whom alone we, as Christians, can come to the Father. As David Jenkins put it: God the Son is God as the personification of love - God who expresses Himself in vulnerability and rejection, God always where we are, being at one with our joy and our pain, at one with our living and our dying - God personifying Love.

And then, first and last, Alpha and Omega, God the Father - the God we do not meet, the God we cannot see, the God whom we often feel we do not know at all - yet even so the God whom we are commanded to love. As David Jenkins put it: God the Father is God greater than great - the mystery who is the source and sustainer of everything: yet whom we do not have the words or the vision or the understanding to take in or comprehend. Who or what is God the Father? No one has ever seen God, but we may all have our own visions of God. More books have been written about God than about anything else in Heaven or earth - and still no one has ever seen God and no one can tell what God is like.

And it is here, within the mystery, that perhaps a glimpse of the truth may be discerned. God is greater than great, too powerful, too substantial for us to be able to understand or describe. But that is not all that God is. We are not simply floating in the void, you and I, lost in the magnificence of this unknowable and indescribable being. God is also there with us in the shape of Jesus, whom we CAN see, whom we CAN know, who knows us and loves us and is always with us, wherever we are. And God is there in the spirit as the Holy Spirit, continually infusing us with the power to get things done. We cannot walk with God the Father, because he is beyond us in the mist, beyond our understanding. But we can walk and we do walk with God the Son and with God the Holy Spirit, for they are here with us, wherever we are and whatever we are doing. The magic of the Holy Trinity is that, while God the Father may be beyond our understanding, God the Son and God the Holy Spirit are not beyond our understanding. They are here and now - with us and available. God is not a distant dream. In the person of Jesus and in the breathing of the Holy Spirit, God is with us all the time.

And that, I truly believe, is how it is. In the person of Jesus and in the breathing of the Holy Spirit, God is with us all the time, here to be prayed to, here to be consulted, here to lead, guide, comfort and console. And, if you ask me what we should do, I think the answer is this. We should pray to the God we know and, as we do so, seek to learn more about the God who is beyond our understanding, the God we cannot yet know, the God we cannot yet see. It was Pope John Paul who said that it is in prayer that Jesus leads us to His Father. He also said that it is through prayer that the Holy Spirit transforms our lives. God is Father, Son and Holy Spirit. But Jesus and the Holy Spirit are the God we know, are the God who is with us all the time: and we must pray to them and listen to them and work at getting to know them. The more we do that, the more we get to know them, the greater chance, I think, we will have of learning more.

Have I been with you all this time? Trinity Sunday

St John. Ch 14. v 8.

"Go forth, therefore, and make all nations my disciples. Baptise men everywhere in the name of the Father and the Son and the Holy Spirit: and teach them to observe all that I have commanded you". This passage, from the last few words of St Matthew's Gospel, is Jesus' only reported reference to the Holy Trinity and is the first time the Holy Trinity is mentioned in the Bible. The concept of the Holy Trinity, the assertion of a faith in Three Persons and One God, Father, Son and Holy Spirit, is one of the fundamental elements of Christian belief: and it involves, of course, the assertion, as a basic Article of Faith, that Christ was the Son of God, a true part of God, in the world and in human form, a man who was literally divine: and I choose this passage as my principal text to day, since today is Trinity Sunday, the day when we commemorate the Holy Trinity: and I want to link it with another passage, this time from St John, Ch 14, which was the chosen Gospel for the day about two weeks ago, a passage which is much better known. Jesus had been talking about his Father: and Philip, the apostle, who did not understand what Jesus meant, blurted out: "Lord, show us the Father and we ask no more". Jesus answered: "Have I been with you all this time and have you not known me Philip? He who has seen me has seen the Father".

Baptise men everywhere in the name of the Father, Son and Holy Spirit. Have I been with you all this time and have you not known me? He who has seen me has seen the Father.

In your dream, you are standing at the top of a long field, looking down the hill into the shallow valley beneath. You are alone, the sun is shining. You are waiting for something, you do not quite know what. As you look down this hill, you see

116

Jesus approaching, coming towards you, walking slowly, but purposefully. Who is this man? Who is this man?

Consider what we know. This is the man who spent his life doing good, the man who gave us the Sermon on the Mount, which is the finest, and most complete, description ever given of how life should be lived. This is the man who devoted his life to telling his contemporaries about God, God's nature and God's works. This is the man who, all through his life, sought nothing for himself, but served others tirelessly and asked no credit for it. This is the man who healed those, whom the medical science of the day could do nothing to help: and who, when he did so, felt that virtue had gone out of him. This is the man who foretold his own death and, knowing what lay in store for him, went out and suffered it without complaint, forgiving those who killed him, even as they applied the torture. This is the man who died and rose from the dead, being seen by hundreds of people and proving to the doubters that his resurrection was a reality. And this is the man who said he was the Son of God. Who is this man? Baptise all men in the name of the Father, SON and Holy Spirit. Have I been with you all this time and have you not known me Philip? He who has seen me has seen the Father.

These passages are two of many occasions recorded in the Gospels where Jesus appears to spell out His real identity: and they are passages, which are the very foundations of the Church's teaching that Christ was the Son of God, a part of God, another face of God. There are professing Christians who will not accept that Christ was divine. But they are, I think, a very small minority. After all, if you do not accept that Christ was divine, what conceivable reason can there be to worship him?

Who is this man? Is he just a great prophet, as the Muslims believe? Is he just a remarkable man, who says remarkable things and uses remarkable words? Or is he more than that, which is what the Christian Church teaches and has always taught and believed? I ask the question because we have to make a choice:

and the whole pattern of our lives, beliefs and hopes may depend on the choice we make.

We are not dealing in fiction here. That we know. For there can be no doubt, can there, that Jesus lived. History testifies to that and no one contradicts it. The evidence about how he lived is clear and incontrovertible. So is the evidence about the substance of what he said. Who is this man? We have to ask: is it possible that a man, who lived as Jesus lived and preached what Jesus preached, a man who lived a life and preached a message of unimpeachable purity and probity, could claim to be the Son of God, as he did claim, and then go on to prove it by rising from the dead, is it possible that such a man could be anything other than that which he claimed to be? For, if he claimed to be the Son of God and was not, he must have been a blasphemer and charlatan of the worst order: and it simply cannot be that a man, who lived as he lived and taught what he taught, could be such a thing. Either he was a fraud and we cannot believe a word he said: or else he was what he claimed to be and we should believe everything he said. I do not think there can be any halfway house between those two conclusions.

You may be convinced. You may not be convinced. I am - but you may not be. It is your business. To reach a conclusion on the question takes many people many years. It takes some a lifetime to reach a decision. But you cannot ignore the question. To ignore the question is like going to a restaurant and refusing to look at the menu. If you refuse to look at the menu, you cannot know what is available, what is there for you: and you need to know whether there is anything there for you, and, if there is anything, what it is. For, if Jesus was not telling us the truth, there is nothing to live for, no long-term purpose in life, no prospect of anything hereafter. We live in the gloom of knowing that our time here is short and the end of it is the end of everything. But, if Jesus was telling us the truth, if God exists and if God saw to it that His Son, a part of him, came to this planet and lived a human life in order to bring us to the salvation which he promised us, then we have enormous cause for rejoicing, for rejoicing at the knowledge of what lies ahead. If the gate of glory has been opened and death is seen to be the pathway to that gate, then we can rejoice in the assurance of God's love and at the prospect of joys to come when life is over. We can and should live our lives with the clear and perceived purpose of finding our way to the God who has been so good to us. We can and should keep our eyes fixed on Christ and put our entire trust in him: and live our lives on the foundation of that trust. As we go about our affairs day by day, either Christ is with us and in us - or else he is not. He said that He would be. The Church teaches that he is. I believe he is. That is why I am standing here. Do you?

In your dream, you are standing at the top of a long field, looking down into the shallow valley beneath. The sun is shining. You are alone, waiting for something, you do not quite know what. As you look down this hill, you see Jesus approaching, coming towards you, walking slowly but purposefully. Who is this man? Who is this man?

And, as you stand there in your dream and ask yourself that question, it may be, just may be, that you will hear, at the back of your mind, at the very edge of your perception, a still small voice: Have I been with you all this time and have you not known me Philip? He who has seen me has seen the Father.

Peace

St John. Ch 14 v 27

From St Luke, Ch 11, verse 9: Ask and it shall be given you. Seek and ye shall find. Knock and it shall be opened unto you: and from today's second reading, St John, Ch 14, verse 27. "Peace I leave with you. My peace I give unto you. Let not your heart be troubled, neither let it be afraid".

My peace I give unto you. We pray to God as The God of Peace and we refer to Christ as the prince of peace. We use this wording every time we come to church. But what do we mean? And what is the peace that Christ has left with us? He was clearly not speaking of world peace, peace between nations, peace between believers. Indeed, in Chapter 12 of St Luke's gospel, Jesus is reported as having said: "Suppose ye that I have come to give peace on earth? I tell you, Nay; but rather division. For, from henceforth, there shall be five in one house divided, three against two and two against three; and he went on to say that all the relatives would be divided, one against the other and that the day would come, when his followers would be hated for spreading his gospel and that men would teach that those, who killed his followers, would be doing God service. And he was right about that, terrifyingly right. More blood has been shed on this unhappy earth of ours in what were seen as religious causes than for any other cause. Catholics and Protestants massacred and burned one another to death in our market places for what they believed to be Christ's sake five hundred years ago: and Muslims are murdering one another in the streets of Baghdad and claiming to do it in the name of the one true God even today. In our own churches today, we Christians argue and claw each other to pieces over gender and sexual practices, even refusing to take Communion together because of these disputes. Our God has not been the God of Peace and Christ has not been the prince of Peace – not then and not now. We claim that we have a Gospel to proclaim, but the outside and wondering world is often at a total loss to know what that Gospel is. It does not appear to be a gospel of peace – and we must face this and try to find out where we are and what we are talking about.

What we have, through our faith, is peace of a different kind altogether. Christ, through his life, teaching, death and resurrection, has given us the means to attain eternal life with God. That, I believe, was the purpose for which He came here: and that, I believe, is the object He achieved. He has given us what that great prayer, the general Thanksgiving, called "The means of Grace and the hope of Glory", a chance, as individuals, to find what has been called "The peace of God which passeth all understanding" .The message, the Gospel, the promise is that, if we commit our lives to Christ while we are here, we and those we love will, at our death, gain the chance of access to a realm beyond our own, the chance of access to eternal peace with God. What that place, that existence, is like, we cannot see, we cannot know, we cannot guess. But that is the promise – the chance to get there after our death and peace of mind, confidence, if you like, that this is our inheritance, if we seek it.

But it is all very well being told that you have a chance of an inheritance, if you seek it. The burning question is How do I seek it? And where do I look? Or, as the lawyer asked Jesus in a well-told story: What must I do to inherit eternal life?

And how I wish that I could give you an answer to that. It is the question that has tantalised seekers after God since time began. But I can make a start with a story, which some of you will know, the story of the priest, who had an appointment to see his bishop at a stated time and arrived late. "I am sorry, my Lord" he said "I have always put great faith in my watch". "You don't want great faith in your watch" the bishop replied "You need good works in it". I suspect that, when we are seeking the road to eternal life, it is good works that we will need. We can say that we believe without, probably, being very sure what our beliefs really are. We can say "Lord Lord" as much as we like and with a faith as deep as the deepest oceans. But Jesus, I suspect, told us the truth, when He said "Not everyone that saith unto me Lord Lord shall enter into the kingdom of Heaven, but he that doeth the will of my Father, which is in Heaven". And our task on this earth is to strive to find out what God's will for us is: and then go out and get on with doing it.

Ah Yes, you will say, that's all very well, but how do I know what God's will for me is? My answer is that you will never know, until you try to find out: and you try to find out by prayer, by seeking Communion with Christ, by listening and by trying to love others as you know that Christ has loved you. Do you remember that wonderful passage in John Bunyan's Pilgrim's Progress, where Mr Christian and Evangelist meet and Mr Christian is in the dark and does not know which way to go? Evangelist says "Why standest thou still?" and Mr Christian answers "Because I know not whither to go". Then said Evangelist, pointing into the darkness across a very wide field: "Seest thou yonder wicket gate?" He answered "No". "Seest thou then yonder shining light?" "I think I do". And Evangelist says "Keep that light in your eye and go directly up thereto. So shalt thou find the gate, whereon, when thou knockest, it shall be told thee what thou shalt do". This is how it probably is for all of us. We start in ignorance and proceed to uncertainty, but, if we have any sense, we ask the way. We ask the way and we start to listen and we go on listening and find, in time, that we are learning. And, as we seek to learn the truth and find ourselves truly searching through the darkness, we will, in the distance, descry that half-seen shining light. If we follow the shining light, we will find the gate. If we open the gate, we will find what we are looking for. It may not be easy and it will probably not be quick. It may require effort, prayer at a deep level and very careful thought. It is likely to require integrity, selflessness and a loving heart: and we will find, in the end, what it is that God wants of us. What God wants of you will probably be very different from what God wants of me, because we are all very different, with different skills, different characters and different backgrounds But, if you ask and if you listen, you will learn what it is that Christ wants of you. It is a personal pilgrimage in which you are never alone and in which you will be always learning. And it may very well be the most satisfying journey of your life. I cannot tell you what the destination will be and I cannot tell you how long it will take you to get there. But the end is the Peace, the peace of mind, which Christ has given to you and given to all of us. Ask and it shall be given you. Seek and ye shall find. Knock and it shall be opened unto you.

Everyone Who Invokes
the Name of the Lord

St Paul Epistle to Romans. Ch 14. v 27

I want to ask you a question this morning. It is a question about what you believe. Maybe it matters. Maybe it doesn't. But I want to ask it just the same. It is this. Do you believe that a devout Muslim, who worships the God he has been told about and lives a good and loving life in his family and in his community, has the chance of achieving eternal life with God, when he dies? We believe that a devout Christian, who worships the God he has been told about and lives a good and loving life in his family and in his community, has the chance of achieving eternal life with God. Do we believe the same for the devout Muslim? I have, over the past months, asked this question of a number of churchgoers from parishes other than our own: and the answer has been almost unanimously Yes, yes he does. Whether or not it is what the Church of England teaches, I do not know. I think it depends on what church you attend and whom you listen to. And, because I think it matters enormously to all of us, who care about our Church, I want to share some thoughts with you about this issue – and today's reading from St Paul's letter to the Christians in Rome may help us in this – or it may not. In this passage, Paul writes:- "Everyone who has faith in him will be saved – everyone. There is no distinction between Jew and Greek, because the same Lord is Lord of all. For everyone who calls on the name of the Lord will be saved. How could they call on one in whom they did not believe? And how could they believe in one they had never heard of? How, you may ask, indeed? I think, though, that St Paul, in this passage, when he speaks of The Lord, is speaking of Christ the Son, not of God the Father . And thereby hangs the problem.

You may ask: What does it matter? I have my faith, such as it is. Why should I bother whether the God I believe in will welcome a Muslim into His kingdom? What has that got to do with me? It is a fair question. But I think it matters a lot because we have to know what it is we believe and what sort of a God we believe in. When people ask us, when our children, our friends, our children's friends, ask us what we believe and why we believe it, do we have an answer? And, if so, what is it? Is the God we worship a God, who sent His Son into the world to save only those who had the chance to hear about Christ? Or a God who sent His Son into the world that everyone might be saved? Is the God we worship a God, who gave His Son so that all who commit their lives to Him should have everlasting life? Or so that only those, who believe a particular creed might attain that state? Do we worship a God who loves everyone? Or a God who loves only just the choosing few? I have said this many times before, but we are charged to love God with all our minds. We can hardly pretend to do that, if we always switch our minds off – and stop thinking - whenever His name is mentioned – or can we?

The one person who said No to my question about the devout Muslim was a devout Christian, who does, as many see it it, great work for Christ. He worships regularly at Holy Trinity, Brompton, a very full church, where many people worship and many people come to believe. He runs Alpha courses, takes the Gospel to men and women in prisons, takes great joy in his faith in Christ and is a leader among his people. He had no doubt about the answer to the question. He quoted one of Jesus' most-reported sayings and was firm about it. Jesus, he said, had told his disciples: I am the way, the truth and the life. No man comes to the Father but by me. There is, he said, no room for argument. If you do not accept that Christ was the Son of God and rose from the dead, you cannot reach the Kingdom of Heaven, you cannot attain eternal life: and I fear that there are many churchgoers, who hold and preach the same opinion. I am a layman. I am not a theologian and I have no authority to teach you anything. My only qualification is that I have been a communicant member of this church for many years, I have thought deeply about these issues and have reached some conclusions. I do not say that I am right and he is wrong. If that is his revelation of the loving God our Church proclaims, I cannot assert that he is wrong. I simply say that the truth revealed to me in the revelation I have received is a different revelation that which he has received. We see things differently.

My belief is that Christ was born into this world, and died in this world, to save everyone. His ministry was short-lived (three years at the most, probably) and confined to a small area of rural Palestine, not much larger than Surrey. During His ministry, He never went to Rome or to Athens or to Egypt, let alone China, in all of which places civilisation had been established for generations. He spoke to very few people. He never had the chance to speak to more. He stayed in Palestine, because that was the home of the Jews, who were, and saw themselves as, the chosen people of God, the people to whom God had promised that he would look after them for ever. The Jews believed that they would find eternal life with God, if they obeyed His commands and lived a good life, because that was what they had been taught. The Jews heard Christ's message, virtually no one else did, and He told His disciples to take the word to the rest of the world, which, over time, they and their followers sought to do. But, even today, many millions have never heard the word at all, heard nothing of this one true God and have worshipped Gods with different names and carried on, millions of them, leading good lives according to the culture and upbringing they have learned and received. As St Paul put it in today's reading: How could they call on a God in whom they did not believe? And how could they believe in a God they had never heard of?

The stumbling-block, the ever-present stumbling-block, on which so much so often turns, is the passage, which my friend from Holy Trinity Brompton quoted, relies on and believes – Jesus' reported words "I am the way, the truth and the life. No man comes to the Father but by Me. He, who believes in me, though he were dead, yet shall he live. These words, attributed to Jesus, have been the basis for more fighting and more argument, more carnage and more suffering, than almost any other words in history. They are there in St John's Gospel and are the basis of the faith of millions. But did Jesus say them? What did He mean? And what are we to make of them?

One thing we know for sure is that Jesus did not say those words. The words he used, whatever they were or meant, were spoken in Aramaic, a dialect spoken by those who lived in Palestine at that time. No one wrote the words down at the time and Jesus Himself appears never to have written anything down at all. The words He used were passed on over the years and the first written record of these words appeared in St John's Gospel – and only in St John's Gospel – a gospel, which scholars today say was written by followers of St John in or after 80 AD, generations after they are said to have been spoken. They have been thus handed down and translated and re-translated, so that it is hard to be sure what Jesus actually said, let alone what He actually meant. It may be that Jesus said that belief in Him and in His divinity was essential for any human to build the right relationship with God. But, for what it may be worth, I believe that he may have said something else altogether.

Consider the words we have. "I am the way, the truth and the life. No man comes to the Father but by me". It could mean "If you do not believe that I am the Son of God, the Father will never accept you". It could mean something entirely different. It could mean:- "I am going to die for you all. I am going to take the sins of the world on my own shoulders. My sacrifice will open the gates of Heaven to everyone who does My Father's will. Because of what I am going to do, everyone, whether they have heard about me or not, will have access to eternal life. I am the way, because it is only through my sacrifice that man will be able to come to God. No man comes to the Father but by me. He also said, if the record is right, the words "He who believes in me, though he be dead, yet shall he live". This, I am assured by a Bishop much-respected in our Church, is, in today's use of language, a mistranslation. The Greek words, which are the oldest we have, mean rather "He who commits his life to me and my teaching, though he be dead, yet shall he live" The Gospel , properly understood, does not speak simply of an intellectual, let alone a merely stated, acceptance of any particular doctrine. It speaks of a lifelong commitment to Jesus' teaching and a life lived according to that teaching. As Jesus is reported as saying, in St Matthew's Gospel: Not everyone that saith unto me Lord Lord shall enter into the kingdom of Heaven, but he that doeth the will of my Father, which is in Heaven. To believe, as we use the word, is not enough. It is the commitment, and the acting out of that commitment, which is required of us.

I believe that the devout Muslim worships the same God as you and I, though he calls Him by a different name and uses a different language. He comes to God by a different path from you and me and has learned how to live, how to do God's work, from a different book and through a different culture. He believes that Jesus was a truly great prophet, second only to the prophet Mohammed, who lived 600 years after Jesus, and has learned about God from Mohammed's teaching. He does not say "Lord Lord" to Jesus (He has, after all, been taught not to), but he may well spend his life doing Jesus' Father's will just the same. And if he does spend his life doing God's will, if he does, what then? Do we believe, ought we to believe, that, even if he does that, the loving God we worship will not have him? And will not have him because he has not joined the club? Is this the message Christ was sent to bring? I simply cannot believe that it is.

But one thing I think I know for sure. No man, no matter how devoted to his God he is, no matter how learned in Christ he may be, no matter how holy a life he lives, can shackle Almighty God with rules. Whatever eternal life may be, it is God who decides what will become of us. We cannot know – we can hope, but we cannot know. It is God, who knows what we have done with our time, how much has been love, how much has been self-indulgence, how much has been kindness, how much has been self-interest, the extent to which our minds have been fixed on helping others and the extent to which they have been fixed on helping ourselves. God alone knows the secrets of our hearts. It is what we do that counts and God alone can decide what we have really done. I, and many other churchmen I have met, would kneel down with joy and pray with the devout Muslim: and I suspect, though I do not pretend to know, that the devout Muslim may very well be nearer to God than I am. Who is this God we worship? What does He want of us in this context? We will all have our own answers: and I leave your answers to you. We might yet make the world a better place, if we think about it.

Hate His Wife and Children

St Luke Ch 14. v 26

What are we to make of this morning's chosen Gospel reading? Here is a man, a truly great man, the founder of our faith, the man we worship as the Son of God. And he says: If any man come to me and hate not his wife and children, he cannot be my disciple. This is the man who, a few short chapters earlier in St Luke's Gospel, in the Sermon on the Mount, told us to love our enemies. One day he tells us to love our enemies. The next day he tells us to hate those dearest and closest to us. There looks to be a massive inconsistency here. What are we to make of it?

The first question, I suppose, is to ask whether we should try to make anything of it at all. There are those who will say that it is in the Bible, therefore we should accept it and not question it. But that, obviously, will not do. We are charged to try to love God with all our heart and soul and strength and mind: and we cannot begin to start to love God with all our mind, if we insist on turning it off every time His name is mentioned. And we have to try to work these things out, for, when people ask us what we believe and why we believe it, we need to give them answers. This passage, from today's Gospel reading, is seized on by some, who attack our beliefs, as the basis of an assertion that Jesus preached a gospel of hate rather than a gospel of love: and, if we take the words out of context and do not try to understand them, that is what it looks like. We cannot say that this is a mistranslation. It is not. Neither can we say that Jesus obviously never said it. This is just as authoritative a passage as any other passage in the Gospels and is chosen to be read in our churches quite often, as it has been today. It would be convenient to forget it, to ignore it, but we cannot get away from it. What are we, then, to make of it?

To answer this, I want to go back from Chapter 14, where we find today's reading, to Chapter 10 of St Luke's Gospel, the story of the lawyer, who asked the questions which led to the parable of the Good Samaritan. A lawyer comes to Jesus and asks "What must I do to inherit eternal life?". Jesus replied: "What is written in the law?" and the lawyer replied, perhaps surprisingly, by using Jesus' own words: Thou shalt love the Lord thy God with all thy heart and with all thy soul and with all thy strength and with all thy mind: and thy neighbour as thyself. And Jesus said: Thou hast answered right. Do this and thou shalt live. In a similar story, in St Luke Chapter 18, the questioner goes on to say: I have loved. I still do. I have done this from my youth upwards: and Jesus, perceiving that the man wanted to do more, said: One thing yet you lack. Sell all you have and give it to the poor and follow me. And the man went away sorrowful, because that was asking too much.

The point, I think, lies here. We ask this self-same question which lurks in the back of our minds all the time, we ask, with that lawyer: What must I do to inherit eternal life? What is it that God wants me to do? And Jesus' answer is the same that he gave the lawyer – Live your life with love. Love God with everything you have – and love your neighbour also. He does not add that it is very difficult for ordinary human beings, who live their lives in the real, the ordinary, world to do this, though He knew, and we know, how difficult it is. But that is His command - Love, He says, as I have told you. Do this and you will live. This, if you can manage it or even if you truly try to manage it, will be enough. But for some – and this, I think, is the message of today's Gospel reading - for some it is not enough. To love God and our neighbour, as Jesus has commanded us, is likely to be enough, or more than enough, for most of us. But others feel called to do more: and I understand Jesus to be saying that, if you feel that you are called to do more, to go the whole hog as it were, then you must reject all human ambition, reject all of the world's ordinary trappings, reject all other human relationships and seek, single-mindedly, after God. You must have no wife or husband, you must have no children, you must reject all other responsibilities and diversions and set your mind on God and keep it fixed on Him. This is why men go into monasteries and women into nunneries. This is why the Roman Catholic church forbids its priests to marry and have children. If you find that, for you, loving is not enough and you are called to do more, you must reject all else that this world offers and give your heart, mind and body to Christ – and to Christ alone. And Jesus adds: Do not decide upon this, do not embark upon this, unless you are sure that you have the strength for it and are ready to pay the price for it. Kings do not set out on campaigns, unless they have made their plans and know they will win. Businessmen do not embark on projects without working out the cost first and deciding whether they can afford them. Christ tells us, He tells us in today's Gospel reading. If you feel called to do more than love, as I have commanded you to love, then look and work out whether you can really see it through, whether you can truly pay the price, before you answer the call: and do not follow the call, unless you are sure that you can.

And here, I think, is the explanation for Jesus' words here. He was on his way somewhere and a crowd was following – perhaps a noisy crowd, with some people crying out; "Master, let me follow you". And he turns round and says: "Look, if you really want to follow me, if you really want to be my disciple, then you must be prepared to give up everything else. You must reject the world and its pleasures, you must reject all human relationships which will divert your mind from God. You must take up your cross and follow me. But don't do it, unless you are sure that you can". He has not given that message to all of us. He has only given it to those, who feel that they have to do more than live Christ's loving life. It may be a cop-out: but I do not believe He has given that message to me. In the inimitable words of the late Jack Foster, much-loved former churchwarden here, I am called to be a layman. I am called to try to live a loving life in the real world, to look to my responsibilities in the real world, to keep my promise to love and to cherish the wife I married 45 years ago yesterday, to love and look after the children God has given us and the grandchildren God has given them. I do not think that Christ is asking me to hate them or reject them. I believe He is asking me to look after them and love them – and if that means that I cannot, in this sense, be his disciple, then that is how it has to be. We are all called to something. Some are summoned to a higher calling than others: and we must all respond to the calling we receive. I am called to be a layman, to live in this world as a layman, to look after my responsibilities as a layman and to try to love as a layman. That is why I am here. And while, in the sense of today's Gospel reading, I cannot ever be Jesus' disciple, it is my hope that I and those I know and those I love, who feel the same sort of call as I do, may yet inherit eternal life. I know nothing for certain. I pray often. And I believe that all may yet be well. It may be that you feel the same. Believe me, if you do, you are not alone.

I Thank God that
I Am Not as Other Men are

St Luke Ch 18 v 11

When I was a boy and studied the Bible at school, as we did then, a trap question, to which I did not immediately know the answer, was: Where in the Bible do you find a reference to a fairground? The answer lies in Psalm 16, Verse 7. "The lot is fallen unto me in a fair ground. Yea I have a goodly heritage". The lot is fallen unto me in a fair ground. I have a goodly heritage. Yes, indeed I have. God has been very good to me. I am very lucky as many others have not been lucky: and, in that regard, I thank God that I am not as other men are.

I thank God that I am not as other men are. Thus spoke the Pharisee in today's reading - and I say it too. I do thank God that I am not as other men are. I do it daily. I do it - and so do you - whenever I come to Church, whenever I pray, whenever I join in the Intercessions at our services. I thank God that I am here in Surrey and not a refugee in the Southern Sudan, that I am living in a temperate climate, living without fear of immediate assault by enemies, having more than enough to keep myself and my family in reasonable comfort, having water and food, which they do not, having a livelihood, which they do not, having hopes for the future, which they do not. I thank God, from the bottom of my heart, that I am not as they are. I thank God that I live here, where the weather is tolerant and tolerable, and am not a resident on the East coast of America or in the West Indies, where hurricanes strike and might destroy all that I have ever built up, where ordinary people have to flee for their lives from uncontrollable storms, which can kill and destroy without compunction. I do not have to face these risks and I thank God that I am not as those others are, who do. I thank God that I live here in comparative peace, and am able to worship freely, to worship as I believe

Christ demands of me, that my faith will not cause me to be beaten or killed, because I worship in a way which others disagree with and forbid. I thank God that I am not subject to fundamentalists of my own faith or to fundamentalists of other faiths - as thousands upon thousands of other men are. I thank God that I do not feel the fear that those brothers and sisters of mine feel. I thank God, in that sense, that I am not as they are.

You very probably feel the same way in this regard - and in this, we are not, you and I, disregarding Jesus' command. Jesus, in this passage read from the Gospel this morning, is not telling us to refrain from giving thanks for God's goodness to us. His message is entirely different. It is a message about prayer and its purpose: and it is about passing judgment on other people. There are, in this passage, two men in the Temple. One thanks God that he is not as other men are, because he keeps the rules of his religion and is a better man than the wretched and despised tax-gatherer, who can think of nothing to say except to ask for God's mercy, for he sees himself as a sinner. Jesus tells us that it is the tax-gatherer, who goes home the better justified.

The use of the word "Justified" in this context is a peculiarly accurate translation. A person becomes, literally, the better justified when he is made more just than he was before. There is a lovely short passage in Psalm 143, where the psalmist prays to God saying: "Give ear to my supplications and enter not into judgment with thy servant. For in thy sight shall no man living be justified". God is just - and so would we be, if we did not all fall short of God's pattern for us. It is by prayer, and by getting to know God in prayer, and by doing what God, through our prayer, has required us to do, that we can begin to put ourselves right with God, to become more just than we are, to become "Justified". Both these men, the Pharisee and the tax-gatherer, went to the Temple. The Pharisee told God how proud he was that he was able to keep the rules and do God's will that way. He thought that he was right with God already, that he was just already and did not think he had any need to be further justified. The tax-gatherer thought otherwise. He knew his failings and asked God's forgiveness. He went to the Temple to pray, not to tell the Almighty how good he was, but to pray that he might be forgiven for falling short: and he did, as we should, pray for that: and he went home the better justified. We pray today to make ourselves right with God and we too hope to go home the better justified.

But this is not the end of it. The Pharisee, Jesus tells us, committed the cardinal sin of thinking that he was better than the next man, a better man than the tax-gathering sinner. He thanked God for making him so, but Jesus makes it clear that he has missed the point. We do not do God's work, if we despise our fellow men or if we believe that we are somehow superior to our fellow men. God has made us as we are - men, women, black, white, strong, weak, quick, slow, more intelligent, less intelligent, heterosexual, homosexual. Christ requires of us that we use such skills as we have to develop our abilities and live our lives lovingly in His service. It used to be argued, not so long ago, that those with white skins were somehow superior to those with black skins and therefore better qualified to take charge than they were. We now know that that is entirely untrue. Is it now God's will that it should still be argued that men are somehow superior to women, so that women should not be priests or bishops in our Church? There are still areas in our Church where that foolishness has not yet been abandoned. Is it now God's will that it should be thought that men and women with heterosexual proclivities are somehow superior to those with homosexual proclivities and that the latter are not fit to be priests in His church? Many seem to think so. Do we, heterosexuals if that is what we are, look at homosexuals and thank God that we are not as other men are? Are we acting as Christ would have us act, if that is what we do and we think ourselves somehow better than they? I suspect not.

We all know that some people have greater abilities than others, some in one field and some in another: and those, who have the greater ability, should take charge in the field where they excel. That much is obvious. But the man, who thus takes charge, is not a better man in God's eyes than the man who takes his orders. If I read Jesus' teachings aright, Jesus is telling us that all men are equal in the sight of God: and that what God requires of us is that we use our skills, be they great or small, to the best of our ability, to learn to love God with them and to try to love our neighbour with them. The widow had only her mite to give, but God thought it greater than the rich man's large donation. The tax-gatherer had only his regret at his way of life to offer in his prayers. But he went home the better justified than the Pharisee with all his glory in his own good works. Truly, Jesus tells us, it is the case that he that exalteth himself shall be abased: and that he that humbleth himself shall be exalted. For, in thy sight, O Lord, shall no man living be justified. I truly thank God that I am not as other men are. But that does not mean, and must not be taken to mean, that I believe that I am better than they are. For I am not: and nor are you, are you?

I Will Destroy this Temple

St John Ch 2 v 19

From today's second reading, St John, Ch 2, v.19. I will destroy this temple and build it again in three days. These are Jesus' words, as recalled by St. John – words, you will remember, quoted by others and used against Him at his trial, words which no one, at the time they were spoken, understood at all. It had taken 46 years to rebuild the temple after its destruction by the Babylonian invaders. How could he pull it down and rebuild it in three days? These sounded like the words of a crazy man.

Christ's personal, that is his living, ministry, on which our Christian faith is based, lasted for only about three years. In that time, he spoke to very few people, never travelled outside Palestine, never wrote anything down. He brought a message, a new and urgent message, and, without armies, without megaphones, without publicists and wholly without any support from the State or the authorities, he got his message over and changed the world with it.

Today's readings, containing, as they do, the Old Testament message and the New Testament message, make the point precisely. The old message, the Old Testament message, the Ten Commandments, are the message of a God, who cared for the Jews, His chosen people, and did not appear to want His message spread to anyone else. The Ten Commandments, just about all of them prohibitions (thou shalt not..) gave no instructions about spreading God's word or proclaiming the news of God's existence to anyone outside the Jewish nation and said virtually nothing about loving other people either. The Ten Commandments, hailed by many professing Christians as being the basis of our faith, say a lot of things. But, in the original version, they said nothing about love for our fellow humans at all. And they are the Old Testament message – a fine message so far as it goes, but stopping many, many miles short of the New Testament message, which Jesus came to bring.

The new message, the Christian message, was, and remains, fundamentally different. It was, for those who heard it, entirely new. The Jews believed with their whole heart, that the God, who created the world in seven days, was their God – and their God only. The suggestion that the God of the Jews was the God for the whole world, who cared for the whole of humanity, was, to the Jews of that day unthinkable. He had said: I am the Lord THY God. It was no part of their creed that they should share Him with anyone else.

By the time that Jesus' ministry began, the Old Testament message was well established in Jerusalem. God, the Almighty God, who had created the world in seven days, was the God of the Jews, not of the Romans, not of any of those outsiders they called the Gentiles, not of anyone else at all. The rules, set down in the books of the law in the Old Testament, particularly Leviticus and Deuteronomy, were to be obeyed: and God's will was done by His people by strictly obeying them. Ritual sacrifices were to be made as the law laid down, God was to be worshipped as the rituals required, in the synagogue or in the temple: and God was pleased with the world, so long as His people did what the rules required them to do. This was the message. Keep My commandments and you will be blessed. If, for example, a Jewish mother gave birth to a child, that child should, at some stage, according to the rules, be brought to the Temple to be blessed – and a ritual sacrifice to God, a pair of turtledoves or two young pigeons, was expected. Any parents without turtledoves or pigeons (and I don't suppose that many had them. They might live in trees, but they did not grow on them) could buy them in the temple: and, if they did not have the funds to do this, then moneychangers were waiting in the temple to lend them what they needed. The place where God was to be found, the place where God was to be worshipped, was the Temple: and the continued preservation of the temple and its traditions was the principal concern of the Jewish leadership. They were happy, politically, to play second fiddle to their Roman conquerors so long as those Roman conquerors let them worship in their temple undisturbed - because they believed that God would be pleased with them and protect them, if they did that. That is how it was. That was what they understood the Old Testament message to be.

And that was what Jesus found when, as we heard in today's second reading, Jesus came to Jerusalem and went to the Temple, the place he called "My Father's House". He did not find a place of worship. He found what He called a house of merchandise and he was very angry. He threw the merchants out. He overturned the moneychangers' tables: and he said:" You have desecrated this place. This, my Father's house, was to be a house of prayer. But you have made it a den of thieves": and then he added: "I will destroy this temple and rebuild it in three days": and they thought he was mad. But these words, which sounded like a threat of violence, also sounded like the language of sedition, the threat of which was very dangerous, since it directly affected the uneasy relationship under which the Romans allowed the Jews freedom of worship. These words may well have been the catalyst which led to Jesus' trial and crucifixion.

The problem was that no one understood what Jesus meant. No one, none of his followers, not even the apostles closest to Christ, had any idea about his plans and his purposes. They had given up their lives, their careers, their families, everything that they had held dear, to follow this amazing man. But they did not know who He was or what He planned to do. They did not expect Him to be crucified and were totally shattered when He was. They had not expected Him to die a public and humiliating death – and were totally shattered when He did. And the last thing, absolutely the last thing, they expected was that He should come back from the dead – and they were utterly amazed when He did. And when He did, when He came back from the dead and, after being publicly executed, lived with them, ate with them, talked with them and explained it all to them, then, for the first time, they understood who He was, what He had meant and what He had done: and, inspired by this, they went out and told the world Christ's new message, the New Testament message, which changed the world and still infuses and inspires in our world now. "I will destroy this temple and rebuild it in three days". As St John, the first Christian theologian and Christ's first and best interpreter, puts it: "The Temple he was speaking of was His body. Before his death, his disciples had not understood. But, after his resurrection, they remembered these words and understood what he had said". The miracle of the resurrection made all Jesus' words, hitherto unrecognised and not understood, completely clear.

That message, the New testament message, was and is that God is not just for the Jews alone, but that He is the God for everyone in His creation, Jew, Roman, male and female, white-skinned, black-skinned, everyone. The God I come from, Jesus said, is a God for everyone, a God whose love is available for everyone. I will die for you and, in three days, rise again, and I will redeem you from the burden of your sins, so that, through me, eternal life with God will be a possibility for each one of you. In those three days, between Good Friday and Easter day, in that three-day space, I will make this old temple as irrelevant as old stones. For I, my risen body, built in that three-day space, I will be your new temple. You will no longer have to go to the old temple to find God. You will find Him through me, through my risen body, which will be your new temple: and my risen body, built in that three-day space, will be your way to God. From now on I will for ever be in you and you in me. From now on, I will be for ever the way, the truth and the life: and, from now on, he who commits his life to my Father's work, whether he knows it is my Father's work or not, will never die. The New Testament message is that our task is not to obey the ten commandments and forget everything else. The New Testament message is that our task is to build, through this, our new, temple, a loving relationship with God, to live our lives with love for our fellow man and do all that we do in this world with love in our hearts. This is the message of the New Testament. This is the message of today's church. This is the living hope which Christ has brought us and makes us what we are. Jesus said: I will destroy this temple and rebuild it in three days. And that is precisely what He did – and that is why we are here.

What is a Christian?

St Paul Epistle to Ephesians. Ch 4 v 24.

'If you have learned Christ', writes St Paul to the Ephesians in the passage which has just been read 'You will put away the old man and put on the new man'. You put on the new man, of course, by becoming a Christian, whatever that means. If you have learned Christ, you may, if you choose, become a Christian.

What is a Christian? If someone asks you: 'Are you a Christian?', what is your reply? Is it Yes? Is it No? Is it I don't know? Is it 'I try to be'. Are you a Christian? How do you know yourself to be a Christian? What is a Christian anyway?

In a letter to The Times some weeks ago, Sir Ludovic Kennedy, a well-known man of letters and a thinking and self-professing, as I understand him, atheist, asked that very question. He asked (I paraphrase): Is a Christian a person who believes a number of myths about a man who lived and died 2000 years ago, myths for which there is precious little evidence and which there is really no reason to believe? Or is a Christian a person who lives by the principles said to have been set out by that man, even though he has no belief in those myths? It is a fair question and deserves an answer. Those whose answers were published in the paper provided, as it seemed to me, very little, by way either of answer or of enlightenment. I propose, in my own small and unauthoritative way, to try to answer the question now: and to say something about Jesus Christ in the process.

The word 'Christian' is, of course, a word like any other. It can mean whatever you want it to mean: and, like the word 'Liberal', it has a number of accepted meanings. If you look in the Oxford Dictionary, you will find that a Christian is defined (1) as a person who believes in the religion of Christ: and (2) as a person who lives according to the principles laid down by Christ. So far as the

Dictionary is concerned, either will do. But Sir Ludovic wants an answer. Who is the true Christian? The one who believes, although he does not follow the teaching? Or the one who follows the teaching, but does not believe?

You have, of course, only to ask the question to see that the answer is obvious. Suppose you are a devout Buddhist and live your life according to the principles of that great religion, you will also be living your life, in the sense of doing good or doing ill, according to the principles which Christ laid down - but you would never claim to be a Christian or ever be thought to be one. You can be a humanist or a fine philosopher, determine, for that reason, to live your life as a good man should, and follow, for that reason, principles which seem the right way to you. You will be following the principles which Christ laid down, but you will not think of yourself as, nor will you be thought to be, a Christian. You can be a very good person in this world, even a saintly one, without being a Christian. Many of the noblest spirits in history, many of the noblest spirits in the world today, are not Christians and do not claim to be. They are good people for reasons not connected with any faith in Christ: and, if that is how it is for them, then, though they may be very good people indeed, they are not - or not yet - Christians. They are not the worse for this. They simply do not qualify for the description.

Who then is the true Christian? I do not think there is any mystery in this. If, in St Paul's words, you have 'learned Christ', then you have accepted that Christ was, in some mysterious, incomprehensible way, divine - not just a remarkable man, who used remarkable words and did remarkable things, but a living part of the Almighty God. Sir Ludovic Kennedy's intellect won't allow him to accept this as a possibility. It allows him to accept the message, but not to accept the messenger. But my intellect, such as it is, not only allows me to accept it. It has, over the years, come to compel me to believe it as the truth. This does not make me a better man than Sir Ludovic. But it does perhaps give me an insight into things which he cannot see.

I start from two places - at least they are where I start from now. The first is the opening words of the first letter of St Peter, who, since he was there and saw and heard it all, knew what he was talking about. He wrote: 'Blessed be the God and Father of our Lord Jesus Christ, who, according to his abundant mercy, hath begotten us again unto a living hope by the resurrection of Jesus Christ from the dead', one example, from the pen of a man who changed his life because of his experience, of a volume of effective, convincing, eye-witness evidence of the rebirth of a dead man: and the second starting-point for me are the reported words of Jesus in Ch. 14 of St John's Gospel: 'If you love me, keep my commandments: and I will pray the Father: and he will give you another source of strength, who will be with you for ever - that is the spirit of truth, the Holy Spirit. I will not leave you alone. I will come to you: and then you will know that I am in my Father: and you in me: and I in you'. 'You in me and I in you'.

The nub, the heart of the Christian Faith, in which I believe, is founded on these two propositions. First, Christ was put to death and rose again from the dead. He was not just a remarkable human being. He was, by some miraculous means, a part of God. Second, this part of God is, through the Holy Spirit, in each of us always. There is, as a result of Jesus' sacrifice, a divine spark in each of us, the divine spark which makes our souls immortal, the divine spark, which can give us the strength, if we use it, to see the right way and follow it rejoicing. If you are properly to call yourself a Christian, I think you have to believe in the divinity of Christ: and to believe that, by God's Grace, a spark of the spirit of that divine Christ is an innate part of you. Christians do not believe in an absent God, nor in a distant one. They believe in a Christ who is with them always, who is a very part of them. If you do not believe this, you may be a very good person, as good a person, if not better, than most Christians are. But you cannot call yourself a Christian, in the true sense of the word, unless you believe that a spark of the spirit of the divine Christ is in you.

But it does not, of course, end there. Belief in what Sir Ludovic calls the myths, belief in what I call the revealed truth, is not the whole requirement. If you are to be a true Christian, you not only acknowledge the presence of Christ in you: you go on to do something about it. Christ in you creates duties, brings obligations. If Christ is in you, this means that, day in and day out, Christ walks on your feet, Christ works with your hands, Christ sees through your eyes, Christ thinks with your mind. If you are a Christian and believe that Christ is in you, you must do honour to Christ, as He works through your thinking and through your limbs in and about all that you do. Christ promised that he would be in us - fine. But he also warned us 'Not everyone that saith unto me 'Lord Lord' shall enter into the kingdom of Heaven, but he that doeth the will of my Father which is in Heaven'. If you believe that Christ is in you, but nevertheless ignore His message and go your own way regardless, you are not a true Christian and cannot properly claim to be one. Sir Ludovic Kennedy accepts the message, but rejects the messenger. The would-be Christian, who accepts the messenger, but rejects the message, is no more a true Christian than he who does not believe at all.

If you ask me: What is the message then?, I am afraid you will have to wait till next week or do some thinking for yourself. Week in, week out, teachers and preachers proclaim Christ's message and some listen and some don't. There is someone here every Sunday telling you of Christ's message. You will hear it if you listen to them: and I recommend it. And if you listen to the Christ in you, you will hear it for yourself. I could tell you about it at length and it might take to well past lunchtime, which you would not welcome: and I cannot possibly encapsulate it in a sentence. But Christ's message was a message of unconditional love. He loved us, those of us who were to become His Church, without conditions: and that is how He taught us to love one another. To love without conditions is the highest perfection to which human nature can attain: and to love without conditions, without reserve, is the Christian ideal. It is not in our nature to love in that way: but the Christ in you will help you to learn to do it: and, if you are trying to learn to do it, you will, in Jesus' words, be 'Not far from the kingdom of God'. That is a start. But the message is often complex: and the message for you may very well be very different from the message for me or anyone else. Strive to work with the Christ in you - that is the Christian's duty: and, though it probably takes a lifetime, your prayer must be that you get there in the end.

Who then is the true Christian? My answer is: A Christian is one who, believing the divinity of Christ and that Christ is in him always, commits himself, in his own living, to do, as best he can, what Christ has told him to do. If you ask me: Are you a Christian?, my answer is Yes. If you ask me: Are you a good Christian?, my answer is: I try to be.

We shall not cease from exploration, you and I: and the end of all our exploring will be to arrive where we started and know the place for the first time. I come back to where I started - St Paul writing to the Ephesians. If you have learned Christ, you will put away the old man and put on the new man. And then maybe, in the end, you will become a true Christian too.

Lost Sheep

St Luke. Ch 15 v 7

Today's Gospel reading recounts Jesus' parable of the lost sheep and how whole-heartedly the shepherd struggles to find it and bring it home. He leaves the other ninety nine in the pasture and goes to find the single lost one. That, Jesus says, is how it is with your Father in Heaven and you. "I tell you", He says:" There will be greater joy in Heaven over one sinner that repents than over ninety nine righteous people, who do not need to repent". One sinner that repents? Ninety nine righteous people, who do not need to repent? I have always felt that I understood about the one lost sheep. I thought that we were, all of us, lost sheep and that God spent my life looking to find me. But who on earth, I always wondered, were the ninety nine righteous people, who needed no repentance? Do I know any of them? Who are they? And where can they be found?

We begin our life on this earth, each of us, as a blank canvas. We are born, knowing nothing. We have no faith, no knowledge of God, an innate yearning for our mothers and their love, but nothing else. As we grow older, we start to learn – to listen, to understand, to speak – and, somewhere along the way, someone may teach us about God. Many, very many indeed, hear nothing about God and learn nothing about God. Some learn about God and Jesus Christ. Some learn about God and His prophet Mohammed. Some are taught that there is no God at all. But, as we grow older, we learn to look and see, to enquire and think deeply – and maybe the Holy Spirit comes to us and plants belief in us – and maybe it does not. Sometimes a person is inspired by someone or some special experience and learns to recognise the shepherd and the joy of following him to the open pasture and remaining his companion there. Others do not. Some hear nothing, do not recognise the shepherd, shun the open pasture, make their lives in the excitement of the wilderness and find their happiness and what they see as their fulfilment there. Some reject the shepherd's call, rebel against the whole idea, make for the wilderness and encourage others to join them and make their lives there. You and I, though, are in the open pasture. Someone, some thing, some word, some influence, something other than chance, has brought us there. That is why we are here in church today. We acknowledge the shepherd and try, sometimes but not always, to do His work. At some stage in our lives, God, through the workings of His Holy Spirit, has met us and brought us home. So, when I ask, Who are the ninety nine righteous people who need no repentance, I think I now know who they are – and that answer may surprise you. They are you. You are the sheep who have found the open pasture, who have stayed there and not run amok. You are the people, who have found the shepherd, who come to Communion, who share Christ's body and drink Christ's cup. You are the people who are lit by the Spirit and, consciously or unconsciously, walk with Christ in your everyday lives. I see disbelief on your faces. No, you say, not me. I am not special. I am not righteous. I am as much in need of repentance as anyone else. But I say –Yes, it is you: and I want to tell you why.

The language used in our New Testament, even the new translations, is old-fashioned English, translated at a time when words had different meanings from those we understand now. The words Repentance and Righteous had different meanings then: and, if we want to understand what Jesus was saying, we have to look at what He meant by what He said. The Greek texts, I am assured, use the word Metanoia for what has been translated as Repentance: and Metanoia means something far more fundamental than the word repentance means today. Today we speak of repentance as simply feeling sorry, feeling regret, feeling guilty about what we have done. Metanoia means something entirely different. Metanoia requires a complete change of your life style, a complete change in your thinking, a complete change in your ideas of right and wrong. When you repent, as Jesus used the word, you don't just say sorry and go on your way as though nothing has happened. When you repent as Jesus used the word, you resolve to change your life, to come back to the fold and live there, to turn your thinking upside down and become an entirely different person, who lives in an entirely different way. Again with the word Righteous, we view the word as meaning saintly or holier-than-thou. That is not what it means in the Gospels. In the Gospels, it means accepting the right principles, trying to live right by God, acknowledging that you have a duty to Christ and your neighbour, even if you don't manage to do it all the time. Jesus tells the story of the poor man, who went to the Temple, stood at the back, put his hand on his heart and prayed "God, be merciful to me, a sinner" – and he went home justified, made just by his praying, made righteous by what he had done and said.

The lost sheep, in this parable, is the man who has denied Christ and His ways, done terrible things and seems, in everyone's eyes, to be beyond redemption. Paul was such a man. His letter to Timothy, read this morning, makes the point clearly. "I thank Jesus Christ for judging me worthy of His trust, although in the past I had met Him with abuse and persecution and outrage". Christ Jesus, he says, came into the world to save sinners and I have been the worst of them all – and he had been. Paul was an orthodox Jew, who firmly believed that those, who followed Jesus, were destroying the Jewish faith and the Jewish traditions with which he had grown up. He was furious with them. He hated them with an all-consuming hatred. So, acting, as he saw it, in the name of his God, he hunted them down, persecuted them and rejoiced as he watched them die. That was what he did. That was the sort of man he was. He was as far from God as he could get. And then, when he was that far off and was on his way to Damascus to destroy the Christians there, God met him in His Son on that Damascus road and brought him home. In the days which followed, he underwent a true metanoia, changed his thinking and his life completely and became Jesus' most eloquent and lifelong supporter. Jesus' message in today's Gospel reading, this story of the lost sheep, shows, that, in God's eyes, no one is ever beyond redemption, no matter how vicious and foul their conduct, no matter how much damage they do to others in this world. But for them a true repentance, a true Metanoia, such as Paul experienced, is needed first.

You and I do not need that metanoia. But this does not mean that we can sit still and do nothing. We may have found the open pasture and stayed there: and because we have found the open pasture and stayed there, we may not need that repentance of which Jesus was speaking. But we are sinners still, all of us. We certainly need to exercise a true self-discipline in all that we do and try to refrain from giving way to the temptations which beset us. But even that cannot be enough. We should never cease to listen to the shepherd, to ask ourselves about our faith, to work out what it is that we believe and tell that news to others, both by what we do and by what we say. For the truth is that we were once far off (not as far off as Paul, perhaps, but far off just the same) and that, when we were still far off, God met us in His Son and brought us home. That is why we are here in this church, this church where we share Christ's body – and find that we must try to live His risen life, in this church where we drink Christ's cup – and learn that we must strive to bring life to others. We are, all day and every day, men and women, whom the Spirit lights, who are lit by the Spirit - so we must share that light and strive to give light to the world: and we pray, as in our Communion services we regularly do with those very words, that God, in His infinite goodness will keep us firm in the hope He has set before us, so we and all God's children shall be free and the whole earth live to praise His name. And we ask this through Jesus Christ our Lord and much-loved shepherd. Amen.

Shall We Burn them Up

St Luke Ch 9 v 55

Today's reading contains, at first sight, a most extraordinary story. Here are Jesus and his disciples, on their way to Jerusalem, seeking to spend the night in a village in Samaria: and the Samaritans, who do not like the Jews very much, refuse to let them in: and James and John, two of the senior apostles, say: "Lord, may we call down fire from Heaven to burn them up?" Jesus says No. But what on earth are they thinking of? What nonsense is this?

It is not, in fact, nonsense at all. It sounds like nonsense, but, seen in the context of the time, it is nothing of the sort. But we need to know what is being said and why. The New English Bible puts it as you have heard it read, with little detail, but the Authorised version, back in 1603, put it more fully. In the incident as translated in the Authorised Version, James and John ask: "Lord, wilt Thou that we command fire to come down from Heaven and consume them, even as Elijah did?" and Jesus turned to them and rebuked them, saying:" You know not what manner of spirit you are of. For the Son of Man is not come to destroy men's lives, but to save them". Why these all-important words were left out in the modern translation I do not know. But they were: and, without them, the whole substance of the message of this incident is lost. "Wilt thou that we command fire to come down from Heaven and consume them, even as Elijah did? "You know not what manner of spirit you are of. The Son of Man is come, not to destroy men's lives but to save them".

Apart from Moses, Elijah was the greatest prophet in Jewish history. He was and still is enormously respected and his doings and sayings were, and remain, part of the fabric of the Jewish faith – and calling down fire from Heaven to kill people was one of the great things he was known to have done. There is a rather long story in the first chapter of the second book of Kings, where Elijah called down fire from heaven which burned up over a hundred men, killed them, left their wives widows and their children fatherless, in order to prove that he was a man of God and had the power, in that way, to marshal the strength of God to show his authenticity. The Jewish prophets of the Old Testament were seen to have a direct line to God: and killing what they saw as God's enemies, and the obedient servants of God's enemies, with fire and in other ways was seen as God's way of disposing of those enemies: and the Jews of Jesus' day knew that very well. Thus it was that, if Jesus was a true prophet of the living God, which the disciples saw Him as and believed Him to be, calling down fire from Heaven to destroy his enemies was an orthodox thing for Him to do. Elijah was a great prophet and did it. If Jesus was a great prophet, that was precisely what He was expected to be able to do. The apostles' suggestion was not nonsense at all. It was, in theory at any rate to an orthodox and properly-educated Jew, what was expected in those days of a great prophet who could do great things.

But, not for the first time and certainly not for the last, Jesus would have none of it. And the truth lies – the full import of the story lies – in the passage so curiously omitted from the New English Bible, in the passage omitted from the story in today's chosen reading, in the passage containing Jesus' response to this suggestion. "You know not" He says "What manner of spirit you are of. He is saying: The spirit of the God I come from, the spirit of the God I preach to you, is not the spirit of the God of the Jewish law, which you have been brought up in. I have come with a new message, to tell you of a new spirit. I have come to save men's lives, not to destroy them". It may have been God's will to burn up his enemies then. I am here to tell you that it is not what the God I come from does now.

This is fundamental, this is radical stuff. And, time and again, when we study the Gospels in the light of the context of the time when the events recorded in them occurred, we find Jesus saying the same thing. Remember that Jesus' ministry lasted for no more than three short years, that none of His sayings were recorded at the time and that nothing was written down, so far as we know, till at least thirty years after His death. Yet, even against that background, we find the same theme repeated again and again. His message was that the Jewish Establishment, the priests, the Pharisees and the lawyers, though they had heard God's message and persuaded themselves that they were following it, had got it wrong. Jesus came to save life, not to destroy it. Jesus came to preach a Gospel of a loving God, not a vengeful one, a Gospel of life, not a gospel of death, a Gospel of love, not a gospel of destruction. He called the Jewish leaders a generation of vipers. He called their abuse of the Temple of God, by using it as a market place, an insult to the God, for whose worship it was built. He told them, as He tells us, that our duty in this life is to learn to love our God and to love our neighbours as ourselves. He told us that those duties encapsulate the Ten Commandments: and, in effect, that His Commandments, His law, supersede the Jewish laws, as interpreted in His time by the Jewish leaders.

If we look critically at how Jesus conducted His ministry, we see examples of this all over the place. The story of the Good Samaritan, where the priest and the Levite passed by on the other side, leaving the injured man lying in the road, is another prime example. They passed by on the other side, because the old Jewish law required them to do so, required them to leave, without helping him, a bleeding man injured in the road, because, if you touched a bleeding man, the law classed you as unclean. Only the Samaritan, who was not bound by the Jewish laws, showed his love for his unknown neighbour by helping the victim in that story – and Jesus said that the orthodox Jews should change their ways and follow his example. Almost every one of Jesus' healing miracles involved touching or handling sick people – a thing which the old law did not permit. Take a good look at the detailed laws set out in the books of the law in the Old Testament, in Leviticus and Deuteronomy, and compare them with Jesus' words and actions; and the point is made clearly time and again. He came to preach a new Gospel to those who saw themselves as God's own people – a new Gospel which included, not just the Jews, but the whole world. The men in power recognised His challenge and had him executed. And he trumped their aces, came back from the dead and inspired His followers to go out and change the world. Only God Himself could have done that – and our faith is that Jesus was and is divine, that is a part of God.

But this is not the end of it. It cannot be the end of it, because we need to think and work out what we believe and where we stand. There are many professing Christians, who see the Bible, and the whole Bible, as the revealed word of God: and who assert that, if something is stated in the Bible, it must be right. It may be a convenient stance which saves a lot of argument. But our Church teaches, I think, in this church at any rate, that it cannot be correct. Some of the old rules in the Old Testament, still there in the Bible in black and white, are simply totally inconsistent with what Jesus taught – old rules laid down, probably to preserve public health at a time when the Jewish people were homeless and when medical science had made no progress. And, if they are wholly inconsistent with what Jesus taught, then they cannot possibly be the rules that we, if we are to be Christians, should follow. Some of them are obviously wrong, such as the rule that a bleeding man should be left, unassisted, lying in the road or that a son, who dishonours or disobeys his father, should be stoned to death. Others are less obvious, such as the rule that homosexual conduct is an abomination to the Lord and is utterly forbidden. We are trying to work some of these out and are busy fighting over them and disagreeing about them. And that, I fear, may go on for some time.

But we must make no mistake about it. The God whom Jesus came from, the God of whom Jesus is a part, the God whom Jesus preached, is a God with different characteristics, different commands, from the God of the Old Testament. He is the same God. For God does not change. What has changed is our understanding of God as illuminated by the light of what Jesus taught us about Him. In the same way, our understanding of the world we live in, how it was made and how its people are made, constantly changes, as our knowledge increases and our understanding of Christ's words and teaching becomes clearer also. The God we worship is not a God, who favours vengeance, discrimination and death. He is a God who loves, forgives, understands and supports and who expects us, commands us, to love, forgive, understand and support others also. The disciples, in today's reading, did not understand what manner of spirit they were of – so Jesus told them. In telling them, Jesus has told us too what manner of spirit we are of. He has taught us and shown us how we should live and what His Father wants us to do. This is my command, He said, that you should love one another, yes, that we should love one another. We know what that means. And in this church and in this community, it is what, I truly believe, we try to do.

Such Things as Shall Please Thee

Trinity 10 Collect

Let Thy merciful ears, O Lord, be open to the prayers of Thy humble servants; and, that they may obtain their petitions, make them to ask such things as shall please Thee. Through Jesus Christ our Lord. This short prayer is the Collect for this, the 10th Sunday after Trinity, a prayer which has been used on this Sunday throughout the Anglican Church for over 300 years: and it invites us to consider how we pray and what we pray for.

I have spent the last two weeks enjoying the spotlight of the Olympic Games, a spotlight which has lit up this country, its athletes and its people – and it has been a remarkable experience. The smiles, the enthusiasm, the enormous support for our team have astonished us all, as has the spectacular quality of the athletes, who have competed. On the television screen, it has been noticeable how many competitors have habitually made the sign of the Cross across their chests just before they participate: and I have wondered why they have done this, whether they were briefly praying, which is how it appeared – and, if so, what were they praying for? Were they praying that God should help them win? Or that God should help them to do well? Or were they thanking God for getting them to the start line in this competition and dedicating to His service what they were about to do to? Their answers might differ, but we will never know what they would be.

Today's Collect invites us, when we pray, to ask such things as shall please God and suggests that those prayers are more likely to be favourably answered, if we do pray for such things: and I have often wondered whether, in the sporting field, it is right, indeed if it is fair, to pray to God for victory. After all, if you win, the others lose: and can it be fair competition if God is exclusively on your side? And is God likely to be pleased, if you pray for His help to make you win? I don't think I ever pray to win, though I often find myself silently, and briefly, praying that I won't make a fool of myself. "O God, help me to do well" seems permissible. "O God, help me to do better than the others" may not be. They must surely be no less entitled than I am to God's help in their enterprises, no matter what they believe or where they come from - or whether they feel that they know God or not? If there is a war on and an enemy is threatening to destroy you and kill you all, it is fair enough to pray for victory. But on the sports field? I suggest not.

Many people, I believe, have prayed that these Games, in which so much time, effort, hard work and careful thought have been invested, should be a success: and so far they have been – and have succeeded beyond our wildest dreams. I am not talking about the number of medals won by the British team, though the achievements of the remarkable young Britons who have won them have brought joy to hundreds of thousands of us. I am talking about, and thanking God for, the efforts, the skills, the commitment of all these brilliant young athletes, from all over the world, who have come together and fought each other, often to a standstill, in peace and affection by striving together to hone their skills to a perfect sharpness, until one or other has turned out to be the winner. This sort of sporting stage shows one aspect of humanity at its best, physically truly beautiful young men and women giving all that they are and all that they have, in honourable and thoroughly fair competition. These are wonderful examples of the majesty of the human body and the human spirit.

We should give joyful thanks to God for this – for these remarkable young people are doing God's work in all that they do in this context. We should give glory to God that they can run, jump, throw, swim, row, cycle and balance as they do, for God is glorified by their achievements and the way we marvel at them. So too is God glorified by the spirit in which these amazing things are done. I almost wept, when I saw the competitors in the women's heptathlon, who had spent two full days battling with each other in the seven disciplines, in which they so greatly excel, stooping to embrace and kiss young Jessica Ennis in congratulation for her gold medal and then joining hands, with her and together, in mutual affection and respect and, together as one band, saluting the crowds of supporters which had so joyfully cheered them on. I will fight you today, they say, for that is my destiny. But I will love you while I do it and for ever, because we all are engaged in seeking the same perfection. This, I am sure, is God's will for them: and it is an example, a grand, immediate and public example, to us all.

For Christ taught us, above all else, to love one another: and this is a wonderful example of how it can be done. The love that Christ commanded us to show to one another, the love that St Paul spoke of in his letter to the Corinthians, the love which is essential in all human activities, comes in many forms – and working in teams and engaging in hard and fair competition is one of them. One of the three young women, who had just won a gold medal in the women's cycling pursuit race, a discipline in which there is no chance of success at all without strict and expert teamwork, said of herself and her two team colleagues: "We have come to be like sisters". They train together, strive together, share ambitions together, as a team, sharing the necessary sacrifices called for by the disciplines of intense training: and concern for each other's welfare, joy in each others' company, love for one another, all grow and develop from this. Nothing that is good in this world was ever achieved without sacrifice: and shared sacrifice, as most happily married people learn, is a very common basis for the growth of love.

The love that Christ spoke of comes in many forms. Its essential ingredients, I think, include unselfishness, shared experiences and sacrifice. We find it in marriage, if we are fortunate – but we do not find it there by looking into each other's eyes and sighing meaningfully or by saying "I love you" every day, but by building up a treasure house of shared experiences and mutual respect and by showing, by what we do and by what we say or refrain from saying, that we are living for someone else as well as, or rather than, ourselves. Members of the armed forces, policemen, firefighters, those who live dangerous lives, feel that love and find it in the sharing of dangers, the willingness that colleagues show to sacrifice themselves for their friends. That sort of love can be found in the office, when colleagues decide to embark on a great enterprise, devote all their time to it, work on it together, give and receive respect from each other for the efforts they put in and the long hours and physical and mental energy expended on it – and then finally see it come to success. It is not an original saying, but, as I have said, nothing that is good in this world is ever achieved without sacrifice: and shared sacrifice in a shared pursuit of excellence, be it excellence in a relationship or excellence in sport, is a common foundation for the love I am speaking of.

And so it is, and has, for the past two weeks, been clearly shown on the sports field. Fine young people, who have stumbled from their beds at 4 am, in all climates and in all weathers, day after day and month after month, to train their minds and bodies, sometimes alone, sometimes with others, so as to attain the highest perfection they can in the enterprises they engage in – and now they have come together to our stadia in our country to show their competitors, and to show us, the watchers who stand by, the wonderful things they can do. By their visible and continuous generosity of spirit and by their unselfishness both in winning and in losing, they have shown, time and again, that they do not do it just for themselves, but for their sport, for their team and for their country. This is God's love at work: and the vast crowds' enormous enthusiasm and applause shows how we love them for it. Their achievements, their excellence, give praise to God for the wonders of the human body and the wonders of the human spirit. These past two weeks have shown us that we are all greater than we thought we were and have taught us fresh ways to love one another. Let us thank God for it – for we have been greatly blessed.

The Baptism of Jesus

St Mark Ch 1 v 9

Today's readings have been chosen, because today we are invited to celebrate the baptism of Jesus. We probably do it every year, but I do not remember doing it before. I do not think that I had ever thought very much about the baptism of Jesus, but there is nothing like being asked to preach about something, if you want to get the mind working – and this brings me straight to today's Gospel reading, which is the first seven verses of St Mark's Gospel. St Mark's Gospel, which, chronologically, was the first of the Gospels to be written, tells us of Jesus' ministry. It tells us of nothing else. It contains no history of His early years, no reflections on his birth or ancestry, no philosophy or deep thinking. It begins and ends with the facts, as Mark believed them to be: and the author did not hang about. He starts, at Chapter 1, verse 1, with Jesus' baptism at the hands of John the Baptist. He starts with Jesus' baptism, after which Jesus goes off at once to spend 40 days and nights alone in the wilderness, at the end of which He comes back, selects His apostles and starts His ministry. The trigger for Christ's work and ministry was His baptism. That appears to have been the springboard for all that He did.

As a matter of history, scholars say that Jesus had an ordinary upbringing, had an ordinary education and worked as a carpenter in His father's workshop until he was nearly 30. He then began His ministry, which lasted for three years or so, before the authorities lost patience with Him and had Him killed. Why he left it thus late to start, we cannot know. He is reported to have said that His time had not yet come, but we don't know why. Why he was given so short a time for His work we do not know. Why He felt it necessary to be baptised we do not know. But baptised He was – and, clearly, on the basis of Mark's writing, He had a deep spiritual experience in the course of it, a spiritual experience which sent him off to commune with Himself and His God for many days, an experience which set Him up to begin, to carry out and to complete His ministry

Why did He come to be baptised? Baptism was, at that time, a wholly new concept. Neither the word nor the practice is mentioned anywhere at all in the Old Testament, not in the books of the law, not anywhere. Ceremonial washing of a guest's feet was commonplace, as men wore sandals and the roads were dusty. Ceremonial washing was ordained for the High Priest and his family, because the High Priest spent his time in the holiest parts of the Temple, where special cleanliness was essential. But the Jews did not baptise their children, either shortly after birth or at all. It was a ceremony they simply did not have They knew nothing of the practice. A child would probably be taken to the temple in his first weeks to be presented to the priest and to be circumcised. But baptism with water, whether for adults or for children, was unknown. It looks as if John the Baptist invented it. He was a strange, wild-looking man, living the life of a hermit, who preached the necessity to repent and seek forgiveness of your sins – and he preached this necessity because the Messiah was coming soon. He taught that, as an outward and visible sign of repentance, his followers should be totally immersed in the water and thus symbolically washed clean. And he gained a great following – so great that the authorities in Jerusalem sent a group of holy men out to ask him who he was, asking indeed if he was himself the Messiah or perhaps Elijah, one of the greatest of the Jewish prophets. His answer was No. I am a herald only, a herald for the one who will come after me. I baptise with water only. But he will baptise with the Holy Spirit. Through me, your souls may be made clean for His coming. Through Him, you will receive the spirit of the one true God, which will pervade and enrich your life for ever.

This was strong stuff and John the Baptist clearly had a great impact. His impact was not confined to Judaea either. When St Paul came to Ephesus, which is a very long way from Jerusalem and very difficult to get to, he found followers of Jesus there already. But, when he asked them if they had received the Holy Spirit since they came to believe, they had never heard of it. They had heard of Jesus all right, but the teaching they had received and the baptism they had received were the teaching and baptism of John, whose followers had travelled that far and spread his teaching. Paul quickly put that right and baptised them in the name of Jesus – and thus, as he clearly thought, completed their journey into understanding.

And so I ask you, as Paul asked them: Have you received the Holy Spirit? Do you feel that the Holy Spirit is alive and at work in you? I hope you do – because the Christian Faith, as we teach it now, is that this is how it should be. In our service of baptism, the child is blessed with water, the sign of the cross is made on his forehead and he is baptised in the name of the Father, Son and Holy Spirit. It is not, as a rule, until Confirmation in our Church, that the bishop lays his hands on the candidate's head and says "Receive the Holy Spirit". It is always a dramatic moment, but I have often wondered why it is thought necessary or desirable. We do not teach, so far as I know, that the Holy Spirit cannot be in you until you are confirmed. There are probably plenty of you here, who have not been confirmed – and I certainly do not believe, that, because you have not been through that particular ceremony, the Holy Spirit cannot be in you and part of you. Indeed, it is my firm belief that, whether you realise it or not, the Holy Spirit is in you and a part of you now.

Christ was, we believe, by some miraculous means, a part of God: and this part of God is, through the Holy Spirit, in each of us always. It was Jesus' promise that this would be so, that there would be this divine spark in each of us, which gives us an immortal soul. The Church teaches that, by God's grace, a part of the spirit of that divine Christ is in you, that Christ is with you always and His spirit an innate part of you – Christ in you, never absent, never escaped from, always there. This means that, day in and day out, whether you realise it or not, Christ walks on your feet, Christ works with your hands, Christ sees through your eyes,

Christ hears with your ears, Christ thinks with your mind and Christ speaks with your voice. We should, each of us, strive to do Him honour in this. But, of course, it does not end there. For, if Christ is in you and a part of you, He is in everyone else as well. Christ is in your friends, in your enemies, if you have them, in those you love and like and in those you find you dislike. Christ is in the people you work with, the people you play with, the people you worship with: and in the people who worship in a different language and look to a God with a different name. Christ is in the rich man and the poor man, the strongest man and the weakest man, the criminal and the victim – and Christ's message was that, whatever we do - or do not do- to the least of these – or the greatest of these – we do it, or do not do it, to Him. With Christ thus in us, we are never alone, never truly lost, never without hope, never unloved.

This is our faith – at least, I think it is. And it all began one day in Palestine, when a young man, of whom the world, up to then, knew nothing, went to the river Jordan and was baptised. And in three short years, went out and changed the world. I had not thought very much before about Jesus' baptism or wondered why we should celebrate it. I have now.

The Marriage at Cana

St John Ch 2 v 1

What are we to make of the account you have just heard, in today's reading from St John's Gospel, of Jesus turning water into wine? The historians tell us that St John's Gospel was written sometime about 80 or 90 AD, by which time St John himself was dead. As one of the leading apostles, perhaps the closest to Jesus of all who worked with Him, he had attracted many followers and students, who wanted to learn from him: and no doubt they asked him questions and took deep note of what he taught. It is not thought by historians now that St John personally wrote the gospel attributed to him. The view generally held is that it was a compilation of his teachings, written by a number of his followers some time after his death - and indeed, if you look at the way the work is written, the resounding beauty of some of its language and the lack of chronological order in it, there is clearly good reason for this view. My guess is that one of his students had asked St John which was Jesus' first miracle and that the authors of this book remembered his account and put it in. The other gospels do not report this event - it only appears in St John's gospel, a strange story, written down perhaps as long as sixty years after the event and recounted nowhere else. What are we to make of it?

It is a most extraordinary tale. Jesus was at a family wedding, as was His mother. Some of His disciples were there too, perhaps invited, perhaps not invited. The wine ran out, which was unheard of. Perhaps it ran out because Jesus had brought some uninvited guests with Him. We cannot know. If that was the cause, it may not be a surprise that Jesus was asked to fix it - and the story is that He did, turning some gallons of water - a massive quantity - into delectable wine - a very popular achievement, you would think, of which word might get out rather quickly. After all, if our rector went down to the Dolphin on a Friday night and, instead of buying a round, followed his Master's example and turned water into wine, there would probably be standing room only in this Church for the rest of the year. He'd probably be barred from the pub as well. Yet nobody complained, even though the caterer was done out of a profit. No one seems to have followed Jesus because he could provide free alcohol: and nobody even seems to have asked Him how He did it. Nobody, it seems, ever asked Him to do it again: and nobody ever mentioned it again, until St John told his students of it maybe 50 years later. What are we to make of it? It is also right to remember that performing miracles with inert things was not the way that Jesus is reported to have worked. Just about all of Jesus' reported miracles are miracles affecting troubled people. It was the effect of Jesus' presence and actions on people's minds and bodies, not on people's things, that we read of in the Gospels. There are two ways of seeming to turn water into wine for a party of guests at a wedding. One is to turn water into wine. The other is to make the guests believe that the water is wine, when it is simply water. The authors of the Gospel clearly thought that the story was true. But which method Jesus adopted we will never know. So I ask: if we are to be honest with one another and honest about our faith, what are we to make of this?

Two things we can accept without any real question. Every marriage ceremony celebrated in our Church today speaks of Jesus' presence at this marriage and teaches that Jesus, by His presence there, blessed and approved a monogamous marriage. Monogamy was, by then, strictly enforced by the Jewish laws, so this should come as no surprise. Even so this endorsement is very valuable. The story is also a clear indication that Jesus did not disapprove of the consumption of alcohol - and apparently alcohol in fair quantities. This is no surprise either. Psalm 104, a wonderful hymn of praise to God, gave thanks to God for His gift of wine, describing it as "Wine that maketh glad the heart of man". They drank a lot of it in those days. The reason, of course, was that much, if not all, of the water then was dirty and infected: and that wine was commonly consumed, because clean drinking water was not available. Water was used for washing or cleaning, not for drinking at all. To drink wine was commonplace. To drink water was both rare and unwise. If Jesus' unique and wholly remarkable powers of alchemy enabled Him to make this water safely drinkable, it was truly a demonstration of extraordinary power.

And Jesus had and has this extraordinary power - and it is in this, and in the symbolism of this story, that the importance of this small piece of history seems to me to lie. Whether or not Jesus truly turned ordinary water into excellent wine on that day I do not know - we cannot know. But, whatever He did, it was a ground-breaking demonstration of what He can do for us. For our experience is that, day in and day out, the living Jesus turns the ordinary water that we are into the excellent men and women that we have it in our power to become. We are ordinary, germ-filled, infected water. But Jesus' touch, Jesus' glance, Jesus' influence can transform us, can make good wine of us, no matter how scattered the ingredients may be, no matter how entrenched we are in our unpalatable ways, no matter how convinced we may feel that we are beyond hope of change. Jesus is as present with us, as we go about the place in our ordinary day-to-day lives, as He was present with the guests at the wedding we have heard about: and the alchemy He used then is the same alchemy He uses today and every day. Jesus promised that he would be in us always: and this is the faith which our Church professes: and this, for what it is worth, is what I firmly believe. He is in us and working in us, whether we know it or not, whether we recognise it or not. His touch, his presence, makes us better people: and wherever there is love, wherever there is selflessness, wherever there is true friendship, Jesus has played a great part in making us what we are. We may not realise it. We certainly may not recognise either our condition or its source. But our Church teaches Jesus' Gospel as the gospel of love, the fountain-spring of all that is good and worth-while in us: and I firmly believe that that is what it is.

That is all very well, of course, but it does not end there, does it? We all have it in our power to use our time on this earth to be the living wine that Jesus wants us to be, by developing the talents passed on to us in our genes by our parents, by harnessing the skills given us by them and others in our upbringing and education, and using those talents and skills, if we so choose, for Christ's service. The living wine that we are may be wine of varying vintages or made from different grapes - but we all have it in us to be this living wine just the same. It may consist in physical strength or physical skills. It may consist in intellectual powers, mathematical ability or skill with computers. It may be a talent you have for giving pleasure or smiling so as to put people at their ease. The wine that you are, and which you can serve to others, may be found in some special talent you have for music or for painting or in skill with animals or in green fingers for growing things or arranging flowers. It may be a gift you have for healing or for being good with children or good with old people or with the sick. You may have that invaluable gift of being able to listen. You may have that underrated, but immensely valuable, capacity to love. These are just some of the ingredients we carry with us as we go on our pilgrimage about this earth: and Christ's message to each of us is that we should use these ingredients to become living wine in His service, so that we may bring joy to others and thus, as the psalmist puts it, may also make glad the heart of man.

For the wine that we can become is ours to do what we like with. We can, if we so choose, keep it and all its goodness and flavour for ourselves. We can, if we so choose, let this wine grow rancid through delay and disuse, till it is too late to do any good to anyone. We can, if we so choose, pour this wine, the good part of ourselves, away because we do not want it or do not want to face it or acknowledge it. We can ignore it and pretend it is not there - if we so choose. Or we can use the chance that our ever-loving God, through Jesus, has given us and listen and learn and become the wine He wants us to be, use it for His service and see that all the guests at the wedding have their glasses filled with it. For you, whether you like it or not, are the wine which Christ hopes will, in one way or another, feed his people. We are all at the wedding in Cana. We all have the bottle in our hand. Are we going to pour it out - or not? Well, are we?

One Day in Thy Courts

Psalm 84

There are, I know, many difficult questions which the Church has to face and answer. Our Church, as it is presently set up, is dogged by disagreements on doctrine and practice. Should we have female bishops? I cannot, for the life of me, see why not. But others disagree strongly. Should we allow homosexual priests to serve and minister to us in Christ's name? I cannot see why not. But others disagree strongly. And the various factions seem no closer to agreement or tolerance, nor do the wounds seem to be capable of being easily healed and so the arguments go on. But, though these things are matters of principle and matter a great deal and have to be faced, I do not want to talk about them today. The passages of Scripture appointed for reading today, and the psalm chosen to be sung today, are all, one way or another, concerned with rejoicing: so I want to talk briefly about rejoicing in our faith: and I do not propose to keep you long - a promise which will probably give you cause to start rejoicing at once. Consider the marvellous, but, at first sight, wholly incomprehensible words, which we have all, I hope happily, sung this morning from Psalm 84. One day in Thy courts is better than a thousand. What do they mean? And why do we sing them? Why indeed have we come here today to this service of Matins at all?

It is a very good thing to hold a service of Matins from time to time. I appreciate the views of those who say that a service without the Sacrament of Communion is a service without a centre, But Matins is, or ought to be, a service which we can really enjoy, where we can, joyfully and light-heartedly, rejoice in God our strength. I do not know whether you have enjoyed today's service. No one has yet laughed aloud in it, but at least you should have been smiling. For our purpose in coming here is not to sit uncomfortably in rows and whinge about things. Somebody once said that Christ did not die on the Cross so that we could sit round in small circles and complain about it. No, our purpose in coming here is to rejoice - to rejoice that God has promised us eternal life - and promised us an eternal life worth living for: and it is with this in mind that I offer you those words from Psalm 84 - One day in Thy courts is better than a thousand. I had rather be a doorkeeper in the house of my God than dwell in the tents of ungodliness".

The writer of this Psalm is expressing his joy at God's great goodness in promising, to each of those who listen, an eternal home where God is. He gives thanks for the sure knowledge that death is the pathway to eternal happiness, that, going through the vale of misery, he can use it for a well, that the road to death is lined with the water of life. Thy courts, O Lord, he says, are the most wonderful destination. One day in Thy courts is better than a thousand anywhere else. It is better to be a doorkeeper there, just to have the right to be there sometimes, than live for ever in the palaces of the ungodly, where God is not to be found. O Lord God of Hosts, says the psalmist, blessed is the man that putteth his trust in Thee.

This is the message of Psalm 84. Do we take it in and believe it? Do we, do you, rejoice that you are here? Do you rejoice that those, who have gone before you, and those who will come after you, and you yourself - do you rejoice that God has promised you all eternal life with him after this life is done? If not, why not? This is, after all, the faith which both Old Testament and New have declaimed, ever since they were put together and which countless millions have spent their lives believing. This is the message which Jesus brought us, a message we find not only in this morning's Gospel reading, but all over the Gospels and underpinning everything that Jesus ever taught. What do we find in today's gospel reading? Jesus'words: Fear not, little flock. It is your Father's good pleasure to give you the kingdom. And that kingdom is not, of course, riches or comfort or happiness on earth. It is eternal life in the courts of the Lord when our days here are done. It is the message of St Paul in today's epistle in his letter to the Hebrews about faith. He spoke of the great heroes of Jewish history, Abel, Enoch, Noah, Abraham, Sarah, Isaac, Jacob, Moses: and told those to whom he was writing, that all those great persons died in faith. They were not yet in possession of the things promised, but had seen them far ahead and hailed them and confessed themselves no more than strangers or passing travellers on earth. They were, in faith, longing, looking for, a heavenly country. Their faith was that that heavenly country was there, waiting for them, their true and only final destination. That is what they believed - and, thousands of years after those old heroes had lived and died in that belief, Jesus came from God Himself and told us they were right.

This is, it has to be, the bottom line of our faith. Our faith is, our Church teaches, that, through the sacrifice of Jesus, his death and resurrection, the path to eternal life, the road to the courts of the Lord, is open for all of us. Death is not the end. It never has been. It is the beginning of a new and incomprehensibly joyful new existence, the details of which we cannot now take in or understand, but an existence in which all will be inexpressibly well. I cannot make you rejoice about this, if you are determined not to. I do not use jokes from this pulpit to bring smiles to your faces. I offer you a much more powerful reason for smiling - the good news, which your Church, through me today, invites you to believe, of Jesus' promise of eternal life, for you and all those you love, in the courts of the Lord, of which today's Psalmist wrote. As countless prophets, priests and evangelists have said before any of us were ever thought of, I invite you, from this pulpit, to believe what the Church teaches and to rejoice at it. Our friends in the more fundamentalist churches rejoice at it with gusto, We sometimes call them happy-clappy, a term which we do not think of as complimentary. But happy, at least, in their faith they seem to be. Are we? Are you? You cannot think much of Jesus or the gospel He proclaimed if you cannot bring yourselves to be happy about it. Joyful, the Church teaches, is what God wants us to be. So let me bring you back to the words you have already sung today. How lovely are Thy dwellings, O Lord of Hosts. My soul hath a desire and longing to enter into the courts of the Lord. My heart and my flesh rejoice in the Living God. One day in Thy courts is better than a thousand. I had rather be a doorkeeper in the house of my God than dwell in the tents of ungodliness. O Lord God of hosts, blessed is the man who putteth his trust in Thee. We preach this. We believe in this. Does it make you any happier? If not, I truly cannot guess what will.

The Needle's Eye

St Mark Ch 10 v 25

One of Jesus's best-loved sayings is the one we hear in today's reading from St Mark. "It is easier for a camel to go through the eye of a needle than for a rich man to enter the kingdom of God". Jesus tells us a lot in this passage. The story begins with a young man in a state of anguish who runs after Jesus and asks him "What must I do to inherit eternal life?" : and Jesus answers that he should obey the law, obey the commandments. The young man replies: "I have done this – always": and Jesus, perceiving that the young man feels the need to do more, says "If you want to be my disciple, then sell all you have and give it to the poor and, come, take up your cross and follow me". That's difficult: and the young man goes sadly away, because he has great riches. Jesus says to the disciples: "How difficult it is for those who have riches to enter into the kingdom of God". At this, the disciples express astonishment: and Jesus puts it another way: "How hard it is for those who trust in riches to enter into the kingdom of God. It is easier for a camel to go through the eye of a needle than for a rich man to enter into the kingdom of God". The disciples then express further astonishment. And Jesus says:- "Well, all things are possible with God".

This question "What must I do to inherit eternal life" is asked a number of times in the Gospels: and Jesus' answers are not always the same. In St Luke, Chapter 10, for example, when a lawyer is recorded as asking this question, Jesus answers "What is written in the law?" and the lawyer replies, using Jesus' own words; Thou shalt love the Lord thy God with all thy heart and with all thy soul and with all thy mind and with all thy strength – and thy neighbour as thyself", to which Jesus replies: "Thou hast answered right. Do this and live" and does not make the point that the lawyer's wealth may, or will, disqualify him from entry. The lawyer, in that story, goes on to ask: Who is my neighbour?

And this leads to the parable of the Good Samaritan. Again, in Chapter 14 of St Luke's Gospel, Jesus is reported as saying that, if a man does not hate his father and mother and wife and children, he cannot be Jesus' disciple. That is a hard thing indeed. No wonder the disciples were astonished and asked how anyone could be saved, if these were the conditions.

If we are to understand what Christ said in this context, it is necessary, I think, to consider his words in the light of the context and culture of the time, in which Jesus was speaking. The Jews, from whom Jesus came and to whom Jesus spoke, despite being under Roman colonial authority, were an educated and articulate people, who had come to be commercially successful and who, having been completely destitute, had learned to value money and affluence as a sign of success. They devoutly worshipped their God, who had taught them that they were His chosen people and who had, with His own hand, saved them from their slavery in Egypt. They were grateful to God for that and for bringing them the commercial success they had achieved and the comfort that came with it: and they devoutly thanked Him for it. So it can be no wonder that the disciples were astonished by Jesus' teaching about the need to get rid of personal wealth. However, the fact was that, by then, their worship had become very much a matter of ritual, so that their duty to God had become seen as fulfilled by going to the temple at the right time, doing the prescribed things, saying the right words and going through the right motions. If you go through Jesus' teaching about this issue as set out in the Gospels, you find that His message throughout His ministry was that the Jews were wrong, calamitously and wickedly wrong, almost obsessively to value the accumulation of wealth, to put their trust in riches, as Jesus is reported to have put it, in the way they did: and He spoke about it harshly and often. But what are we, today, in our times and in our culture, to make of it?

Our task in this life, the task of each of us, is to find our way to God. This, for the Christian, means that we have to learn about

Christ, to discover what He wants of us and then go on and do it. And we ask, with the anguished young man, with the lawyer, who asked who his neighbour was, with the crowds who followed Jesus about and asked if they could follow Him, we ask: What must I do to inherit eternal life? And what must my loved ones do to achieve salvation likewise? What is it that God wants me to do? And Jesus' answer is the same that he gave the young man and that He gave the lawyer – obey the commandments and live your life with love in your heart. Love God with everything you have – and love your neighbour also. He knows that it is very difficult for ordinary human beings, who live their lives in the real world to do this. But that is what He asks for. Love, He says, love as I have told you and shown you. Do this and you will live. This, if you can manage it or even if you truly try to manage it, will be enough. But (He goes on) for some, like the young man Mark speaks of, like the crowds who followed Him and said they wanted to be His disciples, it may not be enough. To love God and our neighbour, to live with love in our hearts, is likely, He says, to be enough, or more than enough, for most of us. But, there are others, perhaps very few others, who feel called, are called, to do more: and I understand Jesus, in the Gospels to be saying that, if you feel that you are truly called to do more, to go the whole hog, as it were, then you must reject all human ambition and the wealth that brings, reject all of the world's ordinary trappings, reject all other human relationships and seek, single-mindedly, after God. You must have no wife or husband to distract you, you must have no children to distract you, you must reject all other responsibilities and diversions which may distract you and set your mind on God and keep it fixed on Him. This is why men go into monasteries and women into nunneries. This is why the Roman Catholic Church forbids its priests to marry and have children. If you find that, for you, loving, as Christ set it out, is not going to be enough and that you are called to do more, then you must reject all else that this world offers and give your heart, mind and body to Christ – and to Christ alone. But Jesus adds (and He spells it out in Chapter 14 of St Luke's Gospel) that you should not decide upon this, you should not embark upon this, unless you are sure that you have the strength for it and are ready to pay the price for it. Kings, He said, do not set out on military campaigns, unless they have made their plans and know that they will win. Business men, He said, do not embark upon projects without working out the costs first and deciding whether they can afford them. He says, in Chapter 14 of St Luke,: "If you feel called to do more than live with love in your heart, as I have set it out, then look ahead and work out whether you can really see it through, whether you can truly pay the price, before you answer the call: and do not follow the call, unless you are sure that you can.

Do not follow the call unless you are sure that you can pay the price, unless you are sure that you can follow it through. And most of us, as I see it, are simply not in a position to pay that price or follow that through. In our marriage ceremonies in these days, we invite the young couple to come to church, stand there together in front of their families and friends in what we assert and believe is the presence of God, and say those wonderful words: "All that I am I give to you and all that I have I share with you. In the presence of God I make this vow". Our Church invites them to do this and to take on the responsibilities which go with it: and, if they do this and take on the responsibilities which go with it, I do not believe that Christ then requires them to reject those responsibilities and abandon the things of the world where their responsibilities lie. I do not think that that is the Christian Faith: and, for what it may be worth, I do not think that that is what Christ requires of me. In the inimitable words of the late Jack Foster, a much-loved former churchwarden here, I believe that I am called to be a layman. I am called, I believe, to try to live a loving life in this, the real world, to keep my promise to love and to cherish the wife I married now over 47 years ago, to love and look after the children God has given us and the grandchildren which God has given them. I do not believe that Christ is asking me to reject them. I believe He is asking me to look after them and love them – and, if that means that I cannot, in this sense, be His disciple, then that is how it has to be. Some are summoned to a higher calling than others: and we must all respond to the calling we receive. I, and you too, I suspect, am called to be a layman, to live in this world as a layman, to look after my responsibilities as a layman and to try to love God and my many neighbours as a layman. That is why I am here. It remains my hope, my fervent hope, that I and those I know and those I love, who feel the same sort of call as I do, may yet inherit eternal life. I know nothing for certain. I pray often. And I believe that all may yet be well. It may be that you feel the same. Believe me, if you do, you are not alone.

The One Shall be Taken and the Other Left

St Luke Ch 13 v 5

The walls and towers of a city are, to many of those who live there, a symbol of the stability of the state they live in. The building, known as The twin Towers in New York was such a symbol to many Americans. The walls of Jerusalem were such a symbol to the Jews of Jesus' day. The rebuilding of those walls, after the Jews' exile in Babylon, had been a great event in their history – and a landmark part of those walls was a structure called The Tower of Siloam. Those walls meant the world to the people of Jerusalem and while they stood, all felt safe. And then, one day, unexpectedly, the tower of Siloam fell down. It not only fell. Eighteen people were killed in its fall. The shock waves were felt throughout the city. Why did this tower fall? Why did these people die? Was this God's punishment of the wicked? The people wanted an answer. That was then. On September 11th, today, ten years ago, terrorists, in pursuit of an agenda of their own, piloted airliners, full of passengers, into the twin towers in New York, killing many thousands of people and injuring countless more – the towers fell, a terrible man-made disaster. And, not long afterwards, on Boxing Day 2004, an undersea earthquake off the coast of Sumatra, caused a huge wave to rise and spread across the oceans, killing hundreds of thousands of innocent people – a terrible natural disaster. We see man-made disasters and we see natural disasters: and we ask, as the people of Jesus' day asked WHY? WHY this disaster? And WHY these victims? Why these victims and not others? Thus it is that I offer you today as a text Jesus' words in Chapter 13 of St Luke's Gospel: "These eighteen, upon whom the tower of Siloam fell and slew them, think ye that they were sinners above all men who dwelt in Jerusalem? I tell you No. But, unless you change your ways, you may all likewise perish.".

We can never forget how it was in South-East Asia on the day after Christmas 2004. Men and women were in their homes, in the fields, on the beach, fishing out at sea - and some were taken and others left - apparently indiscriminately, men, women, children (children who could not run fast enough or understand the danger in time), loving families devastated, thousands of children orphaned, a natural disaster of huge proportions, vastly greater than the fall of the tower at Siloam, but the same on a far larger scale. We come to church today, as we did ten years ago, to pray for all suffering people and all bereaved people and to ask why our said-to-be loving God allows these things to happen. I, like you probably, know how that terrible wave happened in South-East Asia. The earth's surface is not a solid mass. It is made up of large pieces, called tectonic plates, which generally fit together rather well. But occasionally pressure from the heat below builds up and causes a plate to shift slightly, which creates an earthquake and great destruction. On that day, this happened under the sea, vast quantities of matter and energy were released into the waters and great waves were created as a result. They flowed in all directions, hit the land with irresistible power and destroyed everyone and everything in their path. We will never know how many died. How, we ask, can a loving God allow this? If He is almighty, could He not prevent it? Could He not, at least, save the innocent children? We need to search in our minds and through our prayers and try to find an answer to this unanswerable question - why must the innocent die?

There are two answers which we simply must reject: and the first is the suggestion that there is no basis for faith in a God who allows this to happen, to say:- "The God I have always believed in is a good and just God. He did not prevent this. A good and just God would have prevented this. So I shall simply stop believing." That is an argument we must reject. Ever since time began, there have been massacres and mayhem: but that did not stop Jesus from telling us about God. Jesus, in today's text, spoke of the tower's fall and the death of the innocent and told us to go on believing. History is crammed with disasters and they did not stop us from believing. In the 1930's and 40's, the Germans tried, as a matter of national political policy, to annihilate the Jews and everyone they thought undesirable and killed millions, but that did not stop us from believing. Thousands of refugees and Aids sufferers die each month in Africa from disease, hunger and civil war -, but that does not stop us from believing. Innocent children are killed in road accidents every day of the week: and these awful things have not stopped us from believing. These events simply give us no cause to abandon our faith – and that is simply not the answer.

Neither can we possibly say that this is God's judgment on sinful man, that this is the work of an avenging God, who has grown sick and tired of man's failure to live up to His requirements, that this is God's punishment of the wicked. This argument, taken up by members of some religious groups, including, I regret to say, some of our own, is directly contrary to Jesus' teaching, wholly contrary to everything which the Christian Church today argues for. Jesus asked that very question:" Do you imagine that the people on whom the tower of Siloam fell were more guilty than all the other people living in Jerusalem? and answered it in six words: I tell you: They were not". That is the gospel, straight from Christ's lips. To attribute to God a desire for vengeance on humans on this earth, a determination to punish the innocent with the guilty, is directly contrary to Jesus' whole message, as it is contrary to the true message of the Church. We believe that Jesus died for our sins, gave Himself for us, so that we might be clear. God does not need tidal waves or natural disasters to pay us back for our sinfulness. To pretend that He does is to misstate the position entirely: and we simply cannot have it.

What then is the answer? I do not know. I wish I did. But there are places where we can start, there are platforms, which will provide a solid ground to set out from. And the best place to set out from is the place where we stood before the twin towers catastrophe and the Boxing Day tsunami occurred. We knew, before these disasters happened, that the world, which God somehow created, was an imperfect world, a world with faults and flaws in it, peopled by men and women with faults and flaws in them. God created a world with defects, with tectonic plates which move, with volcanoes which erupt because of irresistible pressure from below, with winds and storms which can turn to hurricanes and destroy everything in their path. God created a world with risk in it, with adversity in it: and risk and adversity are two of the elements which make our lives what they are. This is the world God made, a world with these defects: and this is the only world we have to live in. If it were otherwise and life offered no risk, no adversity, we would lose everything that makes life worth while. Without adversity, there would be no overcoming of adversity, no chance for the triumph of the human spirit over the challenges of life. Without risk, we would have nothing. We would not know pleasure, but for the risk of unhappiness. We would not know desire, if there was no risk of disappointment. We would not know achievement without the risk of failure. We would not know freedom without the risk of enslavement. We would not know virtue without the risk of evil. We would not know vulnerability without the risks which come from being vulnerable. We would not know love without the risk of rejection and the terrors of loneliness. We would be no better than robots, programmed to sing God's praises: and our belief is that that is not what God wanted us to be. He created human beings with minds to choose what to do with their abilities, living in a world where adversity could be overcome and risk surmounted, a world with evil in it and danger in it, over which victory could be achieved.

This is the world God created. As St John's Gospel puts it:- The world was made by him and without him was not anything made that was made. In him was life: and the life was the light of men: and the light shineth in darkness and the darkness cannot overcome it. Our world, God's world, is a world with light and darkness in it, a world created with light and darkness in it. The darkness cannot overcome the light, but sometimes it comes pretty close to it. I reckon it came pretty close to it on that Boxing Day in South-East Asia and on that terrible day in New York ten years ago. But the darkness has not won: and it is our task to see that it never wins. And we, you and I, can see that it never wins if we respond to such tragedies in the right way. We cannot remake the world to remove the risk, though we may try to make arrangements for the dangers to be reduced. We cannot irremoveably tighten the tectonic plates. We cannot harness the sea or rein in the power of volcanoes or hurricanes. We can never stop wicked men from doing wicked things. What we can do is what Jesus told us to do. He told us to repent or else we might all be lost. And, when he told us to repent, he was not telling us just to say Sorry. The Greek word used is Metanoia, which means a complete change of heart. Jesus told us then, and tells us now that we must continually strive to live our lives as Christ would have us do. It may involve a complete change of heart and great determination. But this is what we must strive for. And we can pray that, in our collective grief at disasters of this kind, we try to renew and make real that half-seen and distant vision that all human beings belong to the same family. Having seen with terrifying clarity how small and vulnerable humanity is in the face of the forces of nature and the forces of evil, may we not also see how small are the things that divide us and how tragic it is that we should spend so much time and effort being at odds with one another. Let us, in our true repentance, seek with all our heart to bring love (that love which Jesus so constantly spoke of) into everything that we do - and maybe then some good will come out of all this. While Christ is still with us, I believe it can.

Harvest

Deuteronomy Ch 28 v.3

Harvest Festival is a time for giving thanks. We give thanks to God at this time because our faith has been rewarded. The farmer's life is a life governed by faith – he ploughs and sows in faith, believing, on the basis of his experience of the seasons, the soil, the weather and the materials he uses, that his efforts will result in a crop which will grow and ripen to be harvested. At the harvest festival, he gives thanks to God that his faith has been rewarded – if it has. So it is with us all, whether we be farmers or not. Whatever field we work in, whatever harvest we seek, whatever seasons, whatever soil, whatever weather we rely on, whatever experience in life it is which moves us to believe that our ventures will succeed, we ought to give thanks to God for the fruition of our hopes and efforts – and, whatever the nature of our harvest, harvest festival is a good time to do it. And it is because we are not solely, or even largely now, a farming community, but a community engaged in all sorts and conditions of work, that I offer as a text words which were traditionally used in our harvest festival services for many years, a passage from Ch 28 of the Book of Deuteronomy: "Blessed shalt thou be in the city and blessed shalt thou be in the field. Blessed shall be the fruit of thy body and the fruit of thy ground". Blessed shalt thou be in the city.

It is not easy to give an orthodox sermon on Harvest Festival Sunday in this year 2007. Some farmers may have had a good year. For many, however, it has been a disaster. They ploughed, they sowed, they tended their fields in faith - and the summer floods, in the Midlands and East Anglia, drowned much of the crop and destroyed it completely – and now the milk and cattle farmers are facing another outbreak of foot and mouth disease, the regulations for the prevention of the spread of which necessarily bring ruin in their train. The farmers thank God, when they see their faith rewarded. When they see their faith go for nothing, I do not know what to tell them. I do not say, I will not say, that they are being punished for their sins - I think that is a wicked falsehood, even if a bishop asserts it - for the sin is not theirs and that is not the way of the God our Church proclaims. But I do not know what to say to them today from this pulpit, other than to express my sorrow and my sympathy and to pray for them in their distress. What I want to do today is talk briefly about those who produce other fruit, who produce a different harvest – about accountants and architects, shopkeepers and postmistresses, school teachers and driving instructors, school governors and schoolchildren, about mothers who care for children and children who care for parents, about doctors and dentists, administrators, civil servants, priests and, yes, lawyers too. For we all have a harvest from the fields where we work, for which we should thank God and part of which, today, just as the farmers do, we should bring to the altar as a mark of our gratitude for God's great goodness towards us.

We all live by faith. Every year, every season in every year, we take steps into the unknown in faith, that is in the belief that they are steps in the right direction and that the purposes we seek to achieve by taking them will be realised. A child learns to sing in faith, believing that the day will come, when her trained voice will enable her to sing well the songs she wants to sing and give pleasure to herself and all those who hear her. A young man works for years to qualify as a solicitor in faith, believing that the day will come, when he can use his training to good purpose in giving the right advice and bring good order to the affairs of his clients and so make a decent living for himself and his family. A school governor undertakes hours of training and puts in hundreds of hours of unpaid work in faith, believing that the school will prosper from what she does and give the children there a sound grounding in the things they need to know. A mother of small children works in the day and gets up in the night in faith, believing that she is doing the right thing and that one day the child will grow to be the person he or she is destined to be. A committed schoolteacher and loving mother gave up her job to study to become a priest and worked hard at it for little reward to become ordained. She did this in faith, believing that she would, in time, find a parish where she would be welcomed by her congregation and that they would become her people. Carol Coslett will be inducted as our priest here in nine days time: and today we rejoice and give thanks that she has committed herself, her family and her life, to us in this community. She has resolved to make us her next life's harvest: and, to some extent (for we will work with her – at least I hope we will) she will be our harvest too. Blessed may she be in the city and blessed may she be in the village also. Let us pray that all will go well for her here.

We never know what will happen tomorrow, what lies waiting for us round the corner. Our faith is that, if we take the right steps into the unknown and keep Christ by our side in whatever we do, the fruit of our ground will be blessed, whatever field we work in and whatever our harvest is to be. And today we think of all things that have gone well for us and give thanks to God for them. For blessed have we been in the city and blessed have we been in the field. How we give thanks is perhaps something we should think about with care. He, who is blessed in the field, the farmer, traditionally brings part of his crop to the altar, a portion for Christ, to show his gratitude. But those of us who have been blessed in the city, those of us in manufacturing or service industries, do not have any tangible part of our harvest to bring. An accountant cannot bring his figures, an architect cannot bring his drawings, a lawyer can bring neither his clients nor his advice. But if, like the farmer, those of us who have been blessed in the city are to lay part of our substance on the altar as an outward and visible sign of our gratitude to God for His goodness, then, perhaps quietly those of us, whose harvest is measured in money, should use the opportunity to bring a cheque in an envelope for an appropriate sum, with which good may be done.

Perhaps we should think about it. Some years ago, in a then prosperous motor industry parish in Coventry, they brought a new car into the sanctuary as their harvest gift. At a gift day, I believe, in Holy Trinity Brompton, a few years back, the successful young

Christians from the city gave £ 150,000 to their Church in one night as a token of their thanks to God for His goodness to them. We here have countless gifts of love to thank God for. Today is not a day for letting pangs of conscience dilute our thankfulness. But, as we rejoice for all those good things and for our Lord's infinite mercy and goodness towards us, let us perhaps take some time to consider in what form our harvest giving may be made next year.

Meanwhile we have been blessed in the field and we have been blessed in the city – and for this may the Lord be praised.

Christ the Unwilling Healer

St Matthew Ch 15 v 26

It is not right to take the children's bread and throw it to the dogs. These are Jesus' words, used by Him in response to a plea by a young mother, a Canaanite, not a Jewess, who begged Him to heal her seriously sick daughter. She approached Him and asked His help and He ignored her. She went on pleading. The disciples suggested that He turn her away. He replies that it was the lost sheep of the house of Israel, not the likes of her, that he had come to help. She asked again. He said that, if He helps her, He is taking the children's food and casting it to the dogs. The woman produces a rather clever answer, whereupon He relents: "Woman, what faith you have. Be it as you wish" – and the girl is healed. This story is well authenticated. It appears in St Mark's gospel also, together with other accounts of Jesus being unwilling to use His healing powers to help the sick and afflicted. I will not take the children's food and cast it to the dogs. It is not how we generally think that Jesus behaved. Indeed it comes as something of a shock to hear such opinions attributed to Him. But this is what the gospels tell us – and, if we are to be honest with ourselves and our belief, we must face it. Jesus here is presented to us as a thoroughly unwilling healer – a man who wants nothing to do with healing at all.

This is the picture which St Mark and St Matthew present to us - a picture of an unwilling healer: and, since we have to face the realities of what we read in the gospels, if we are to find the real Christ and understand the gospels properly, we have to ask ourselves why Jesus, this greatest of all, this infinitely good man, born to live the perfect life as God on earth, was an unwilling healer. For it is so easy, isn't it, to let the Gospels simply shed a rosy glow over our thinking? So easy to avert our eyes from the awkward questions? So easy just to count the blessings and overlook the difficulties? These gospel writers present Jesus, their Jesus, their Master, the man they followed, the man they devoted their lives to, as an unwilling healer: and we have, if we are to be honest in our quest to find the real Christ and not a false one, to ask why.

The answer, I think, is that the Son of God did not come to live with us on earth in order to heal the sick - nor indeed to work miracles of any kind. God could have planned it any way He chose. But he did not choose that way. It would have been easy enough for God to come on earth, do a whole lot of magic tricks, make everyone vote him Top of the Pops or Sports Personality of the year: and go on His way rejoicing. But he did not choose that way: and He did not choose that way because His purposes were different. It was never Jesus' purpose to make people comfortable or to make life easy for anyone. He came to deliver a message, which he knew would bring strife and division. He came to show people how life should be lived - not with magic tricks or milk and honey or comfortable armchairs, but with love poured out to others and iron self-discipline in himself. And because he knew that the demands of the love he spoke of and the bands of the self-discipline he taught were hard to meet and infinitely restrictive in their operation, he knew that strife and division would result from the principles he taught. His healing of the sick was almost an irrelevance. As a loving shepherd, he saw people suffering and, out of his infinite love, sometimes healed them as he passed by. But he generally wanted no one to know about it, I imagine, because he did not want his message diluted. He did not want his people diverted by the outward signs of the exercise of his power into believing that that was all he had come to do: and we must not be diverted by them either. Christ the healer is a very attractive and easily lovable figure. Christ the Son of God, the Christ who demands principled decisions and iron self-discipline, is a much more formidable prospect.

Jesus' message was simple, troublesome and very demanding. You must try to live your life in such a way as will enable you to find your way to God. You must love God with all your heart, mind and strength, doing only what God permits and avoiding what God excludes: and, at the same time, you should love your neighbour as yourself, that is by doing right things to others and refraining from doing wrong things to others. This, since we are humans, involves unconditional loving (which is rare and hard) and massive self-restraint (which is contrary to our nature and also very hard): and, while Jesus showed us an example of how these difficult things can be done, he left, inevitably, a large number of questions unanswered, so that we have to solve them for ourselves. And solve them with love and understanding is what we have to try to do - a course in which we inevitably disagree, which is why we have the strife and division which Jesus told us he would bring. If there was nothing left to argue about, there would be no strife. But there are things left to argue about: and we have strife in plenty. We cannot leave the solutions to Christ the Healer and do nothing ourselves. It is our task, yours and mine, to solve the problems. We can and should pray for guidance - but the answers lie in our own loving and understanding and in our own self-discipline: and we cannot be followers of Christ and run away from that responsibility.

If you ask me what I am talking about, I will tell you. Take, for example, a problem much talked of now, the problem of the loving, committed, homosexual man or woman. Should such a person be allowed to fulfil what he/she feels to be his/her vocation and become a priest? Some say yes. Some say No. Those who say No argue that homosexual activity is contrary to the laws of God and seriously perverse in nature. No one, they say, who is committed to a life of that kind, can ever be in a sufficient state of grace to work as a priest. The argument is strong and has plenty of support in the Bible, if you look for it. Those who say Yes assert that such people have great gifts and pastoral skills, presumably God-given: and that the love they feel for their partners is just as great, their commitment is just as firm and their activities, for them, just as natural as any you will find in the heterosexual community. They argue that such people's capacity for love is great and valuable: and that, if we are to love our fellows as Christ commanded us to do, we must, in our love for them, not deny them the fulfilment they seek in being authorised to carry on this work. The argument is strong and, while it may have less literal Biblical support, it has a wealth of implied biblical support, if you read the gospels with an eye to finding it. We have the responsibility of finding the answer to this, if Christ's work on earth is to be advanced: and the problem will not go away, if we simply refuse to face it. The answer, of course, is to ask what Christ would do, if faced with the problem: and the trouble is that we do not know. No one, in Christ's day knew then what we now know about chromosomes and genes and the make-up of the human body and the human mind, just as no one in Christ's day knew what we now know about the earth being round and revolving on its axis in its orbit round the sun. Christ might have answered that homosexuality was a perversion and that the homosexual life was abhorrent to God. He might have said that homosexual love was just as much a natural instinct implanted by God as heterosexual love. We just don't know. And so we are left with the problem: and so we are left with the strife, strife which we must study and pray to deflect and expunge, problems which we must strive to solve without bitterness and anger and in a truly Christian spirit. For the finding of solutions out of our love for God and our love for our neighbour is what we are pledged to achieve.

This problem, of course, though it may yet shatter our Church, pales into insignificance beside the greater problems of war, world poverty and family breakdown: and what the Christian response should be to them. We don't know for sure what Jesus' answers would be to them either: and again, because we don't know, we disagree, often strongly: and so we have strife and division. But what we must, as Christians, surely always remember is that the fact that we do not know the answer does not mean that there is none or that we should not work at trying to find it. Indeed that is what, in our service to Christ, we are bound to do. And it is here, if I may come back to where I started, that we encounter Christ the true healer. It is through Christ's presence in us, through Christ's boundless ability, through prayer, to lead us to His Father, by the process of working things through with Christ at our side and in our thinking, that we can and must find answers to these difficult questions. It was not, and is not, Christ's mission to heal the sick in body, though He did, can and, sometimes, in His infinite mercy, does. It was, and is, through us, Christ's mission to heal the wounds in the spirit, to help the anguished soul through the healing process towards the answers to the problems of our age. Medical science can cure most of our physical problems now. But no scientific process can answer the spiritual problems which we weak humans daily face. Through faith and prayer and by really trying, we have the power to solve those problems – and Christ the healer is the power by which it can, and will, be done.

The Transfiguration

St Luke Ch 9 v 29

At every service of baptism in these days, it is our practice to pray for the child that he will "Shine as a light in the world to the glory of God the Father" - that he will shine as a light in the world.

The Book of Exodus in today's first reading, describes how Moses' face shone when he spoke to God. St Luke, in his account of the transfiguration of Jesus in today's second reading, describes how Jesus' face shone, when he spoke to God. The placing of these two readings together delivers a clear message. There was, to the Jews, no more important piece of history, no more fundamental incident in the whole of their historic pilgrimage, than the story of the giving of the Ten Commandments, the great tablets of stone, by God himself to His servant Moses: and, when Moses received them, his face shone. When the greatest of their forefathers, the founder of their religion, spoke to God, his face shone - and the Gospel writers went out of their way to attribute the same experience to Jesus. This was the greatest tribute they could possibly pay, in Jewish eyes anyway, to their crucified and risen Master, to describe how Jesus' face shone, when God came to speak to Him. To put Him equal with or above Moses in this way placed Him on a pedestal, which any Jewish reader of the Gospel would immediately understand, which would bring any Jewish reader of the Gospel up short and make him gasp - is this man greater than Moses then?

The account of the transfiguration of Jesus is a strange story. Jesus went with a few disciples out into the countryside in the middle of the night. The disciples went off to sleep, leaving Jesus alone - and, when they woke up, they found Jesus talking to two men, whose faces and bodies were shining, whom they identified as Moses and Elijah, heard God talking and saw Jesus' face shining also. They had this utterly remarkable, miraculous experience - and decided to tell no one about it at all. It is very odd: and the evidence, when you examine it in any critical sense, is very thin. But this is not the point. The point is, as historians and commentators now assert, that the Gospel writers were not necessarily seeking to recount the historical truth. They were seeking to demonstrate that Jesus was the Son of God: and they were seeking to demonstrate that Jesus was the Son of God, because the impact, which Jesus had made on them through the time they had known Him, had been so powerful an impact that they had come to be totally convinced that He was indeed God's son. His impact on them, ordinary Jewish folk with an orthodox Jewish upbringing and religious education behind them, had been so massive that they felt compelled to broadcast any tale which would emphasise His divinity. And the shining of His face when he spoke to God was a story which could not fail to affect every Jewish listener and reader and persuade them of their conviction that Jesus was divine.

I am not saying that the transfiguration of Jesus, as described in the Gospels, did not occur. I do not know. I cannot pretend to know. Maybe it did. Maybe it did not. We, you and I, simply cannot tell. But fifty years ago, I would probably have been drummed out of the Church, certainly banned from the pulpit, for speaking to you in this way. To suggest, in church, that there are passages in the Gospels which are not the literal truth, was considered a serious heresy. People were burned at the stake for much less a few hundred years ago: and there are priests and preachers in the Church of England today, some in parishes very near to here, who will argue, and continue to argue, that the whole of the Bible is, and must be accepted as, the literal truth. It is scarcely two years since a senior retired priest, a former Canon of his cathedral and former Chaplain to the Queen, was banned from preaching in the Church in the town where he now lived, because, from the pulpit, he had questioned the literal accuracy of a particular passage in one of the Gospels. Parishioners had objected, his Parish priest had banned him: and the Bishop supported that ban. The reasons why this devout and experienced priest had put this view forward were of no concern. He appeared to be expressing doubt about the literal truth of the Bible: and that was not permitted. In a sense, that is what I am doing now. I ask you to bear with me.

Jesus told us that the first and great commandment was that we should love the Lord our God with all our heart and soul and strength and mind. Heart, soul, strength and mind are four different things, four different ingredients in the make-up of the human person. To love with the mind requires the enthusiastic involvement of the intellect, the involvement of the thinking process, in our approach to, and our worship of, the God we revere. We cannot, I think, truly love God with our mind, if we insist on suspending our intellectual processes, whenever His name is mentioned or we talk about our faith. When a country goes to war in these days, we want to know why. When our young men are sent to the desert and get killed, we want to know why they were sent there; and what the evidence was which required that they be thus deployed. We want to know these things because we love our country, because we are concerned about its reputation. We cannot, I think, truly love our God or His church or be effective guardians of its reputation or be worth-while evangelists for it, unless we allow our brains, which are probably the most wonderful things that God has given us, to become involved in our search for Him. To refuse to use our minds in searching for answers to the difficult questions God has posed for us is to do Him a serious disservice. Surely our Lord deserves better at our hands than that.

The Bible is not a book. It is a library, containing 66 books, 39 of the Old Testament and 27 of the New Testament, books chosen, probably lovingly, by experts about 1400 years ago. Why some were included and some excluded may be known to scholars, but, like so many other things, are not known to you and me. 66 books there are, making up the best-loved and most-read and most-commented-upon library in history. There are 66 books in the Bible. There must be 66000 and more books about it, examining its contents, seeking for its meaning, considering the purposes for which its contents were written and who its authors were, what they knew and what they believed: and seeking out what its messages truly are. The vast majority of these books have been written, over many years, by scholars - devout men of deep belief and great learning, many of whom have spent their lives in study and in prayer. Most of them were Christ's devoted servants. Do we serve God, do we show our love for the God, who was their inspiration, by refusing even to think about considering what they wrote? Do we show our love for God by closing our minds to all their thinking and by a continuing unwillingness to move an inch beyond what appears to be the literal meaning of the much-translated words which we find in the Bible which we use? It is far easier to sit and say nothing, simply to stay put and pretend that the difficult questions do not matter. But, if we are to love God with all our mind, can we properly do that? Do we love God with all our mind by just switching our mind off? That is a question, which you and I, each individually for ourselves, must answer: and if the answer is Yes, I will not engage in further study or questioning, is it your faith, which leads you to that answer? Or is it something else?

I was reading this week a short article by Alan Webster, formerly dean of St Pauls, whose 11-year-old grandson had been prepared by his Parish priest for confirmation and had, in his confirmation classes, been told about the problems faced by the Church over the election of the new apparently homosexual Bishop in New Hampshire. Grandfather asked grandson: "What did you decide about him?": and the answer was: "I said I needed time to think it out". The Dean's comment was:- Would that "Thinking it out" could become normal for both young and old. It remains an open question which parts of our scriptures are true literal history and which are not. "We have" wrote the Dean "to think it out": and he quoted Cardinal Newman's words, which are very apposite:- "In a higher world" wrote the Cardinal "It is otherwise. But here below, to live is to change: and to be perfect is to have changed often".

It is a common saying for us that we live and learn. Because we learn, we change. If we learn what is right, we change for the better. But, if we switch our minds off, we cannot learn at all. Our faith cannot require us to believe or speak out for facts, which we can see to be demonstrably untrue. That is not good for us. It is also manifestly bad for the Church we love. God does not change. But the more we can learn about the God we worship, the more we will change - and the more we will change for the better. Which brings me back to the point where I started. The point is that the Gospel writers, and the apostles who informed them, believed, beyond any doubting, that the Jesus, whom they had known and seen and followed, was the Messiah foretold in their scriptures, was the Son of God, was divine. Their experience of Him, seeing Him risen, had persuaded them of the undeniable truth of that - and that was the truth they felt impelled to spread abroad to the listening and the unlistening world. And that is our Faith. The more questions we ask about it, the more we will know: and the more we know, the more effectively we will be able to live the life and spread the word - which is our task. Our faces may not shine. We probably don't want them to. But we may become a source of light, may we not? And then perhaps we will shine as a light in the world to the glory of God the Father, which is what, at our baptism, someone may have prayed that we should do.

All Saints Day

Today is All Saints Day, the day when we remember all the saints, who have no specific day of their own. I know the names of a few of them, but only a few: and I have some idea of what a few of them did - but again only a few. There are hundreds of them down the ages, great servants of Christ and His church, people who did great good and lived good and godly lives. They served their Lord as He deserved and today is their day. I cannot tell you who they were. All I know is that their numbers include all sorts and conditions of men and women - black and white, male and female, rich and poor, strong and weak, fast and slow, red-haired, dark-haired, blonde-haired, bald - and, very probably, whether anyone has taken account of it or not, heterosexual and homosexual - all sorts and conditions of men and women, who are unified in that highest common factor, that they served Christ without reservation throughout their lives and did Him great honour.

Some years ago, I was a guest at a Christian men's breakfast meeting in Ashtead. There were about 40 men there, varying in age, I would guess, between 27 and 77, a mixed group of Roman Catholics, Anglicans and Baptists, who met once a month for breakfast and worship and worked together from time to time. There were two priests there, a Roman Catholic and an Anglican: and Grace was said before we sat down to eat by a Baptist layman, who thanked God for our food and our fellowship and added: "But, Lord, most of all, we thank you for sending us Christ, your son, who unites us". "Thank God for Christ who unites us" he said: and I wondered. I wondered, because, like, I imagine, many of you, I am sorely troubled by the things which seem to disunite us, the quarrels in our Church about the appointment of women as bishops and the sexual orientation of priests, the apparently unbridgeable chasms between those, who welcome good people to the priesthood, regardless of their gender and sexual proclivities, and those who would forbid this status to women or homosexuals. I know the arguments on both sides: and I accept the good faith of some of those with whom I personally disagree: and, as a layman, I ask you, as thinking Christians, what we are to do. I ask this question today, on All Saints Day, the day when we remember the multitude and huge diversity of these great people, who have served God in their lives and. regardless of their gender or sexual orientation, have been honoured for it.

Our Church is a great institution, said to be the Body of Christ on earth. This is what Christ told us to be: and it is unacceptable to me - I find it offensive - that this great body of ours should be made to split into different pieces on issues such as this. My belief is that God caused us to be made as we are, all different, all with varying abilities, all with differing hopes, differing aims, differing approaches to the realities of life. God caused us to be made this way and looks to each of us, each to fulfil ourselves by the differing service we can give Him. Our approach to our faith, yours and mine, is an approach brought about by our introduction to, and our understanding of, the faith which we profess: and it is the fact, as well as what you might expect, that, because our introductions were different, so our understandings will be different also. In a word, we do not all believe exactly the same things. Our approaches are different, our understandings are different, our beliefs are different. But it is Christ who unites us. We are united because we look to Him, because it is to Him that we turn to try to find out what we ought to do. That is surely how it should be.

Archbishop Rowan Williams put it simply in an address he gave some years ago. The trouble, he said, with this Church of ours (I paraphrase) is that there are far too many Christians saying: "The Church is me", the people who say: "I know what I believe. I am convinced that what I believe is the truth – and, since it is the truth, it must be right". The truth is that the Church is us - all of us - and we must work and worship in harmony together. We may not go to the same church building and we may not follow the same rituals. But we must work and worship in harmony just the same. The Christian men, who entertained me in Ashtead on the day I told you of, belong to different denominations. The Roman Catholics have been brought up to believe, believe passionately and will never be dissuaded, that, at the Communion rail, the bread and the wine are, by a miracle, physically transformed into the Body and Blood of Christ. They are taught and believe that they are eating and drinking Christ's flesh and Christ's blood. Their firm belief in this alchemy is an integral part of their faith. To them it is the truth and they believe they must be right. The Anglicans generally believe that the bread and wine are symbolic only: and Roman Catholics generally see no substance whatever in our Communion services for this reason. Our faiths, our understanding, our approaches on this vital issue are entirely different and contradictory. Each firmly and honestly believes that the other is wrong. The truth is that both are right.

Let me put it another way. God, Christ, through the Holy Spirit, has revealed Himself to each of us in different ways and at different times. We are different. His way of making Himself known to us is different. We all have, each of us, a different revelation. We are, each of us, bound to serve Him in accordance with the revelation of Him, which we have experienced - and that means that we do different things and worship in different ways. The black tribes in Africa, for example, speak a different language in their worship from the white tribes in that continent. Their faith is founded on a different culture, they use a different ritual, a ritual developed with them, and taking into account their culture, to enable them to express their love and their commitment to the Christ we all serve. If you went to their church, you would not understand the language, you would not feel at home with the ritual. You would probably find that they believed different things and emphasised different things. If they came to your church, they would have the same experience. But Christ unites you just the same.

The evangelical movement in our Church do not worship in the same way as we do here. Some call them happy-clappy, a phrase which I greatly dislike, a phrase which, in my view, is derisory and demeaning. But it is the way the Christ, who has revealed Himself to them, calls on them to worship. We are more sedate in our worship here, because that is the way that Christ has called upon us to worship. We are both right to worship in this way. Their beliefs are based very much more on the literal truth of our translation of the Bible than mine are, perhaps more than yours are. But, if that is their revelation of the Christ we all worship, then that is a view which is right for them just as our views are right for us. I am convinced that, if we each of us worship in the way we feel called on to do, in accordance with the revelation we have received, neither of us is wrong. We are both right. Their revelation may move them to believe that an active homosexual cannot be an acceptable priest or that a woman cannot be an acceptable bishop. I entirely disagree, because my revelation of Christ and his requirements is different from theirs. Their views are, for the moment, right for them. My views are, for the moment, right for me. Our task, each of us, is, by work and prayer and study, using our intellects to overcome our prejudices, fully to work out what we believe the truth is: and then to pursue our quest for Christ on the basis of the truth we have thus discovered. But the fact that we truly believe something which they do not does not mean that either of us is wrong and must change our thinking. The truth is that, for the moment at least, we are both right and we must each worship as we are called to do, as part of the same organisation, as part of the same body.

But, if we are one organisation, one body, we must have rules. Rules may be good, they may be bad, they may be changed. But, if made, they must be obeyed, or else the organisation collapses. There has been a rule, ever since the Church began, that active homosexuals should not be priests and that women cannot be bishops. I regret those rules and I would like to see them changed. But, while it remains the rule, it should be followed. I think there is a strong case for saying that this issue should be a local matter, for local decision by the country or diocese, rather than by the Anglican Communion as a whole: and maybe the rules can be changed to allow for that. But that has not happened yet. The rules will have to be changed before that becomes permissible. Meanwhile we must remain one active and loving body. The campaigners should campaign within the body, the argument should continue within the body: and the body, strengthened by the love which fuels the argument, should remain healthy and whole, one Church, one Faith, one Lord. Let us be what we ought to be, a great cloud of witnesses, striving to live Christ's Gospel, sharing our faith and continually thanking God for Christ who unites us. We are united because it is to Him that we look. What we must do, all of us, is continue to look to Him and, as we do so, go out and show the world that one body is what we are.

Jumping Shoes

Genesis. Ch 2 v 7

You are no longer aliens in a foreign land, but fellow-citizens with God's people, members of God's household. So wrote St Paul to the Christians of Ephesus – and maybe they were what he said they were. But are we? Are you? Do you feel that you are members of God's household? There are tens of thousands who say: I am not a member. I am not qualified. What must I do to join this company? They feel that they want to be a part of it, but don't know how to start. In trying to answer that, I offer two texts today, one from the Bible, one from elsewhere. From the Bible, I offer, from Genesis, Ch 2, the Jews' traditional account of the creation of man. "But there went up a mist from the earth and watered the whole face of the ground. And the Lord God formed man from the dust of the ground and breathed into his nostrils the breath of life. And man became a living soul". My second text is some words from the writings of a 13th Century mystic named Meister Ekhart, a divine much quoted in books on mysticism: "Up then, noble soul. Put on thy jumping shoes, which are intellect and love. Overleap thine understanding and spring into the heart of God".

When God made you, He made you a living soul. Your duty to God, my duty to God, in this life is so to conduct ourselves that our souls truly live and that we find our way to the God who made us. We find our way to God by seeking to learn about what God is and where He may be found: and we need to try to understand what God is to be able to get near Him. But this is where our principal difficulty lies. For God has no dimensions- is almost wholly indecipherable. More books have been written about God than about anything else in Heaven or earth. But even so no one has ever seen God and no one knows what God is like. If we search the Bible, we will find all sorts of records of what God is said to have done, but almost no record at all of what God is like. When Moses asked God: "How will I and the people recognise you?", he got the answer: "I am that I am. Tell them I am hath sent me unto you" – a powerful answer, but not helpful to the real seeker after truth.

The disciples asked Jesus the same question, but in another way. They asked how they should pray – and, in giving them an answer, Jesus told them a lot about God. He gave them, gave us, the Lord's prayer, which tells us a lot about God , when we think about it. It tells us that we should address God as we would a parent, that God is in a place called Heaven, that He has a name which should be treated as holy, that He has a kingdom which will come for us, that He has a will which we should follow. Jesus tells us that the provision of our daily needs is in God's gift and that the forgiving of our offences is in God's gift also, that He can keep us from temptation and keep us from harm and that power and glory are His for ever. These are descriptions of a sort: and to those of us who ask what God is like, these answers get us some way, but not very far. We have effectively no information as to what God is like, no inkling of an understanding of God's true nature. The picture I see in my mind of genuine seekers after truth trying to understand God is a picture of energetic tracker dogs sniffing at an impenetrable wire fence, trying vainly to get inside, running here and trying to dig there, barking at the sudden scent, but never getting through to the mystery within.

All of which brings me to Meister Ekhart. "Up then, noble soul. Put on thy jumping shoes, which are intellect and love. Overleap thine understanding and spring into the heart of God". You can jump the fence, he says, and spring straight into the heart of God, if you put on your jumping shoes. Use, he says, those two gifts, which God has given you, and overcome the handicap of your restricted understanding. Harness your intellect. Harness your power to love and overleap the fence which impedes your understanding. For you can reach God without knowing what He is like and without understanding His nature – and that is the process which we call Faith.

The first of your jumping shoes is your intellect. Harness your intellect, says the prophet, and see where it takes you. God gave you the gift of reasoning: and you owe it to Him to use it in your quest to find Him. We use our intellect, I would suggest, in trying to define what it is that we believe: and that should not be difficult because we recite it by heart whenever we come to church. We often tend, I think, to stop thinking about it because we find it so easy to recite. But the Creed sets out what it is that we say that we believe: and it provides, I find, an invaluable foundation for what our reason tells us about God. I believe in God, the Father almighty, maker of Heaven and earth, and in Jesus Christ His only Son, our Lord. Do you believe that? I don't need to know whether you believe that or not. But you need to know, don't you? Who was conceived by the Holy Ghost. Born of the Virgin Mary. Do you believe that? I don't need to know whether you believe that or not. But you need to know, don't you? The Apostles' Creed lists about eighteen short sentences, each a clear statement of fact. Each of these unequivocal and direct sentences, recited in our churches daily and weekly, one after the other, month in and month out, is thinking fodder for our intellects to work on. Do you believe this statement? if so, why? If not, why not?

The prophet invites you to use your intellect to question these things as an invaluable road map in your quest for God. For the more you think about the details of your faith, think about what it is that you believe, the more strongly founded it will be. The more you think about it, the more you will know about it – and, if thinking about it creates doubts about parts of it, then face the things you do doubt, confirm your belief in the things you don't doubt, work out which is which and see your faith grow stronger.

That is the first of your jumping shoes. But you need two. To use your brain and reason about God is not enough on its own. You need a second shoe. That second shoe is Love, an activity about which Christians speak a great deal without necessarily being sure what it is they mean - Love God? Love your neighbour? Love your family? Love your enemy? Love whom? Love how? What sort of loving will enable us to spring into the heart of God?

The love he speaks of – indeed the love that Christ spoke of– lies, I believe, in true selflessness, the losing of yourself in your concern for others. Love is the noblest of all human feelings – and its nobility lies, I believe, in the absence from it of self-concern and self-advantage. This was the hallmark of everything that Jesus did: and Jesus' command was, not so much to "Love others", but "Love others as I have loved you". It is by love such as that, I believe, that the soul is raised beyond the ordinary human level – and you do not have to live in particular circumstances or be out of the ordinary in your situation in life to do that.

We all deal with other people in the course of our daily lives – in dealing with the wants and situations of our families, in dealing with those we work for or work with, in the way we treat everyone we encounter along the way. In all our dealings, in everything we do, we meet people who have Christ in them and who personify Christ to us – and the chance to treat such people, such ordinary people, with the love which Christ would show to them is a chance we experience every day. And this, I think, is the second activity of which the prophet speaks. Live like that with love for your fellow man in your heart: and you will be on the way to doing what Christ commanded all of us to do.

These are the jumping shoes then – intellect and love. With these you can jump over the fence of your restricted understanding of the nature of God and spring straight into

God's heart – and remember this. You are to God of all things the most valuable. God thought it worth while to give you an immortal soul. He also thought it worth while to come to this world in the person of His Son to give that soul eternal redemption and a place with Him in the life to come. It was not for nothing that man became a living soul. For God gave you the chance to become immortal- if you choose. Up then, noble soul. Put on thy jumping shoes, which are intellect and love. Overleap thine understanding and spring into the heart of God. For, you see, you are already a member of God's household. You have been one all the time. For that is what God made you to be.

There is a Lad Here

St John Ch 6. v 9

Jesus Christ, who founded our Church and on whose life, death and teaching our faith is based, did many remarkable things in the course of His short life: and one of the more remarkable, and one of the best authenticated, was His miracle in the feeding of the five thousand, which has been read to us this evening. Thousands of people had flocked into the countryside to hear the teacher speak. The evening came and there was nothing to eat. What shall we do? asked His followers. One of them answered: There is a lad here with five loaves and two small fishes, but what is that among so many? They left it to Jesus, as they always did. And he fed all five thousand with the five loaves and the two small fishes: and there was more than enough for everyone. There is a lad here, they said, with five loaves and two small fishes. There is a lad here. The story of the feeding of the five thousand is full of meaning, some obvious, some less so. Large numbers of people are in need of sustenance - and Christ feeds them. Large numbers of people have gone far out of their way to find the truth from a new teacher - and Christ provides what they are looking for. Large numbers of people are hungry for wisdom, for food, for whatever - and Christ answers their need. Large numbers of people are seeking enlightenment as to what they need for a fulfilled life - and Christ gives them no magic potions, no complicated recipes, no elaborate messages, but just the basic stuff of life, bread and fish, the things they know, the things which are familiar: and the food they need is found in that. You have needs. Christ will satisfy them. You are lost. Christ will keep you safe. You are hungry. Christ will feed you. The symbolism is there for all to see: and God be praised, for it can all be true, true today and every day, if you truly look for it. But I want, briefly today, to speak of something else, of another aspect of this remarkable tale.

There is a lad here. We have no idea who he was. He was probably the son of a local shopkeeper, who had heard that the crowds were coming to hear the teacher and thought they might want to buy some food, and sent his son out with a few supplies in search of customers. This lad answered Christ's call. He did not have much to sell and he did not know how this man would use what little he brought. He did not think himself important. He did not think he had anything with him of any particular value. He simply offered what little he had - it was such a little thing, just five loaves and two small fishes - but Christ took it and used it to feed the multitude, took it and used it for God's purposes. This boy, this offering and its use have been recorded and are remembered two thousand years later. He and his merchandise have gone down in history. It cannot be what he expected.

It was such a little thing. When I think of this, I am reminded of another story in the Bible. If you have a Bible at home, and I hope you do, you will find it in Chapter 5 of the Second book of Kings, the story of Elisha and Naaman, the foreign general. Elisha was the prophet of the one true God in Israel, who did great work in God's name: and the mighty King of Syria, a powerful and rich state to the North, had heard of his skills. He had a Secretary of State, his general Naaman, who had leprosy, a disease which finished a man completely: and he wrote to the King of Israel, asking him to find Naaman a cure. The King of Israel received the letter and was greatly disturbed. "I cannot cure leprosy" he said: "The King of Syria is picking a quarrel with me": and he was very worried. But Elisha heard of this and sent the king a message, saying "Send this man to me. I'll show him what God can do". So Naaman came - with heaps of silver and gold and a great chariot and a whole army of servants. But Elisha did not care a penny about his silver and his gold. He did not even go and see him, but simply sent a messenger with a message: "Go and wash in the river Jordan seven times - and you will be healed". This made Naaman very angry. He said: "I thought he would at least come out to me and stand and call on the name of his God and strike his hand over the leprosy and cure it all. Are not Abana and Pharpar, rivers of Damascus, better than all the waters of Israel? May I not wash in them and be clean?" and he went away in a rage. But one of his staff said to him:" If the prophet had asked you to do some great thing to make yourself better, you would surely have done it. All he has asked is a little thing. Why not give it a try?". And Naaman did what Elisha had suggested - only a little thing, a very little thing: and he was healed. There is much more to the story than that – read it if you get a chance - but I will leave it there. God works through great things: and God works through little things. He uses important people: and he uses people who do not know how important they are. He works with the rich man's fortune. He works with the pensioner's pittance. He demands great things of us. He demands little things of us: and sometimes He does great work with the little things. Naaman was greatly changed, wholly cured, by the little thing. Five thousand people were fed by the little thing. There is a big lesson there for all of us.

We meet in Church today to worship Christ: and, at the same time, to give thanks for the founding of the Brockham Scout troop and the seventy years, through which it has flourished. We thank God today for those who founded it, those who worked to keep its spirit alive and all those who willingly gave their time and efforts to see that it did well. If you had asked them about it, they would probably say that it was really nothing at all, worthwhile work maybe, but a very little thing just the same. I am sure that they gave a great deal of thought to it all, for little that is good is achieved without hard work and a great deal of thought, but they would still have said that it was a very little thing - five loaves and two small fishes maybe and not an ounce more. But the good that Christ has done with the service they gave is probably incalculable.

And it can be the same for all of us, can it not? We all have loaves and fishes in our hands, talents passed on to us in our genes by our parents or by them and others in our upbringing and education, talents being developed in the schools and in the Scouts, talents which can be used, if we so choose, for Christ's service. Our loaves and fishes are all different - but we all have them. They may consist in physical things - strength, being able to run fast, leadership skills. They may consist in intellectual things, mathematical ability, skill with computers, communication skills. It may be that you have a talent for giving pleasure or smiling so as to put people at their ease or making others happy. Your loaves and fishes may consist in some special talent for music or for painting or in skill with animals or in green fingers for growing things. You may have a gift of organising things and be able to help to run your troop or your community. You may have a gift of healing or be good with children or good with old people or good with the sick. You may have that most valuable gift of being able to listen. You may have that underrated, but immensely valuable, capacity to love. These are just examples of the loaves and fishes we carry in our hands and hearts as we go on our pilgrimage about this earth: and Christ's message to each of us is that we should develop them and use them lovingly, loving Christ in one another, which is how we start to love God, which is what we are charged to do.

But, remember this, our loaves and fishes are ours - ours to do what we like with. We can eat the loaves and fishes ourselves, keep them for our own use and maybe grow fat through consuming them - if we so choose. We can, if we so choose, throw them away because the burden of carrying them is too great - and thus waste them altogether - if we so choose. We can put off a decision till tomorrow and wait - until the loaves are stale and the fish are dry and of no use to anyone - if we so choose. But we can, if we so choose, do what that lad did - do what the founders of your troop did - and put our loaves and fishes into Christ's hands, however little and unimportant we think they are, and see them used by Him to feed the multitude - and, in doing that, find that, which we all so earnestly desire, true fulfilment for ourselves.

The last thing that lad imagined would be that he would go down in history and be remembered two thousand years later for his merchandise. But he did and he is: and it could happen to you too. You do not carry bread and fish with you. You have other talents. You carry other gifts. You will know what they are. Christ calls you, as He called that lad, to put them in His hands and let you, through Him, use them for his purposes. You see, there is a lad here: and that lad is you, isn't he?

Inasmuch as You Did it Unto One of the Least

St Matthew Ch 25 v 40

"Inasmuch as you did it unto one of the least of these my brethren, you did it unto me". You did it unto me.

The message of today's second reading is that we should love one another by being good to others and by looking after them, whatever their need: and I offer you two texts this morning, both about love, one from the Bible, one from elsewhere. From elsewhere, I offer six lines from an unremarked 17th Century poet, William Cartwright:-

"There are two births. The first, when light
First strikes the new awakened sense,
The other, when two souls unite
And we must count our life from thence.
When you loved me and I loved you,
Then both of us were born anew".

And, from the Bible, I offer Jesus' words to Nicodemus in St Johns's Gospel, Ch 3: "Unless a man has been born over again, he cannot see the kingdom of God". When you loved me and I loved you, then both of us were born anew. Unless a man has been born over again, he cannot see the kingdom of God.

Those of us, who have had the immense good fortune in this life to have fallen in love and found that love returned, are, or ought to be, no strangers to the concept of being born again. Truly to fall in love is to undergo a spiritual change, in which you instinctively feel that everything is new, that you are facing in a different direction, that your priorities and desires are utterly changed. You feel reborn, that somehow you are starting all over again on a different stage and under different lights. It is a spiritual rebirth.

The coming of Jesus, both into the world in His own day and into your life and mine in our day, is much the same. When Jesus came then, and when He comes now, the spiritual life of everyone He touches is utterly changed. Our belief, as Christians, is that God chose to be born on earth, chose to live life as a human being, chose to sacrifice that life for our redemption and, by His choice, has caused His Spirit to be in us, an integral part of each of us. Through Christ we are all reborn. As Christians, we are each of us committed to the conviction that Christ is in us, a living part of each of us. As Jesus Himself said:- "From henceforth I am in My Father and you in Me and I in you".

"Christ in you". This is the gift you and I have, in this rebirth, received – the invisible gift which makes all things new for us. "Christ in you" – always there, never absent, never at rest, often forgotten, often ignored, never escaped from. Christ's presence in us is the reality of our faith – and once we accept this amazing and transforming truth, things for us can never be the same again.

For the fact that Christ is in us is not just an article of belief which we can put in the cupboard and forget about, something kept in reserve like the savings in the Building Society. Christ's presence in us every day makes demands of us as to how we should live and as to what we should do. It demands of us that we should try to live as Christ would live, that we should approach our problems as Christ would approach them – and do our work as Christ would do it, with integrity and with love. For Christ is not only in you. He is in everyone you meet, in everyone you speak with, in everyone who is affected by the decisions you make. Christ is in your family, your colleagues, your employer, your employees. Christ is in your neighbours, in your customers, in your competitors. Christ is in the public whom you serve, in your friends, in your enemies, if you have them. Christ is in everyone whose life you touch, in everyone whose life touches you: and His words from today's Gospel ring inescapably in your ears: "Inasmuch as you did it unto one of the least of these my brethren, you did it unto me". You did it unto me.

This is the gift you and I have received as Christians, the gift which you and I are called to pass on to others, the gift of Christ in you, Christ a living part of you. This means that, day in and day out, Christ walks on your feet, Christ acts with your body, Christ works with your hands, Christ speaks with your voice, Christ thinks with your mind, Christ at work in you as you set about all that you do. That is why no Christian is ever alone, that is why our faith is so exciting: and the fact that Christ is in us surely makes it our duty, by word and by example, to try in our lives to do what we perceive to be the will of God for us, to use our bodies for the right purposes and not the wrong ones, and to follow the straight path, wherever it leads. Inasmuch as you did it unto one of the least of these my brethren, you did it unto me.

Easily said, you may say, not so easily done. How are we, ordinary people with ordinary frailties and ordinary uncertainties, how is it possible for us to do all this and get it right? Where can we, with all our doubts and weaknesses, find the strength to do God's will? The Scriptures give us the answer to that too.

This is a passage of which I have spoken to you before. But it lives in my mind as the answer to this question, one of the most powerful pieces of imagery in the whole of the Old Testament, the story, in the First Book of Kings, of Elijah on his approach to Mount Horeb. When Elijah was in despair, he went to find his God, he set out to find where God would be, and, on the way, lay down exhausted and went to sleep: and an angel brought him meat and drink and said "Arise and eat. For the journey is too great for thee". And the passage records that he went in the strength of that meat 40 days and 40 nights unto Horeb, the Mount of God –and he found God there in the still small voice and found again the strength to do God's will. In the strength of what meat are you and I to make our way to the holy mountain? In the strength of what meat are you and I to exercise our calling to be doers of God's will? Jesus gave us the answer. "Verily verily

I say unto you, except ye eat the flesh of the Son of Man and drink His blood, ye have no life in you. Whoso eateth My flesh and drinketh my blood hath eternal life and I will raise him up at the last day. For my flesh is meat indeed and My blood is drink indeed. He that eateth My flesh and drinketh My blood dwelleth in Me and I in him". Christ in you. You reborn in Christ.

And it is this, the body and blood of Jesus, which we, as Christians, will this morning share in our Communion Service, which perfects the gift of Christ in us. It is this that is the meat for our journey on Christ's feet through this difficult and demanding world, the meat which, day by day, gives us the strength and the perception to go on our way rejoicing and to strive to do God's will in our lives. We have His promise and we have the means. All we need is the resolve.

Do you ask "Why me?" I have. Do you say "I cannot do this. These demands are too great for me"? I have. The answer is that Christ has chosen you and, since Christ has chosen you, nothing is now beyond your compass. The angel's message to Elijah was "Arise and eat. For the journey is too great for thee". The Gospel's message for the Christian is that, with the body and blood of Jesus, no journey is now too great for you. For you are special. God thought it worth while to give you an immortal soul. He also thought it worth while to come Himself, in the person of His Son, and die a dreadful death upon a cross, so that you might be redeemed. It was for you that the victory of the cross was won. It was so that He might be an ever-present part of you that Jesus died. You are.... Reborn, reborn to do God's will – and, inasmuch as you do it unto one of the least of these His brethren, you do it unto Him.

Is it Love?

St Paul Epistle to Romans. Ch 13. v 14

I offer you three texts this morning, one from St John's Gospel, Ch 12, one from St Paul's letter to the Romans Ch 13 and one from St Matthew's Gospel, Ch 24. The text from St John tells of certain Greeks, who came to Jerusalem to worship at the feast. "The same came to Philip and desired of him, saying "Sir, we would see Jesus". The text from St Paul is a clarion call. "The night" he says "Is far spent. The day is at hand. Let us therefore cast away the works of darkness and let us put on the armour of light. Let us walk honestly, as in the day – not in rioting and drunkenness, not in chambering and wantonness, nor in strife and envying. But put ye on the Lord Jesus and make not provision for the flesh to fulfil the lusts thereof." The text from St Matthew is a warning. "There shall arise false Christs and false prophets, who shall show great signs and wonders". "Sir, we would see Jesus". "Put ye on the Lord Jesus". There shall arise false Christs and false prophets, who shall show great signs and wonders".

Our task, yours and mine, in this life, I firmly believe, is to find our way to God – and if we can, to bring others with us. It is for that purpose that we come into the world. There are diversions, good diversions, along the way – and we serve God in those diversions by caring for our families, by caring for our neighbours and in making our way in the world and in all the good and familiar things of life. But our task, our lifelong quest, is to find our way to God. It is because we seek the way to God that we are here – and Jesus' message to us is the same as it was to His disciples – "I am the way". Jesus has told us:" Let my spirit be in you. Follow me. That is the way". St Paul talks to us as well as to the Romans, when he says:- "Put on the Lord Jesus" – and, like the Greeks St John speaks of, we too would see Jesus. But we cannot, as St Paul requires us, "Put on the Lord Jesus" and we cannot, like those Greeks, "See Jesus", unless it is the real Jesus that we seek and the real Jesus which we find. For there shall arise false Christs and false prophets, who shall show great signs and wonders.

I want to share some thoughts with you today about this because I am worried – for I don't know whether some, who call themselves Christians, see the real Jesus any more, even when they truly think they do. When Jesus was asked: "What shall I do to inherit eternal life?", which is the question we ask when we seek for the real Jesus, He replied:" What is written in the law?": and when the lawyer, who had asked the question, answered: "Thou shalt love the Lord thy God with all thy heart and with all thy soul and with all thy mind and with all thy strength – and thy neighbour as thyself", Jesus said "Thou hast answered right. Do this and live". Love God. Love your neighbour. Do this and live. What worries me today is that there seems to be a general view in and around the Church in many places that, so long as we claim to be acting out of love in whatever we do, then just about anything goes, because, if it is done out of love, it must be what Christ wants of us, regardless of what we are actually doing and regardless of what its results may be.

Jesus' command to us was :- "Love one another as I have loved you" – and His love for us and the love He seeks from us can be very different from the love which we refer to in the ordinary use of our language today. When we talk of loving someone in our language in these days, it means feeling real affection for them or being physically drawn to them in some way. Loving God is not like that at all. We love God by single-mindedly seeking our destiny in His service and by concentrating all that we have and all that we are in seeking after Him. Christ's command was that we should strive to love God with all our heart, with all our soul, with all our mind and with all our strength – and heart, soul, mind and strength are four very different things. We love God with all our heart by harnessing our emotions in God's service rather than our own. We love God with all our soul by developing our spiritual selves in God's service rather than in our own. We love God with all our mind by fully and energetically applying our intellect in seeking out God's will, rather than our own, and doing it. We love God with all our strength by dedicating our bodies to God and by using our physical powers and abilities in God's service rather than in our own. Christ requires of us that we develop the necessary discipline to commit our emotions, our spiritual selves, our intellect and our bodily strength and abilities, all four of them, for God's service: and not for our own, unless God's purposes and our own truly coincide.

We do not love God with all our heart, do we, if we let our emotions run riot in inappropriate ways, even if we say that it is love which takes us there? We do not love God with all our soul, do we, if we allow ourselves to be led into spiritual by-ways, where the real Christ is not to be found, even if we say that it is love which takes us there? We do not love God with all our mind, do we, if we let hysteria or mindlessness overtake us in what we claim to be our search for the true Christ, even if we say that it is love which takes us there? We do not love God with all our strength, do we, if we abuse or misuse our bodies in what we claim to be God's work, even if we say that it is love which takes us there? If we lose control of our minds or of our bodies, we may say that it is God's work and we may say that we see Jesus in the doing of it – but we may be casting off the armour of light and putting on the works of darkness. We may be getting it wrong. We may be listening to a false Christ.

Our Christian duty is to find out the true Christ's will and do it, even if it is painful, demanding and inconvenient. If we do what we like and then seek to justify our actions by persuading ourselves that it is Christ's will, we may be doing the Devil's work and not Christ's work at all. If we are to live according to our faith, it is vital that we adapt our life style to match our faith, not adapt our faith to match our life style. So, in the same way, we must seek to ascertain the real will for us of the real Christ – and then try to do it – not do what is purely self-indulgent for ourselves and then justify it by claiming that it is all done out of love and that that is why Christ has willed it for us.

Should we think about all this? Perhaps we should.

His Family Have Been Informed

Remembrance Sunday

The boast of heraldry, the pomp of power, and all that beauty, all
that wealth, e'er gave, await alike the inevitable hour. The paths
of glory lead but to the grave. When Thomas Gray wrote those
unforgettable lines on a long warm slow summer's evening, nearly
250 years ago in a country churchyard, he was not thinking
of those who died in war. Today we are thinking of those who
die in war – and in our day, day after day, often, too often, on the
evening Television News, we hear the newsreader tell us of the
death of a young serviceman in Afghanistan and add the grim
words: "His family have been informed". There is usually no
further comment. "His family have been informed" brings a sort
of public closure. We breathe again. It's not my son, my daughter:
and we go back to life as it was before. But it is always someone's
son or daughter, not mine, just someone else's. There is always a
family, left with inconsolable grief. It is someone else's son or
daughter, who took the paths of glory, knowing full well that it
might be the grave that they led to: and it is always someone else,
who has been informed.

Who are these young servicemen, who, knowing where they
lead, thus, of their own accord, choose the paths of glory? I read
a very moving account of them some time ago and share it with
you now, for these are the men and women we are talking about,
the men and women we are remembering today. Forgive me if you
have heard it before. In Afghanistan, it said, the average age of the
military man is just 19 years. He is a short-haired, tight-muscled
kid who, under normal circumstances, is considered by society as
half man, half boy. Not yet dry behind the ears, just old enough to
buy a beer, but old enough to die for his country. He never really
cared much for work and he would rather wax his own car than
wash his father's, but he has never collected unemployment benefit

either. He is a few years out of comprehensive school; he was probably an average student, pursued some form of sporting activity, drives a ten year old jalopy, and has a steady girl friend that either broke up with him when he left, or swears to be waiting when he returns from half a world away. He listens to rock and roll or rap or jazz - and a 155mm howitzer.

He is 10 or 15 pounds lighter now than he was at home because he is working or fighting from before dawn to well after dusk. He has trouble spelling, thus letter writing is a pain for him, but he can field strip a rifle in 30 seconds and reassemble it in less time in the dark. He can tell you all about a machine gun or grenade launcher and use either one effectively if he must. He digs foxholes and latrines and can apply first aid like a professional. He can march until he is told to stop, or stop until he is told to march. He obeys orders instantly and without hesitation, but he is not short of spirit or individual dignity. He is self-sufficient. He has two sets of fatigues. He washes one and wears the other. He keeps his canteens full and his feet dry. He sometimes forgets to brush his teeth, but never to clean his rifle. He can cook his own meals, mend his own clothes and fix his own hurts. If you're thirsty, he'll share his water with you; if you're hungry, his food. He'll even split his ammunition with you in the midst of battle when you run low. He has learned to use his hands like weapons and weapons like they were his hands. He can save your life – or take it, because that is his job. He will often do twice the work of a civilian, draw half the pay and still find ironic humour in it all. He has seen more suffering and death than most people that you'll ever meet. He has wept in public and in private for friends who have fallen in combat and is unashamed. He feels every note of the National Anthem vibrate through his body while standing rigidly at attention, while tempering the burning desire to square away those around him, who haven't bothered to stand, remove their hat, or even stop talking. Yet, even so, day in and day out, far from home, he fights to defend their right to be disrespectful.

And now, just as in earlier wars and earlier generations, he is paying the price for what he has been told is, what he believes to be, our freedom, yours and mine. He is not just a boy. He is not a boy at all. He is the British fighting man that has kept this country free for over 200 years. He asks nothing in return, except our support and our understanding. Remember him, think of him, for he has earned our respect and admiration with his sweat and his blood. And it is not just the young men. There are young women out there, in the front line, doing the same job – and I remember reading, not long ago, of a young woman, a corporal, I think, in the Royal Army Medical Corps, who crawled out under fire to a young man whose leg had been shattered by a bomb and tended his wounds, yes, and held his hand, though the bullets were flying all around her – and would not come back, refused to come back, to safety until he had been rescued. These are the young men and women we are thinking of today, the young people, who chose the paths of glory, the young people, whose families may be the next to be informed: and they don't half deserve to be remembered.

But what should we do, you and I, what should our answer be to this their sacrifice? Christ answered that question in the passage from St John's Gospel you heard read this morning. "This is my commandment" He said:" That you love one another as I have loved you. Greater love hath no man than this that a man lay down his life for his friends.". I want briefly to try to tell you what I think He meant by that: and, in trying to do so, I want you to have a particular picture in mind. It is a well-known picture, showing an event in the first Queen Elizabeth's time, depicting Sir Walter Raleigh, in doublet and hose, taking off his cloak and laying it on the road in the mud, so that Queen Elizabeth could walk down the path without getting her feet wet. Out of love and respect for her, he laid down his cloak for his queen. He laid down his cloak for his friend. In the same way, today, we invite our young people to lay down their lives for each other. In this church now, whenever we have a wedding, we ask the young couple, in the presence of their friends and families, to stand by the chancel steps, look each other in the eye and say those wonderful words; "All that I am I give to you and all that I have I share with you within the love of God, Father Son and Holy Spirit". And they say it and they mean it. And what they are saying to each other is that, as Sir Walter Raleigh laid down his cloak, so they will each lay their life down on the road for the other and use it to keep their loved one safe and well. I lay down my life before you, they say, so that it is yours to use, ours to use together. Christ tells us that the greatest love you can show for your friend is to lay down your life for him. He is not telling us to commit suicide. He is not telling us to get ourselves killed. He is saying that, if you truly love your friend and want to show that love, you lay your life down in the road for your friend so that it may be used for his/her benefit. For Jesus it was different. He knew that his destiny was literally to die for His friends – as He did on the Cross and won eternal life, or the chance of it, for all of us by doing so. But He does not ask the same of us. We are, He said, to show our love for Him by following His command that we should love one another. We love one another by laying our lives in the road for our friends, by thus leading our lives with love in our hearts. We lay our lives down in the road for the friends we love by letting them see and know that our lives are to be spent in loving and caring for them – and then by living out that reality. Christ does not ask us to die in His service. On the contrary, He asks us to live in His service – and to serve Him, for as long as we live, by loving as He has commanded us. That is what He is asking us to do.

But it cannot be the same for everyone: and, for those young people fighting in Afghanistan, living your life with love in your heart has an extra dimension. Living your life with love in your heart, if you are civilians, as we are, may be demanding, but it is not dangerous. But, for serving soldiers, sailors and airmen, it is very dangerous indeed. For they run the risk of death daily. That danger is their constant companion: and each of them is prepared, daily and without reservation, to lay down, and sometimes lose, their life for their friends. They don't lay down their lives in the road for their friends, as we do in this place, if we obey Christ's command. They lay it down for their friends on the battlefield, because that is where they are: and that is what you do, when you are on the battlefield. Men and women, some of whom we remember today, have done that in wars since time began: and today they are remembered at war memorials all over the world. But we ought to remember them, not just for their victories, not just for their bravery or their skill at arms. We ought to remember them for the love they felt for their fellow fighters and fellow citizens, for the love they felt for their friends, for the love which moved them to go to fight for their country, for the love which put them in the predicament which brought about their deaths. Every day, as fighting men and women have always done, as these young people give their service in the barren fields of Afghanistan, they are showing the love for their friends, which Christ commanded them to show. We need, thank God, no guns in Buckland. But, on easier ground and a fairer playing field, we can, perhaps, follow their example, love one another, and give them our support, our respect and our prayers. But, above all, we must not forget them. We must keep them in our hearts, remember them and thank them for what they do and the spirit in which they do it. For they are all heroes, whether they live or die – and that surely is the least we owe them.

Lord, we pray Thee, hold our troops in your loving hands. Protect them, as they protect us. Bless them and their families for the selfless acts they perform for us in what they see to be our time of need: and teach us, through all the changes and chances of this fleeting world, to try, as they do, to love one another, as you have commanded us. Through Jesus Christ our Lord. Amen.

Remembrance Sunday

I am one of the many, now alive today, who have never suffered directly from the ravages of war. I am lucky in this, as many of us alive today are lucky in this. No close relative of mine was killed in the Second World War, which ended nearly sixty years ago. No close relative of mine was killed in Malaya or Korea, though some I knew suffered as a result of the fighting in those places. No one I knew was killed or injured in Kosovo or the Falkland Islands, in Northern Ireland or in Viet-nam or in Iraq. No one I know has been killed by terrorists - yet. I am lucky, very lucky in this: and I am aware of it.

It was in 1974, as I recall it, on a warm summer's evening in Chambers in the Temple, when this was brought home to me. I had just finished a consultation with a QC I knew quite well and had noticed a strange card on his mantlepiece. I looked more closely and saw it was a piece of card with a small glass phial attached. In the phial was some dark powder: and above the phial were the letters "A.P. In remembrance". He saw what I was looking at and told me his story.

"I was" he said "21 years old, a newly fledged officer in the Navy. We were at sea and I was on watch with my friend, Albert Parsons, who had joined up with me. We had trained together and been posted to the same ship. We were in the North Sea. It was 1943. We had often spoken together of our hopes for the future, he and I. We both had plans to go into the Law. He was warm-hearted and ambitious and extremely able: we had shared great trials and dangers together and somehow come through them. We had shared happy times together too: and we were very close friends. We were on watch together and chatting, as we so often did, when he suddenly pushed me very hard to one side, knocked me over and threw himself on top of me: and, as he did so, the shell he had sensed approaching, exploded a few feet from where we had been standing. I was merely stunned. He was killed outright. Had he dived to the ground without pausing to push me out of the way, he would have lived. He gave his life for me. Because of our friendship, his parents asked me if I would like to keep a small portion of his ashes: and, as you see, I still have them on my mantlepiece. I never go into Court without thinking of him, for I have spent my working life in the career which he had himself hoped for. His memory has been with me in everything I have done. "A.P. In Remembrance".

"A.P. In Remembrance". He gave his life for me. His memory has been with me in everything I have done. How often have we heard that said in the context of Remembrance Sunday? How often have we marvelled at the instinctive and selfless actions of others, who, out of love somehow felt but never expressed and probably never consciously perceived, have given their lives that others may live? How often have we heard, but perhaps not thought fully through, that shattering sentence of Jesus, that "Greater love hath no man than this, that a man lay down his life for his friends "?

His memory has been with me in everything I have done. We cannot bring the dead back, you and I. Even if we knew them, we cannot bring them back. But we can, even if we did not know them, strive to keep their memory with us in everything we do: for most of what we do, whether it be worshipping in this lovely church, whether it be playing golf in the autumn sunshine, whether it be kissing our small grandchildren goodnight and thinking happy thoughts about the golden future which we hope for them, most of what we do is only possible for us because of the sacrifice of those who died in war. Nothing that is good in this world was ever achieved without sacrifice. We can keep their memory with us by seeing to it that their sacrifice is not wasted, that their early and untimely deaths have not gone for nothing.

The day before yesterday the sacrifice was in North Africa, in Europe, in the North Sea. Yesterday the sacrifice was in Viet-nam, in the Falkland Islands, in Yugoslavia. Today the sacrifice has been, today the sacrifice still is in Iraq. Whether our soldiers' presence in Iraq was lawful or unlawful, whether the decision to go in there with force was right or wrong will be a matter for argument, among those who wish to argue, for years to come: and the contradictory verdicts of history will be for our grandchildren, when they are adults, to consider. What we know is that the soldiers and the administrators and the peacekeepers are now trying to do good in that unhappy land and are risking and giving their lives in the process, so that others may live in peace. It was a moral vision which sent them there, a moral vision which saw, or claimed to see, the good and the honourable throwing out the evil and the corrupt, a moral vision which saw, or claimed to see, kindness and justice replacing tyranny and oppression. It was a moral vision. It was a moral vision.

In his immensely powerful sermon in the Remembrance Service at St Paul's last year, when we thought that the war in Iraq was over, Archbishop Rowan Williams said this:-

"As we look out at a still uncertain and dangerous landscape, as we think of the soldiers and civilians, the UN personnel and the relief workers who have died, we think of that moral vision and we have to acknowledge that a moral vision is harder to convert into reality than we should like. We never know in advance quite what the cost, the cost in human lives and human misery, of that vision is going to be.

There are "he went on (and I paraphrase now)" Two responses that simply will not do. We cannot say:" This is your business, not mine. I was against going in there in the first place. It is a matter of principle now. You made the mess. You sort it out". That response will not do. It needs a massive effort from all people of goodwill to change the world into a less unbearable place. And we must all take part in that effort, all work at making that effort, for otherwise no good can be done at all. But equally we cannot say:" I've got quite enough to do cleaning up this mess and I haven't got time to listen to you preaching about your principles. Stop preaching and let me get on with it". That will not do either. We have to go back and test what has happened in the light of the original moral vision. We have to find out what we have learned. We cannot just put this complicated and tragic history aside without asking if our values and commitments are right values and right commitments: and whether we should persevere with them or let them go."

"Today", he said "In church, all we can do is pause briefly in the presence of God. We give thanks for many lives of skill and bravery and patience - the lives of the servicemen and women whom we mourn: and the lives too of peacemakers and community builders of all kinds: and those who bore the cost without choosing or volunteering, those swept up in the unplanned death and terror that all conflict brings. But we can do more than that. We can pause to think a little about what it means, and what it costs, to turn vision into reality, what it means, and what it costs, when we try, by using other people's efforts and other people's trust, to turn our principles into practice for other peoples' lives, what it means and what it costs to go to war. We cannot pay back what we owe to the dead unless we stop and think about these things."

And this is, is it not, what we, as professing Christians, should be doing today. Remembrance Sunday is not only about marching in lines with old comrades, remembering distant battles, calling back the sound of distant trumpets and distant gunfire, though all that is very important still.

Remembrance Sunday is here to remind us of those, who gave their lives in the hope that a better world, a safer world, a world with more justice, more kindness, more honour in it might be built from the ashes they left behind them. They have left it to us, to you, who grew up in that safer world, to do the work, to build the peace, to bring the justice, to live with the honour: and, in the end, to turn the moral vision into reality. We can't do it, you and I, on our own. But we can make a difference, if we use these few moments in God's presence seriously to consider what we can do to make things better: and to pray that God will take all the good things which have been done, together with all the suffering, all the pain, all the bereavement and all the anxiety: and, through us and those we can influence, use it all to bring reconciliation and renewal for us and for all the nations of the Earth.

A.P in remembrance. He gave his life for me. His memory has been with me in everything I have done. Is it enough to remember? Is this not also the time to ask: What effort should I make in return?

Joe Strudwick

Remembrance Sunday

There is, I think, no tragedy more poignant, no event more likely to bring the tears to our eyes, than the untimely death of a boy or girl, a young man or a young woman, in the prime of youth - the hope cut off, the promise unfulfilled, the now-never-to-be-achieved full flowering. Whether the death be the death of one in a dangerous venture to rescue a fellow-soldier in Afghanistan, or the death of twenty nine in the explosion of a terrorist bomb in Northern Ireland, or the deaths of tens of thousands in the appalling rain-soaked fields of Northern France now ninety six years ago, there is no consolation, no healing, save by the passage of time.

It is with this in mind, on this Remembrance Sunday, that I offer you as a text five words from this morning's reading from Chapter 17 of the 1ˢᵗ Book of Samuel: "Thou art but a youth". Thou art but a youth. You may not immediately recognise the words, but the story will be familiar. The Philistines had gathered to fight against Israel. Goliath, their champion, came and defied Israel's army and mocked Israel's God: and there was great fear and dismay. David, who was a shepherd boy and too young to join the army, was sent by his father to take food to his brothers, who were serving soldiers - and he saw and heard what Goliath said and did.

"And David said unto Saul: "Let no man's heart fail because of him. Thy servant will go and fight against this Philistine". And Saul said to David: "Thou art not able to go against this Philistine to fight with him. For thou art but a youth and he a man of war". Thou art but a youth.

David killed Goliath as we all know. He killed the enemy and became a hero. He became king and founded a dynasty, the family into which Jesus, the Son of God, was later born. If Goliath had killed David, he would never have become a hero and no one would ever have heard of him. He would have fathered no children and founded no dynasty. The Lord delivered David out of the hand of the Philistine and gave him the victory. Countless others have been less fortunate. In all the years which have passed since David fought Goliath, countless Goliaths have risen and fallen - and countless Davids likewise. Some were tall and strong like Goliath. Some were small and frail like David. Some were Jews, some Gentiles, some white-skinned, some black-skinned, some of noble birth, some of no known parentage, all races, all languages, all creeds, all classes, all nations. They have but two things in common, these endless ranks of fighting men and women. Each died in battle: and each was but a youth.

I want to tell you about a particular youth. Some of you may know of him, others will not. His name was Valentine Strudwick, though his friends all called him Joe. He came from Holmwood, just a few miles from here, and ran away from home and joined the army in January 1915. He joined the 8th Battalion of the Rifle Brigade and, in March 1915, after only six weeks training, was sent to France. Early in that summer, he was invalided home, badly gassed and shell-shocked and spent three months in hospital in Kent. He then discharged himself from hospital, made his own way back to France to rejoin his regiment and was sent back to the front in the Ypres salient, where it met the Ypres canal. On the 14th January 1916, he was killed in action. To those who know the terrible story of the endless carnage on that front, now some 96 years ago, the story is familiar. He was one of many thousands. What is remarkable about Joe Strudwick is his age. For he joined the army when he was still only 14. He was hardly 15 when he discharged himself from hospital and went back to fight. He died one month short of his 16th birthday. He was the second youngest British soldier to die in the 1st World War. His grave is in the Essex Farm cemetery, which lies by the Ypres Canal, just outside the town. He was but a youth. But for his death in battle, he might have survived the war and done great things. He might have founded a dynasty. He might have done what David did, have been what David was. But he never had the chance because he died at the age of 15. Next time you visit Waitrose in Dorking, take the time to cross the road and look at the War Memorial. They have recently re-inked the names on it, so that you can read them: and you will find Joe Strudwick there, second from the top in the right hand column. The memorial won't tell you anything about him - merely his name, V. J. Strudwick. But you will know - and you may remember. Today is a little over 3 years short of the centenary of his death. Thou are but a youth.

The guns roar no more by the Ypres Canal. It is quiet there now: and the Essex Farm cemetery, where Joe Strudwick lies with nearly 2000 others, is green and well cared for. Hard by that cemetery you will find, should you go there, a strange ramshackle structure, embedded in a mound of earth. It is an old dugout, which was used as a medical station by units of the Royal Canadian Medical Corps between 1915 and 1917 and has been preserved. One of the doctors who served there was Dr John Macrae: and it was there, one evening in May 1915 during a quiet spell in the battle, that John Macrae sat on the edge of that dugout, looking out across the field, which was to become the Essex Farm cemetery. The larks were singing. The poppies were flowering: and it was there, in the quiet of that early summer evening, that he wrote the poem "In Flanders Fields", which some of you will know and which has been read at this morning's service and is set out in your service sheets, a heart-wrenching poem, expressing, in words more plangent and more powerful than any I can muster, the tragedy and the challenge of Remembrance Sunday.

"In Flanders fields the poppies blow
Between the crosses, row on row,
That mark our place: and in the sky
The larks, still bravely singing, fly
Scarce heard amid the guns below.

We are the Dead. Short days ago
We lived, felt dawn, saw sunset glow,
Loved and were loved – and now we lie
In Flanders fields.

Take up our quarrel with the foe.
To you, from failing hands, we throw
The torch. Be yours to hold it high.
If ye break faith with us who die,
We shall not sleep, though poppies grow
In Flanders fields".

As he wrote those unforgettable lines, he had youths like Joe
Strudwick in his thoughts and, in his mind's eye, the crosses, row
on row, in what was soon to become the Essex Farm cemetery.
He himself died in battle in France before the war was done. He
cannot have been more than 25 years old. Thou are but a youth.

And across the years, my friends, down 96 years of tormented
history, John Macrae and Joe Strudwick are talking to you and me.
For it is our world now - our world to make better or to make
worse, our world to make war or to make peace, our world to bring
justice or injustice, our world to bring liberty or licence, our world
to bring freedom or tyranny. They gave all that they had. Their
message is that we owe it to them to give all that we have to try to
do what is right and to undo what is wrong in this world of ours.
For we do not celebrate Remembrance Sunday to rejoice at the
victories, let alone to glorify the killing. We celebrate Remembrance
Sunday to remember the dead and to remind ourselves what it was
that they died for. They gave their lives that those, who came after
them, you and I, your children and grandchildren and my children
and grandchildren, might have the chance to grow and flourish in
peace and freedom. That was what they had grown up with. They
fought and died, so that we might do the same.

The freedom from tyranny, which we now enjoy, is ours
because it has been bought and paid for in two World Wars and

in many smaller conflicts since - a fearful price, paid by hundreds of thousands of youths, ordinary men and women, some of whom we remember with love, but most of whom we will never know, who went out and died in the hope that a better world might come of it. The task of building that better world is the torch which their failing, their dying, hands have passed to us. We owe it to them to do what they never had the chance to do and build the world they never had the chance to build. For the carnage will surely have been purposeless, the sacrifice will have been vain, our remembrance of the dead will be no more than an empty gesture, if we use the freedom, which they died to preserve for us, simply to turn our backs and do nothing in the face of all those things which we know to be so wrong in our world today.

A fearful price has been paid for our freedom. The yearly challenge of Remembrance Sunday surely is that we are all asked to do something in return - isn't it?

Where Your Treasure is

St Luke Ch 12 v 34

Where your treasure is, there will your heart be also. I have never known anybody give credit to Christ for being a great poet. But it is wholly remarkable, when we consider the extraordinarily beautiful words and ideas, which sprang, all those years ago, from the lips of this amazing man. The parable of the sower, for example, or his words about the lilies of the field will stand comparison with anything which any of our great poets have come up with – and this wonderful sentence, so short and so compelling, is one of His greatest. Of course, He did not say those words. He said something in Aramaic, which someone remembered and wrote down in Greek or Hebrew, and which has been translated by English poets hundreds of years ago into the words in our Authorised version. But the original words and original ideas must have come from a mind without parallel – and they are a glorious part of our Christian heritage. But what did He mean? What is His message?

The message appears to be: During your life on earth, do what is right rather than strive to accumulate riches: and you will get your reward in the next life, when it comes. Riches here are temporary and will go stale. Your reward in Heaven will last for ever. Do not fix your mind, your heart, on transitory delights, for they are here today and gone tomorrow. Let it be your greatest desire to seek eternal life with God. Let that be the treasure you seek for. If you limit your aims to seeking riches here, your heart will be enmeshed in this world. If you seek riches with God, your spirit will be in communion with Him – a condition which will complete the circle and make it your desire to do what is right in this life. That will be your treasure. That is where your heart will be.

It all sounds so good and so easy, but all we have to do is look round the corner or search under a stone or two: and the difficult questions begin. I have been thinking, in the last week or two, about a terrible story, which was in all the papers, of some young people in Cornwall. There was a man in St Austell, a weak-willed, mentally disabled man, with a reading age of 6 and an intellect to match it. He lived in a flat for the disabled – and a small group of young people, led by a man of 24 and a young woman of 17, moved in on him, took over the flat, humiliated him over a period of months, tortured him, took every advantage of him and ended up throwing him 100 feet to his death from a railway viaduct – and, according to the evidence, laughed as they did it. They are in prison now – and rightly too, I suppose. But this happened in a small town in Cornwall, a country town, a community like Dorking or Reigate and no bigger. How can this happen? Should someone not have stopped this? Did no one know? Did they say, in that attractive town, "It is not my business"? and mind their own business and so do nothing. What should we say to these things? Would we, should we, have interfered, had it happened in our community? What would we have done? It is all very well to say: Do what is right in this life. It is all very well for us, in the comfort of our community here, to talk of our treasure and our heart. But what do we say of those young people and the dreadful things they did? What do we say or think about their treasure and their heart? Do we say: They are wicked and have received the punishment they deserve. and close our eyes then and forget about them? What does Christ say to us and to them about what has happened? And what should we do?

That is the ever-sitting-on-my-shoulder question, isn't it? What must I do? Not everyone, said Jesus, that saith unto me Lord Lord shall enter into the kingdom of Heaven, but he that doeth the will of my father, which is in Heaven. And it is hard to find out what God's will for us truly is. When the lawyer asked Jesus: What must I do to inherit eternal life? Jesus answered: Obey the law. When the lawyer replied: I do that, but I feel I should do more, Jesus replied: Ah well then, if you want to do more than that, then sell all that you have, give the proceeds to the poor and come, follow me: and the lawyer went away sorrowful. When we ask: What must I do to inherit eternal life? What is Christ's answer to us?

If I could answer that question, I would have the solution to the problems of the world. The only answer I can give is that we should pray, listen and use our God-given brains to think with. We have, as thinking human beings, been created with skills and potential skills: and I believe that our task on this earth is to develop those skills and use them for Christ's service. This involves doing, in Christ's service, what we are good at. It serves no purpose to devote our lives to things we are not good at. It is an old story, but maybe a true one, of a wealthy young man I read of, who wanted to follow Christ with all his heart and felt himself called to work in a hospital in a poor village in Africa. He volunteered, was flown out and put to work. The difficulty was that he had no healing skills, no medical experience and was not very strong. There was nothing he could usefully do, except get things wrong: and he soon fell ill with worry as well as disease, found himself eating the food which the starving inhabitants needed and occupying a hospital bed needed by others. He relieved no one's burdens. He simply created new ones – and, when he recovered, he was, at great expense, flown home. His desire to help, though genuine, was in reality totally misplaced. There was nothing there that he could usefully do. But, when he returned home and recovered his senses, he prayed, listened and thought about his predicament. He decided to do something useful. He studied finance and made himself an expert in the investing market and contrived to turn his wealth into a great fortune, so that he was able to give large sums of money regularly to the very charity, to whom he had made himself such a burden earlier. As a result of his gifts, the charity were able to pay for more doctors and nurses and more medicines and more treatment for the people he had wanted to help. Thus, though he was far more comfortable than he would have been in Africa, he did a great deal more good than he would have done, had he stayed there. He had developed his skills and come to use them for Christ's service. We should, in our own way and with our own skills, try to do the same.

I am no good (I often wish I was) at going to young people with bad habits and teaching them to do what is right. I cannot go to cruel youths in Cornwall or anywhere else and turn them from their terrible ways, because I do not know how to do it. I would only create greater resentment and cause greater alienation. But there are people, some trained for it and some not, who have that skill and can do it and it is, in the real world, far better to support them and let them do the work, so that it can be done effectively. I do not think that God's will is done by finding a problem and making it worse, even if the exercise involves personal hardship and sacrifice. I think that God's will is done by watching and listening, finding and understanding: and then either solving it yourself or finding and supporting people who can solve it and can get it right. And we must remember that we have responsibilities. We have wives, husbands, children, who look to us for comfort, company and support. We promise, in our marriage ceremonies, to love and to cherish till death us do part. "All that I am I give to you and all that I have I share with you" is what we in our Church invite our new wives and husbands to say to each other: and that is hardly consistent with an indication that we should physically leave them and go elsewhere to tend the poor and needy. If we create responsibilities for ourselves (as Christ encourages us to do) and engage in good enterprises (as Christ also encourages us to do) I reckon our first duty is to look after those we have helped to create, those we are directly responsible for: and I believe that we serve Christ best by serving them first.

But we must not be blinded by these primary duties. There is a real world with troubled people in it, who are our brothers and sisters in Christ, even though we did not create them: and we must develop our skills and use them to help those troubled people too. It cannot be God's will that we should look to ourselves and those close to us alone. We must be mindful of, and pray for, those cruel young people in Cornwall. Christ died for them as well as for us: and the ever-loving Saviour unceasingly holds out his arms to them in love and prays "Father, forgive them for they know not what they do". And so, surely, should we. We pray for them and use our skills, such as they are, to try to create a world, where people will learn to love one another. This, I think, is Christ's command. Do not seek for yourself treasure upon earth, where moth and rust will corrupt and thieves break through and steal. Seek for yourself rather treasure in heaven, where neither moth nor rust can corrupt and where thieves do not break through and steal: and let your heart be where your treasure is.

Whence Hath it Tares?

St Mark Ch 13 v 25

Whence hath it tares? Some enemy hath done this. Consider these words from today's second reading: and consider further Jesus' well-known words from St Luke Chapter 12. Watch therefore. For be ye well assured that, if the good man of the house had known at what time the thief would come, he would have watched - and would not have suffered his goods to be broken through. It is a long way from today's reading - but I will come back to it in the end.

Whence hath it tares? Some enemy hath done this. Tares are not much spoken of these days. But, in their prime meaning, tares are weeds which grow amongst the corn in the cornfield. They adversely affect the growth of the corn and, because they look rather like the real thing, are difficult to separate from the true crop. Today's second reading, the parable of the wheat and the tares, contains, I think, not only the Bible's only reference to tares, but also Jesus' first recorded reference to the devil in the course of His ministry - and it is one of very few occasions in the Gospels when we find Him recorded as using that term at all. We do not speak much about the devil in our Church these days either, though our fundamentalist friends speak of him rather more frequently. I want to share some brief thoughts on the topic with you this morning. Who and what is the devil? What, if anything, should we do about him?

One of the cornerstones of Jesus' teaching lay in his words: From henceforth I am always in you and you in me. He said it a number of times and in a number of ways and it was fundamental to his message. I have always believed - and have said so many times since I started to share thoughts with you in the shape of sermons on Sundays - that Jesus is in each of us and an inherent part of each of us. Jesus is in each of us and never apart from us.

He works with our hands, sees with our eyes, thinks with our minds, partakes in all our actions. That is part of the basis of the faith I hold, that Jesus is always there with us, whatever we are doing and wherever we are. But unhappily, I think, that is not all. I also believe that the devil, whatever the devil or Satan is, is sometimes in us too. Just as the conflict between good and evil goes on daily in the world, so the struggle between right and wrong goes on daily in each of us. For some, including many who call ourselves Christians, temptation may come less frequently. For others, things are sometimes very different and the urge to do something wrong meets little resistance. I do not see the devil, as he is sometimes portrayed, as a kind of wicked dwarf-like creature with a twinkle in his eye, horns on his head and a sharp arrow in his hand. I see him as the beast within, the quiet voice always tempting, always seeking to persuade that it does not matter what you do, the siren song promising easy and unwise enchantments, the beckoning finger calling us to spiritual death. The devil is no more physically visible to us now than Jesus is. But the quiet voice, the siren song and the beckoning finger are there, at work in us, just as Jesus is there, at work in us, also. And just as the fight between them goes on in the world without much let-up for either side, so the conflict within us goes on daily without much let-up also.

I want to tell you three short stories. The first is of the son of a friend of mine, one of the nicest of men. One of his sons, well brought up and well educated, a University graduate with a good job and great prospects in the City, found the pressure of work more testing than he could conveniently manage and started to use cannabis to ease his mind. It did ease his mind, but not enough - and one day, on the urging of a colleague, he tried heroin, which seemed to ease his mind much better - and he went on trying heroin till he became addicted to it and could not manage without it. He spent all his money on it, borrowed more when his funds ran out and soon found himself owing more than he could ever find. He deteriorated physically, left his work and suffered a complete physical and mental breakdown. His father used all his own savings to pay off his son's debts and to pay for his son's treatment. The young man is better now after utter degradation and determined self-discipline. But the promise of his youth has gone, the family savings have gone and he has felt bound to go and live and work abroad. It had all seemed so good. Now all is lost. What went wrong? Whence hath it tares? Some enemy hath done this.

The second story is of another man, a fine and well-respected man who was the manager of a large bank. He had a customer who was a racehorse trainer, who recommended a bet on a particular horse he trained. The manager put on a £ 20 bet at 10-1. The horse won and the manager was pleased with his profit. He followed his customer's advice a few more times and always won. Betting became an exciting pastime and soon turned into a major preoccupation. He started to lose - and the more he lost, the more he wagered: and the more he wagered, the more he lost. To cover his losses, he took money from the bank he managed, carefully concealing his activities - and, when he had taken over £ 200,000 with no possible hope of repaying it, his defalcations were discovered, he was sacked and prosecuted and sent to prison. His wife was left penniless and divorced him and he found he had lost everything. It had all seemed so good. Now all was lost. What went wrong? Whence hath it tares? Some enemy hath done this.

The third is of a young man you may have read about. He came from a cheerful and hard-working family in Leeds, from parents well-known and liked in the community, followers of Islam as it happens, and liked and respected for that and other reasons. Their son was 19, good-natured and popular, seemingly well-adjusted and having the prospect of a good life ahead of him. He became keen on his religion, went abroad for a spell, studied at a religious school in Pakistan, came home and resumed a cheerful and, it seemed, ordinary life. He went to a mosque often and he visited friends often. His family had high hopes for him. And then, one day, on a planned venture, he went with three friends to London with a rucksack full of explosive and killed himself and a number of others in an underground train, when he detonated the bomb. His parents are beside themselves with grief. Their son is gone. He is not just dead. He is branded as a murderer and a terrorist. Their life in their community is over, indeed their life is over for they have lost their beloved son, they are in personal danger and who will speak to them? It had all seemed so good. Now all is lost. What went wrong? Whence hath it tares? Some enemy hath done this.

These are familiar stories. Some of them happen more often than others, but you don't read about them in the papers much because, for the most part, they are commonplace, they are no longer news. But we see these things around us - broken marriages, young people on drugs, trusted employees stealing in the course of their work, terrible things done out of some false belief that these things are required by some vengeful and demanding God - and we have to ask ourselves why they occur and what we can do about them. Our loving God is still there through all this misery; and the bleeding Christ stands by with pitying eyes, watching and powerless to intervene, unless we let Him in to do so. I ask, as you must ask: what can we do to make things better? And I pause, as you must pause, to think about these things. And as I paused and thought about these things, there came into my mind some words from Chapter 5 of the first epistle of St Peter, words which became familiar to me long ago during my schooldays: "Brethren", wrote St Peter "Be sober, be vigilant, because your adversary the devil, as a roaring lion, walketh about, seeking whom he may devour, whom resist, steadfast in the faith". Brethren, be sober, be vigilant, because your adversary, the devil, as a roaring lion, walketh about, seeking whom he may devour, whom resist, steadfast in the faith. Whence hath it tares? Some enemy hath done this. Be sober, be vigilant, because your adversary the devil, as a roaring lion, walketh about. Some enemy hath done this. Your adversary the devil. Some enemy. Your adversary.

Whence hath it tares? Some enemy hath done this. We are all responsible in this life for ourselves and, many of us, for others who are younger than we are. It is a lifelong and important task, both for us and for those for whom we are responsible. But, by God's grace, this is a battle we can win. For, for us all, Jesus' command is clear. We find it in St Luke Chapter 12 and all over the Gospels. Be alert, said Jesus. Be ready for your enemy - and resist him when he comes. For we are all at risk - there is no one who is not. You know who your enemy is, but you never know when or where or in what form he will come. He may be recognisable, he may be unrecognised. He may come - and you not know that he has been. He may come at any time - and you not know it until it is too late. Watch therefore. For be ye well assured that, if the good man of the house had known at what time the thief would come, he would have watched and would not have suffered his goods to be broken through.

What Manner of Man is this? (3)

St Mark Ch 4 v 41

"Blessed be the God and Father of our Lord Jesus Christ, who, according to his abundant mercy, hath begotten us again unto a living hope by the resurrection of Jesus Christ from the dead – to an inheritance incorruptible and undefiled, which fadeth not away, reserved in heaven for you". So wrote St Peter, who was there on Easter Day - and I will come back to what he said. But I want to take, as a text today and not for the first time, some other words, spoken by Peter on a very different occasion during Jesus' ministry: "What manner of man" he asked:" is this that the winds and the sea obey him?"

- What manner of man is this? The story, where this question is asked, appears in three of the gospels. Jesus and his disciples are in a boat on the lake at Galilee, crossing from one side to the other. The principal disciples are professional fishermen, professional sailors, who know this rather small piece of inland water like the back of their hands. Jesus has spent his early life as a carpenter – neither a fisherman nor a sailor. The fishermen are sailing the boat. Jesus is asleep. A storm comes up and the water gets very rough. The fishermen panic. They wake him up – help us Lord or we sink. He wakes up, calms the waters and goes back to sleep again. Any sailor worth his salt would have said Don't panic, Master. We'll look after you. Yet this lot wake him up and ask him to save them. It tells us a great deal about them and a great deal about the awe in which they held him. And they ask, as we ask, What manner of man is this that the wind and the sea obey him? And we might ask too – what manner of men were they, that these sailors looked to a carpenter to save them from the storm.

Who was this Jesus? Try to answer the question: and the immediate answer is that we know virtually nothing about him. We have no idea what he looked like, tall or short, dark or fair, hairy or smooth – for we have no pictures and no contemporary descriptions. We know that he had worked as a carpenter in his father's workshop till he was about thirty, became an itinerant preacher then and ministered for about three years before they killed him. We know that he could read and write, but know nothing of his education. Was he top of the class? In the middle? Did he play games? Did he have a sense of humour? Was he popular? Did he have friends? What did they think of him and his ministry? We know nothing of his early years at all. It has been suggested that he had a brother, perhaps two, and possibly a sister. But we do not know. We don't know what became of his father. We know that his mother was beside the cross when he died. But what his parents did during his short ministry, what they thought about it, what he said to them about it and what became of them after it, we have no idea. We have no idea who paid for his ministry, who paid the bills during the three years or so that he worked at it, whether he had any visible means of support. We believe that there were women in his group, but we do not know what he thought of them or what he said to them. We do not know how he would have reacted if somebody had physically attacked his mother in his presence, what he would have done if the law had required him to fight in a war, what he thought about marital happiness and unhappiness, what he thought about sexual matters. We know nothing of his personal habits, what he liked to eat and drink, what his personal preferences were. He wrote nothing down about his beliefs and his teachings and seems to have seen to it that nobody else wrote anything down either until thirty years and more after he died. He wrote no letters which have survived. He left no visible record of any kind. We know more about our county councillors (and that is precious little) than we know about this man. Yet we don't just vote for this man. Two thousand years after his death, we commemorate this man, we worship this man. Yet, in just about every respect which today we consider important in a human being, we seem to know nothing at all. Who is this man? What are we doing here?

Well may we ask – and well we must answer. For people are curious about our faith, want to know what it is that we believe and why we believe it. We are required, are we not, to learn to love God with all our heart, soul, strength and mind – and we cannot, can we, begin to love God with all our mind, if we insist on turning it off whenever his name is mentioned. We need answers, both for others and for ourselves – so we ask, as we are bound to ask, as the disciples asked: What manner of man is this? What manner of man is this?

What I want to put before you is this. This man was born in questionable circumstances into a peasant family in a small province, which was part of the Roman Empire and of no particular importance. He seemed to be no one in particular, born nowhere in particular. If he was anything special, nobody knew about it, except perhaps his mother. When he was about thirty, he became an itinerant preacher, working almost exclusively in a small country area in Palestine. He gathered a small group of followers, none of whom were influential or well-known, and none of whom had the faintest idea of what was going on. He preached a new Gospel, a gospel of a loving God, a loving father figure, whom he claimed to know. He told us of a God who loved us with an unending and unequivocal love. He wanted that love to overwhelm us. He wanted us to find that love irresistible. But the Romans, who were masters of the world and certainly masters of Palestine, took virtually no notice of him at all. The leading Jews, his own people, loathed him for his teaching, since he said that they were dogmatic and superficial and were not living as God wanted them to live. After about three years of this, the Jewish leaders had him arrested, watched his supporters, such as they were, run away, and, after a mockery of a trial, had him most painfully put to death in public. If it was Jesus' hope to convert the world to his gospel in his lifetime, he failed completely. Indeed, in reality, he had never had a chance of success. Palestine was a small, unregarded, province of the Roman Empire. There was nobody there with any influence at all. He was talking to the wrong people in the wrong place and three short years were nowhere near enough time. The project, if that was what it was, was doomed to failure from the outset, doomed to failure and blown to pieces. And blown to pieces it should have been - the teacher killed, the disciples baffled, ignorant, terrified and scattered, the message dead in the water. By any ordinary standards, according to any ordinary expectations, Jesus would have disappeared within a week and stayed forgotten – a tiny blip on the landscape of history at best, lost at once to sight and memory, nothing remaining.

And so it should have been. But it was not. For, amid all the argument and all the speculation, there is one thing we know – and know for absolutely certain: and that is that, contrary to all the odds and every expectation, he did not disappear and was not forgotten. The cause may have been lost, the army scattered, the message simply never understood. But the one thing we know for certain is that he was not forgotten. Within weeks of the apparent destruction of all that Jesus had lived for, their scattered ranks now suddenly united, their fears now suddenly put aside, these weak-kneed fishermen, who had looked to a carpenter to save them from the storm, were setting the world on fire with the very gospel, from which they had so recently fled. Now, all of a sudden, they believed. Now, all of a sudden, they were inspired to tell to the world this amazing message, which, before, they had never begun to understand. Now, all of a sudden, they had the strength, the assurance and the words to proclaim this message to the housetops, the strength and the assurance to give their lives and go to their deaths for the message their master had given them. And that fire, which they began, did not just flare up, sputter and die. It took hold, a mighty hold, overcame the Roman Empire and spread throughout the world. And this was so because something had happened, an event so momentous, so startling, that it had, almost in an instant, changed these timorous and uncertain weaklings into giants for their cause. And, when people ask you what it was that transformed these men and the world they lived in, the answer must be that it can only have been one thing, the thing they asserted, the thing they had seen with their eyes and felt with their hands, the thing which no one in his right mind was likely to believe but which they knew, without doubt, to be true, because they had seen it, God's miracle that Jesus had risen from the dead. You see, they now knew without any doubt what manner of man this was. They knew that this man was the true Son of God, who, wherever they were, would now always be with them. Life was now changed for them for ever, because they now knew the truth about this man.

And so it is with us. For we now know the truth about this man also. Ask yourselves. What else, what event other than the true perceived resurrection, which they asserted, can have caused this change in these men and given them the power, the understanding, the words, the determination, to give their lives and go to their deaths proclaiming this man's divinity? Nothing else. And if, like me, you ask yourself this question and cannot find any other answer, give thanks to God in whatever way you choose and remember the words of St Peter, with which I began. Blessed be the God and Father of Our Lord Jesus Christ, who, according to his abundant mercy, hath begotten us again unto a living hope by the resurrection of Jesus Christ from the dead – to an inheritance incorruptible and undefiled, which fadeth not away, reserved in heaven... for you. It is not a myth, you see. It is the truth. There is no other explanation. Christ is risen. He is risen indeed. I wish you all a very happy Easter.

Towering Inferno

St John Ch 1 v 19

Some of you may remember the film "The Towering Inferno", a film about a massive skyscraper, where a small fire started in a basement and finished by consuming most of the vast building and killing many of those inside, particularly those dining in the restaurant on the top floor. The film, like all disaster movies, began by showing the ordinary lives of people living and working in that building, while we, who watched, knew that catastrophe was about to consume them all. We knew, because we knew what the film was about, that fire would begin and fire would spread. The people living and working in the building did not know - and part of the fascination of the film to us lay in our foreknowledge and their ignorance.

It is with the same fascination that, in today's Gospel reading, we watch and listen to the Jews at the time when Jesus was growing into manhood, watch the Jews and their priests and leaders, watch them living and working in Jerusalem in the shadow of what we know was about to happen to them. They did not know what was about to happen to them - but we do: and the passage chosen for today's reading makes the point for us precisely. There was John the Baptist, a very unorthodox man, curiously dressed and attracting many followers, preaching a new message about something which was about to happen. Who was he? Did he know something which they did not know? What was it? We know the answer, but they did not. Watch this space and see the story unfold.

This is the record of John. The Jews sent priests and Levites and asked John the Baptist who he was. Are you the Christ? they asked. No, he said, I am not. Are you Elijah then or one of the prophets? No, he said, I am not. Who are you then, they asked. We have been sent here to find an answer and must give one to those who sent us: and he replied: "I am the voice of one crying in the wilderness. Make straight the way of the Lord". "Someone is coming, someone far greater than I, someone beside whom I am nothing at all. Make the way ready for Him".

But they did not get the message and they did not understand. Maybe they were too set in their ways. Maybe they felt that they had the power and control and did not want to lose it. Maybe they genuinely wanted to do something about it, but did not know what was to be done. But, whatever the reason was, they did nothing. Jesus came to them. The Son of God came to them. He walked about their land, walked about their streets, entered their houses, taught in their synagogues, talked to their people, took their children in his arms, looked them in the eye: and, save for a few, a very few, they saw nothing and recognised nothing. The world was about to be set on fire with the Gospel of Christ, set on fire with the living Word of the living God: and, like the guests in the top-floor restaurant in the skyscraper where the inferno was about to take hold, they carried on with life as it had always been: and did..nothing. They did nothing because they did not know that anything was happening. They saw no smoke. They smelt no flames. Things were as they had always been.

That is how it was for them. Is it any different for us? The world beyond the Church tends to see only what the media show it: and the view of our Church, from outside, is that, like the Jews in Jerusalem, we too are carrying on with life as it has always been: and, as a Church, to the outside world, we too seem to be doing.. nothing. The world outside sees no smoke. The world outside smells no flames. For those of us on the inside, our church can be, for many is, on fire with the Gospel of Christ. It is, for some of us on the inside, on fire with the living word of the living God. But, outside these walls, does it show? Outside these walls, does anyone care? I fear, perhaps, very few. And, if, outside these walls, we appear inactive, we do not have the excuse which the Jews had for their inactivity. They did not know that the world was about to catch fire. They did not know that there was smoke to see and that there were flames to smell. We do. We know that Jesus was not just another baby in a stable. We know that the man in the crowd was not just another passer-by. We know that that baby is the Son of God. We know that that young man in the crowd is Christ the King. We know that the world has been irrevocably changed by His presence here. We know that our relationship with God is established and complete because of it. The Jews of Jesus' day did not know these things. We do. If we act as the Jews did, do no better than they did, there is no excuse for us - no excuse of any kind at all.

Rowan Williams is a great Archbishop. He calls for a new moral lead from the Church: and he strives to give it. He is a very good man, a very learned man and a very articulate man. But in these days, when people talk in short sentences if they want to be understood, and soundbites seem to have replaced logical argument, I do not know how many people inside or outside the Church are listening to him. I hope that many are. But I fear that the concentration will remain on the continuing disputes and the peripheral arguments, because the inner truths are thought to be too difficult for ordinary minds to embrace: and many people simply do not want to be bothered with them. We are, I fear, going to act just like the Jews in today's Gospel reading. We will ask the questions. We will hear the answers. We may even find our way to an understanding we can take back to those who sent us. But will we do any more? The Archbishop preaches the Gospel to the outside world. But what do we do and say? Do we give him the support he needs? Do we give him any support at all? Do we tell anyone about our faith and why we have it? Do we let anyone see that we have a faith? And that it matters to us? Or is it going to go on, as it has always gone on, just seeing that we get the organisation right, just go on being "The sort of thing we don't like to talk about in public "? These are uncomfortable questions. But we have to face them. For we are the Church's ambassadors, the Church's spokesmen and spokeswomen in the world. And, if we do nothing, the Gospel is left unappreciated and unloved, like a beached whale on a sandy shore, huge, moribund and silent: and that is not what Jesus was born for: and it is certainly not what he died for.

What shall we do then? What can we do? The first thing we should do, I would suggest, is respond to Isaiah's call in today's Old Testament reading, praise God and rejoice. Praise the Lord, he said, call upon His name, declare His doings outside these walls, tell his doings among the people. Cry out and shout. For great is the Holy One in the midst of thee. We can share our faith by allowing ourselves to be seen, by people outside these walls, to have that faith and by being heard, outside these walls, to rejoice in the fact that we have it. For, make no mistake about it, the Gospel we hear contains the best of good news. Our faith is, our Church teaches, that, through the sacrifice of Jesus, his death and resurrection, the path to eternal life, the road to the courts of the Lord, is open for all of us, if we choose it. Death is not the end. It is, for all who share our faith and for many many others beside, who do God's work in the world, even if they don't know that they are doing it, the beginning of a new and incomprehensibly joyful existence, the details of which we cannot now take in or understand, but an existence in which all will be inexpressibly well. And that is surely something to rejoice about.

So can you, will you, let others know that you have your faith and, outside these walls, rejoice about it? I am not asking you to dance and sing and throw your arms about. That may be more ostentatious that you think right. But is it too much to ask that we openly show ourselves to have a faith and be happy about the fact that we have it? I cannot make you rejoice about anything, if you are determined not to. I do not tell jokes from this pulpit to bring smiles to your faces. I offer you, as the Church offers you, as the Gospel offers you, a much more powerful reason for smiling - the good news, which your Church, through our Rector every day and through me today, invites you to believe, of Jesus' promise of the chance of eternal life, for you and all those you love, in the place, whatever we choose to call it, where God is. As countless prophets, priests and evangelists have said before any of us were ever thought of, I invite you, from this pulpit, to believe what the Church teaches and openly to rejoice at that belief. Remember, after all, that our purpose in coming here is not to sit uncomfortably in rows and whinge about things. Somebody once said that Christ did not die on the cross, so that we could sit round in small circles and moan about it. We should openly rejoice that we have our Faith and let the world see that we have the inner happiness, which comes from that faith. Some of our friends in the more fundamentalist Christian Churches seem to be able to rejoice at it with gusto. We sometimes call them happy-clappy, a term which we do not think of as complimentary. But happy, at least, in their faith some of them seem to be. Are we? Are you? You cannot think much of Jesus or the gospel He proclaimed, if you cannot bring yourselves to be happy about it. I urge you to think on these things.

In our carol service in this church, we sometimes sing an old 16th century carol, one verse of which begins with these words:-

"Stupendous babe, my God and King, Thy praises will I ever sing.

In joyful accents raise my voice: and in the praise of God rejoice".

Stupendous babe indeed! We ought to be stupefied, we ought to be knocked sideways by the greatness of Christ and the generosity of God's love. We ought to rejoice wholeheartedly that we are sufficiently alive to take part: and we should let the world know what it is that we have, so that they may come and join us. Then, perhaps, this Christmas, when we sing "O come, all ye faithful, joyful and triumphant" and truly mean it, we will truly be doing Christ's work.

Wedding Address

To love without conditions, without reservations, is the highest perfection to which human nature can attain. It is how Christ loved us. It is how He taught us to love one another. To love unconditionally is the Christian ideal. But, as human beings, we are not generally very good at it. If we were good at it, the world would be a better place. So, when we find this love, we should cherish it and work at it. For we do not find it often. For those who have fought in war, we know that it is sometimes found in battle, the love that will cause a man to lay down his life for his friend. But, if we look at the ordinary incidents of life, it is, I think, only in a true marriage between two equal and loving participants that we find ourselves brought the closest that we ever come to this Christian ideal - this Christian ideal of unconditional loving and the unconditional giving, which goes with it, which together raise our human nature to its highest pinnacle.

Christ, who set the Christian standard, could have done anything, gone anywhere. He could have ruled the world, been master of the universe. He CHOSE to do neither, but to live humbly and to die alone and in agony, so as to save His people for ever - and He made that choice out of unconditional love for the people of his time - whom he knew - and for you and me, whom he did not know. We cannot match that love, you and I. We cannot hope to, though the Mother Teresas of this world have a go at it. But, in Christian marriage and in Christian parenthood, we come closer to it than in any other occasions in our lives - and we honour and respect Christian marriage and rejoice at it for that reason.

You two are at that stage now, now and here, as you sit together in this, the Church of Christ on your wedding day. Now you love unconditionally. It is, for each of you, now, in this defining moment, your complete desire unconditionally to give to the other all that you are and unconditionally to share with the other all that you have. This is Christian love at its zenith. This is as near to the mind of Christ as, save in parenthood, in which we hope you will be blessed, you are likely ever to attain.

It will not stay the same. As you become accustomed to being together, to being a married couple, your feelings for each other will unconsciously change. Your love for each other will deepen as your understanding of each other develops, as your instinctive trust in each other grows. Up till now, you have merely been playing with the bricks of a relationship. Today, here, in your present state of mind and in this hallowed building, you are laying the foundations and putting in the reinforcement, which will be the basis for the structure, which will be your life: and, on the foundation laid today, may you build a superstructure perfect in its parts and a source of continuing joy and satisfaction, as you build it, to you both. Take care to build it strongly. For, inevitably, storms will come, storms of tragedy or misunderstanding or disappointment, and your building must be proof against them. Every joyful shared experience will add new strength to that building. Every problem, faced together and shared and solved together, will add greater substance to it. As the treasure house of your shared experiences grows ever richer, so will the building, which today you are starting to construct, grow ever stronger. It is our prayer today that the structure of your life together will be sound, loving and long-lasting: and that the day will come, when others, not yet born and not yet thought of, will look at what you have built together and what you have done together and resolve to follow your example and do what you have done. And, when you hear what they say and realise what they think, your thoughts will go back to this day, to this chapel, to this beginning: and you will know that you have done a great thing. Make that your aim, for the testing times will come. We all have them - cracks in the plasterwork, leaks in the roof, a tile blown off in a storm. But because your foundation is strong, your structure will survive: and that foundation is the firm, loving and public commitment which you are both making now, the mindset which has brought you to this point, the unconditional loving, of which I have already too long been speaking. As the years pass and as the structure grows, never never allow yourselves to forget how you felt today, how it felt to feel as you feel today. For it is the unconditional love you feel now which is and will be the basis for all that you will do together and all that you will build together from this day forward.

Before I end, there is one piece of symbolism, which I would wish to share with you. When this service is over and you leave this building to start upon your new life together, you will turn away from the altar and make for the West door, which leads to the outside world, where your life together will be spent. As you go down that centre aisle, that outside world lies ahead of you: and you walk, side by side, towards it between the ranks of your friends, old and young, who love you and wish you well. But, as you make that turn and take that short walk, which, side by side, marks the beginning of your journey, there is one thing, which you will no longer see, because, by then, it is behind you - the sign of Christ, the emblem of love, the Cross upon that altar there. As, from this place, you set out together on your journey through life, you have, whether you are conscious of it or not, you will always have, the strength of the Cross behind you - and that strength will always be with you, will never desert you, no matter how high you fly, no matter how far you fall.

So make your vows now, in the presence of God, for that is your desire: and go on your way in His strength, wholly confident in your love for each other. It is our prayer that God will bless you both and bring you to great things.

Jubilee Service

Christ's words from today's second reading, St Matthew's Gospel Ch 20, v 26. "Whoever will be chief among you, let him be the one who serves you.". If you will be chief among the people, you must serve them. We meet in church today to give thanks to God for our Queen, for the triumphant and joyful sixty years of her reign and for the deep and continuing faith in Christ, which has strengthened and upheld her commitment to her country over all that time. It is an amazing record.

Our Queen was born, the first child of the then Duke and Duchess of York, on the 21st April 1926. There was no expectation then that she would ever be Queen. The heir apparent was her father's elder brother, who seemed a very likely successor . But that was not to be. She lived through the abdication crisis when she was 10 years old and realised what it meant for her. She was a teenager in London throughout the blitz. She watched her parents at work throughout the war, seeing them sharing their people's dangers and sadnesses every day: and she learned the craft of kingship from them through those difficult years: and she learned well. On April 21st 1947, her 21st birthday, while touring South Africa with her parents, her destiny now approaching, she broadcast, in a light and girlish voice, a remarkable message to the world. She publicly called upon the peoples of the Commonwealth, and especially the youth of those countries, to join her in building a better world – and her words were and are words of true inspiration. "If" she said (and it is a 21-year-old speaking) "If we all go forward together with an unwavering faith, a high courage and a quiet heart, we shall be able to make of this ancient Commonwealth, which we all love so dearly, an even grander thing - more free, more prosperous, more happy and a more powerful influence for good in the world – than it has been in the greatest days of our forefathers. To accomplish that, we must give nothing less than the whole of ourselves. There is a motto which has been borne by many of my ancestors- a noble motto "I serve". Those words were an inspiration to many bygone heirs to the Throne, when they made their dedication as knights as they came to manhood. I, a woman, cannot do quite as they did. But, through the inventions of science, I can do what was not possible for any of them. I can make my solemn act of dedication with a whole Empire listening."

And, with a whole empire listening, she said this:-" I should like to make my dedication now. It is very simple. I declare before you all that my whole life, whether it be long or short, shall be devoted to your service and the service of our great imperial family to which we all belong. But I shall not have strength to carry out this resolution alone, unless you join in it with me, as I now invite you to do. God help me to make good my vow: and God bless all of you who are willing to share in it"." I declare before you all that my whole life, whether it be long or short, shall be devoted to your service". Some words for a 21-year-old. She was 21 then. She is 86 now. She has lived, and lives still, a life of loving and unceasing service to her people. The vow she told us of, all those years ago, has been kept to the letter. We thank her: and we thank God for giving her the strength to do all that she has done.

But we must do more, must we not, than simply say Thank you? All those years ago, a young princess invited us to join her in a great and historic enterprise, to make the world a better place. The fact that we are celebrating a diamond jubilee does not mean that the enterprise is over. Her Majesty will not stop: and neither should we. It is a challenge which brings us straight to today's second reading from St Matthew. Jesus said "Whoever will be great among you, let him be your servant. If you will be chief among the people, you must serve them". Her Majesty said: "I make this solemn vow. My whole life, be it long or short, will be devoted to your service": and it has been. Our Queen has taken Christ's words, vowed to follow them and done what she promised. In this reading we find the mother of the apostles James and John asking Jesus to place them on his left and right hand in

257

God's kingdom. She had seen her sons leave their careers, their homes and families, give up everything they had and follow Jesus in His ministry. She was upset by this and wanted to see them suitably rewarded – what mother would not? But Jesus used this request as an opportunity to tell us something fundamental: and, if we look, we will see what the Christian Gospel, in this context, is.

Jesus' answer to this lady was that it was not in His power to decide who would inherit eternal life. But He made it clear that there was eternal life with God after death for those for whom God provided it. This is one of a number of passages in St Matthew's Gospel where Christ tells us of life with God after death and how to achieve it, the most dramatic of which is His great and memorable parable of the labourers in the vineyard, where He spelt it out in words of one syllable. It is a passage which many of you will know. A landowner hired labourers for his vineyard and promised them a penny for the day's work. They went off to work. He later hired other men, some at 9 am, some at midday, some at 3 pm and some an hour before sunset, when the work was due to stop: and, at the end of the day, he gave them all the same wage – the same penny for the day which those who had worked all day had contracted for: but also the same to those who had done much less work, even those who had turned up just before the work ended. It looked unfair. Those who had laboured all day complained – and why not? Goodness knows what the Civil Service Unions would make of it today. But Christ said:- "The Kingdom of Heaven is like this. God is free to do what He likes with His own creatures. It is God who judges.".

In this passage, Christ assures us that there is life after death, telling us in the clearest terms about eternal life with God and what we must do to achieve it. God is the landowner. The world is the vineyard. The payment is our reward. We are set, all of us in our lives on earth, to do God's work in the vineyard. Some spend all their lives doing God's work in the vineyard. Others are called to it later. Some only join in the hour before sunset.

But, Christ says, no matter when you start, no matter how much or how little of God's work you may have done, even if you only start to do His work an hour before the sun sets on your life, God may reward you with the wages due to those who spent their whole lives in His service. Jesus' promise is that you may, if you have, in any way at all, done His work, have your place with Him, when you move on.

What must we do then to inherit eternal life? Christ told us "Not everyone that saith unto me Lord Lord shall enter into the Kingdom of Heaven, but he that doeth the will of my Father, who is in Heaven". He is telling us that it is what we do which counts, not what we say. The true message is that, whether we come to it early or late, we must spend our time on this earth doing whatever it is that God calls us to do. And, if you ask what it is that God calls you to do, Christ's answer is always the same – that you must do what our Queen has done, that you must serve – serve others and show your love for God and your neighbour by and through the service that you give. The Christian message is that you show your love for God by striving to develop the skills, whatever they may be, that God has given you and by using them lovingly for the service of others whatever your position in life has come to be.

Her Majesty, our Queen, did just that. She took a vow in public on her 21st birthday that that was what she would do and kept it. We must seek to do what she has done, find out what God wants of us and go out and do it. It may be grand work, leading the country, building a cathedral, preaching to tens of thousands in Wembley Stadium. It may be smaller work, building a family, leading your children in the right way, ministering to someone in need down the road, cleaning the church at the week-end, or simply showing, to those who come within your circle, the example of a loving life lived with honour and integrity. The only way we know of discovering what God wants of us is to look at Christ's example and follow Him. Communion with Christ, learning His language, letting our thoughts run in the same stream as His spirit – this is the only way of finding out what God wants us to do. I cannot tell you how to earn eternal life with God. No one on earth can do that. But what we have is Christ's promise that there is eternal life with God and that, if we do God's work, even without knowing it, we, with St John and St James, with our noble and gracious Queen and with countless others, who have set us examples which we can follow, have a chance of finding a welcome there. So let us today thank our Queen by resolving to join her in her continuing enterprise and strive, each of us, to do what we can to make the world a better place. We will, if we get it right, be doing God's work at the same time.

.

The Christian and the Courts

This is a talk I was asked to give, in, I think, 1993, as part of a series of Lent lectures at Holy Trinity Church, Guildford on the subject of a Christian at work. It was entitled "The Christian and the Courts"

A Lenten Address

Do you want a Christian in the Courts? And, if so, what do you want him to do?

It is a fairly ordinary Friday morning at the Guildford Crown Court down by the river – your Crown Court, where those, who commit crime in your city, are tried and sentenced. In the first case listed, the Defendant has pleaded guilty to all charges. There were four victims of this offender's crimes – a 19-year-old shop assistant, a 60-year-old taxi driver and two police officers. The offender had been shoplifting and had been caught by the 19-year-old shop assistant, a slightly-built young woman, who had spoken to, and tried to apprehend, the thief. The thief had resisted, struck her in the face and bitten her hand, causing a nasty mark, some pain and slight bleeding. Having broken free and run out into, and down, the road, the offender got into a taxi. The taxi-driver, suspecting, rightly, that his fare was drunk and probably unlikely to pay him, refused to carry his would-be customer, whereupon the thief jumped out on to the pavement, picked up a brick and struck the taxi with it three times, badly denting the nearside wing. When the driver came round to stop this onslaught, he was heavily struck in the chest with the brick. The offender then ran off, pursued by a young policeman, who arrested the thief after a struggle, in which he was kicked on the knee and shins and bitten on the hand. He took the offender to the police station, where the custody sergeant was also attacked and bitten on the forearm, before the offender was finally placed in a cell. The whole incident had taken less than 15 minutes from start to finish.

Who was this offender? She was a woman of 23 with three children, all aged under 5. The children all had different fathers, the oldest child being a child of a teenage sexual relationship with an unidentified youth, the second being the child of her first husband, from whom she was now divorced, and the third child being the child of her second husband, who had just started serving a sentence of eighteen months imprisonment for burglary. She had a Council flat less than 3 miles from this church, which was clean and tidy, if rather sparsely furnished. The children were clean and generally well cared for: and she was a loving mother to them all and very fond of them and very kind to them. She had no money other than the slender sums which the State provided: and no prospect of paid work, because she could find and pay no one to look after the children. She did not take drugs. She did not batter the children. She had no close friends. She was inclined to spend much of the little money she had on drink, when things got on top of her, as they often did – and when she was drunk, she was very, very drunk and lost control of herself completely, being inclined, when in that state, to use considerable violence to anyone who got in her way. She had been before the Courts for similar offences many times before and had been placed on Probation three times (each time she had failed to co-operate after a few weeks) and had been to prison on one occasion for a month or so.

That is who she was. You will not have read about her case in the newspapers, first because such cases are fairly commonplace and merit no particular mention, even in the local Press: and second, because she is, in reality, fictitious. I cannot speak in public about individual cases, but those who know what happens down at the Crown Court will recognise her as typical, an amalgam of a number of Friday morning pleas of Guilty in your Crown Court, neither exaggerated nor understated. The Courts are full of young people like that – young men, who became fathers in their teens, young women who became mothers in their teens, with responsibilities they cannot handle and needing skills they do not have and do not know how to acquire, ever inclined to run away from their pressing problems by taking drink or drugs and running amok when they lose control because of these things.

What is the Christian to do with a woman like her? Probation has failed three times, despite enormous efforts by good-hearted and skilled Probation officers. For the will to co-operate may not last for long: and Probation is often powerless without co-operation. I cannot fine her because she has no money, I cannot order her to do Community Service, because drunkards are very disruptive in Community Service schemes, and anyway she cannot get anyone to look after the children. If I send her to prison, the children will be taken into care and may stay there. She herself was taken into care when she was young: and part of her rootlessness springs from that. She is a loving mother: and her children are well-loved children: and to break the bond between mother and child, even temporarily, is a last resort and may do much more harm than good to her and to them – and, in the final event, to you too.

The shop assistant is shocked and hurt. Her mother is angry and her father is very angry. They both call for severe action. The taxi-driver is shocked and hurt. He was off work for 5 days and has lost earnings and his no-claims bonus. His wife is very angry and calls for severe action, as do his colleagues. Taxi-drivers are in a very vulnerable position and need to be protected by the law. The police too are entitled to be protected from these things and are entitled to look to the Courts for firm action, when they are physically injured, If the Courts are seen to do nothing, then someone will, sooner or later, take the law into their own hands and exact their own revenge. And what happens then? So do you want a Christian in the Courts? And what do you want him to do? What do you want him to do with this offender?

Some of you will think the answer obvious – but I am sure that those of you, who see the answer as obvious, would be in profound disagreement with each other if we stopped to discuss it. Christ might have looked her in the eye and told her to go and sin no more – and she might have sinned no more and she might have been back on the bottle within a fortnight. I don't know. But I cannot tell her to go and sin no more – and she would ignore it if I did: and you would criticise me – and do so rightly – if I took that course.

So what is the Christian in the Courts to do? The challenge which Christ throws out to those of us who work in the Courts is clear and unequivocal: and it has to be faced squarely. St Matthew, Ch 7, v.1. "Judge not that ye be not judged. For with what judgment ye judge, ye shall be judged: and with what measure ye mete, it shall be measured to you again". And, just in case there is any doubt about the identity of those, upon whom we are called to pass judgment, Jesus gave us the answer in that unforgettable passage in St Matthew, Ch 25:-

"Then shall the King say unto them on His right hand: "Come ye blessed of My Father, inherit the kingdom prepared for you from the foundation of the world. For I was an-hungered and ye gave me meat. I was thirsty and ye gave me drink. I was a stranger and ye took me in. Naked and ye clothed me. I was sick and ye visited me. I was in prison and ye came unto me". Then shall the righteous say; "Lord, when saw we Thee an-hungered and fed Thee? Or thirsty and gave Thee drink? When saw we Thee a stranger and took Thee in? Or naked and clothed Thee? Or when saw we Thee sick or in prison and came unto Thee? ". And the King shall answer and say unto them: "Verily I say unto you, inasmuch as ye have done it unto one of the least of these my brethren, ye have done it unto me".

Then shall He say unto them on His left hand: "Depart from me, ye cursed, into everlasting fire, prepared for the devil and his angels. For I was an-hungered and ye gave me no meat. I was thirsty and ye gave me no drink. I was a stranger and ye took me not in. Naked and ye clothed me not. Sick and in prison and ye visited me not". Then shall they also answer Him saying: "Lord, when saw we Thee an-hungered or athirst or a stranger or naked or sick or in prison and did not minister unto Thee?": and the King shall answer them, saying: "Verily I say unto you, inasmuch as ye did it not to one of the least of these, ye did it not to Me".

For the Christian there is no escape from this. I call myself a Christian because I feel myself conscious of the presence of Christ in me. Christ is present in everyone – at least that is what I believe. What distinguishes the Christian from the non-Christian is that the Christian feels himself conscious of the presence of Christ in him: and the non-Christian does not. For some, the presence of Christ is unknown and unsuspected. Others acknowledge the existence of Christ, but feel that He is irrelevant or at so great a distance that His existence can have no impact on their lives. Others see Christ as close at hand or round the corner, but yet somehow out of reach. The Christian is the one, who feels conscious of the presence of Christ in him and of the ability of the Holy Spirit, when all other conditions are met, to work through him. That is my belief: and that is how I feel. It has not always been so. It has taken many years of gradual discovery to bring me to this point. But this is where I am now – irregular, inadequate, constantly falling short, but unable now to free myself from the meshes of His service, whose service is perfect freedom.

Please do not misunderstand me. I do not see myself as God's messenger, riding a winged horse through the ranks of the evil-doers, carrying a flaming torch and breathing the breath of righteousness into their souls. Nothing is further from the reality. Nor do I claim to have an open telephone line, which will tell me what God's will is or where absolute truth lies. Again nothing is further from the reality. I am just an ordinary human being like you, with a wife and children and a home like you, and my ordinary human failings, trying, on the basis of such education as I have and over 30 years full-time experience in the law and in the problems of those who go to law, to do a difficult job properly and in accordance with the principles I believe in and which I am expected to apply. It is just that, as a Christian, I feel myself conscious of having the advantage of never being out of reach of the well: and, whenever I am thirsty, I can go and drink at it – and possibly relieve, at the same time and to some small extent, the thirst of one of the least of these Christ's brethren.

No. I believe myself to be a Christian because I feel myself conscious of the presence of Christ in me. And Christ, of course, is not only in me. He is in you too. Christ is in you and in every one of you and in everyone you come across, in everyone who is affected by what you do, in every one of the least of these your brethren. Christ is in everyone, queen and subject, left and right, rich man, poor man, beggar man, thief. Christ is in the murderer's victim and the rapist's victim. He is in the murderer and the rapist also, though He may be very deeply concealed. Christ is in those you love, in those you do not love. Christ is in your colleagues, your employer, your employees, your customers, your rivals. Christ is in the public whom you serve, the people whom you meet, the users of the products you make and sell. Whatever you do about your work or omit to do, it is done or omitted to be done to the least of these your brethren: and, as Christ says, inasmuch as you did it to one of the least of these, you did it to Him. There is no escape from this. To the Christian in the Courts, there is no escape either. Christ is in the man in the dock. Inasmuch as you do it to him, albeit one of the least of these your brethren, you do it to Christ also.

I did not become a Judge by whim or by accident. After proper investigation, I was considered fit for the appointment: and I was appointed by HM the Queen, acting on the advice of the Lord Chancellor. When I take my seat on the Bench in the morning, I sit beneath the Royal Arms, as all judges do in every Court in this land: and, when I was appointed, I took an oath in the following terms:- "I do swear by Almighty God that I will well and truly serve our Sovereign Lady The Queen in the office of a Circuit Judge and I will do right to all manner of people after the laws and usages of this realm without fear or favour, affection or ill-will".

"Judge not that ye be not judged. For with what judgment ye judge, ye shall be judged". "I will do right to all manner of people without fear or favour, affection or ill-will". I see no conflict between these two obligations, no conflict between my duty as a Christian and my duty as a Judge. Indeed I think the duties are the same. Christ requires of me that I shall do right to all manner of people, that I do so fearlessly and honourably, insofar as I am able, and without ill-will, that is without enmity and in no spirit of revenge: and my oath of office requires exactly the same thing. The difficulty lies, as the difficulty always lies, in putting the principle into practice.

For the task of doing right to all manner of people means exactly what it says: and "All manner of people" embrace much more than the Defendant in the dock alone. Christ is in the Defendant and the Defendant's family. Christ is in the victim and the victim's family. Christ is in the policeman, who labours and risks his life to prevent crime: and in the Probation Officer, who seeks to look after the offender after sentence or release. Christ is in the person who will be this offender's next victim, if this offender goes free – and in that person's family. Christ is in the child, who may be the next victim of the child abuser's wickedness. Christ is in the old lady, who is afraid to go out at night because she does not feel safe in the street. Christ is in those we are there to protect as well as in those we have to sentence. That is what makes it difficult. That is how it is for you in your job. That is how it is for me in mine.

Judge not, that ye be not judged. For with what measure ye mete, it shall be measured to you again. I will do right to all manner of people without fear or favour, affection or ill-will. I will try to do that: and so will my colleagues. But think about it. Do you really want a Christian in the Courts? And, if so, what do you want him to do?

Lightning Source UK Ltd.
Milton Keynes UK
UKOW04f0640091013

218741UK00001B/39/P